Wives, Mistresses and Matriarchs

Wives, Mistresses and Matriarchs

Asian women today

Louise Williams

Weidenfeld & Nicolson
LONDON

First published in Great Britain in 1998
by Weidenfeld & Nicolson

© 1998 Louise Williams

ISBN 0 297 81701 9

Set in 11/13pt Arrus by DOCUPRO, Sydney

Printed in Great Britain by Clays Ltd,
St Ives plc

Weidenfeld & Nicolson

The Orion Publishing Group Ltd
Orion House
5 Upper Saint Martin's Lane
London, WC2H 9EA

To my mother, Margaret Ann Williams,
and my late grandmother, Edith Jane McKenzie

Contents

Author's note

Material from several of these interviews has previously appeared in my book, *On the Wire*, published by Simon & Schuster. Other material previously published in the *Sydney Morning Herald* has also been incorporated into this book.

Introducing Yurnilawati:
the only child

When Yurnilawati's mother went back home to the village of her birth, her five children in tow, the old ladies would sit around clucking sympathetically over her misfortune. 'What a pity she had only one child,' they would mutter, the brood of five clearly in view. 'My mother would feel hurt, I know,' says Yurnilawati. 'But it was always the same, every time she brought us home, they would always say the same thing.'

The village lies in the soft foothills which run down to the west coast of the Indonesian island of Sumatra. This is clan territory, where the *adat*, or cultural rules of the Minang people still govern daily life. The *adat* was born with the famous Minang queen in Bukittinggi (High Mountains) further inland, but followed the clans south as they sought out new rice fields and clear streams. 'It is so beautiful,' says Yurnilawati wistfully. 'Life still revolves around the river. The water is so clean and fresh and every day people sit on the banks washing and talking.'

In her mother's village it was only Yurnilawati the people saw, and not her mother's four sons.

Yurnilawati was the only girl, the sole heiress to the family rice fields, the modest village home and the gold jewellery hoarded by the rural villagers. She knew her mother really loved the boys, but she is understanding about their rejection. The *adat* stated that boys were destined to be cast out of the family home at the age of 12 and could only return to the village as adults as 'honoured guests' in the home of their wives or sisters. This was a matriarchal village and, as such, it was only Yurnilawati who carried with her the future of the clan. Like all the little girls she was her family's princess, worthy of special food, worthy of her parents' trust and of their priority in distributing the limited advantages they could bestow upon their children.

In those days, she says, the village was reached by foot, over three river crossings; the sky vast and blue overhead, the lush hills pulsating with the soft din of the tropical jungle which wrapped itself tightly around the rice fields, thick and moist.

In this village the women owned it all.

The reasoning behind the *adat* which gave the women authority was simple, Yurnilawati says. A man is mobile, a woman with children is not. So it is her security which must be assured for the sake of the clan's future. She must have a home in which to bring up her children, she must have rice fields from which she can feed them. That way, she will never be vulnerable to a man's fickle attentions or his wandering ambitions.

It was not, explains Yurnilawati, a kind of power struggle between the women and the men.

'A woman was always there to come home to, the men would always have a place to stay. Women, we thought, were a kind of heaven.'

As a sister she already knew that she must offer shelter to her brothers, should they need it, for the rest of their lives. She would show her brothers respect by taking their advice, over that of her husband, in the raising of her children, just as her mother's brother had been sought out for his views on Yurnilawati's education. And she would consult her brothers first should she decide to sell the family home or the family rice fields.

Yurnilawati, herself, was born further south in Palembang, outside the reach of the clan lands. But, like the millions of Minang people who have fanned out across Indonesia in search of their fortunes, the *adat* was carefully protected within the home and the village was regularly visited where the lessons were reinforced. Both her parents were merchants in the local market of a provincial town. Her father had asked her mother to give up her business when the children were young, she says.

'My mother refused, she said she wanted to have her own money. So he had his business and she had hers, there were no further questions about that.'

Both her parents were from Padang clans, so the pressure to give birth to a girl was strongly felt. In 1962 their first child was born: a girl.

'My father was so proud, there is a lot of prestige attached to a first-born girl, and my parents said she was just so beautiful,' she says.

Just after her first birthday their baby died. She had been running a high fever and went into convulsions in a town without modern hospital emergency facilities. Within five minutes she was dead in her mother's arms, just like that, she says.

'My mother told me that my father almost went mad with grief. Finally, my mother took him away travelling to try to make him forget.'

On that trip across Java, Yurnilawati's mother fell pregnant again. When the child was born it was a boy. 'I think my father was disappointed,' she says. So when Yurnilawati was born two years later she was smothered with attention, overshadowing her older brother and the three boys who followed in her wake. 'I think it was a combination of the culture which valued girls more highly and my own parents' tragedy,' she says of her upbringing. 'Oh, yes,' she says, laughing, 'I was so spoilt, I was Daddy's spoilt little girl'.

But she didn't even realise until she was about eight years old that other little girls were not the princesses of their own homes.

For decades a steady stream of anthropologists have been trekking through the Minang villages, raking over every detail of daily life in a society which seems to operate in reverse of the rest of the patriarchal world. Particularly fascinating to early European visitors to the region was the high divorce rate and the right of Minang women to 'upgrade' or exchange husbands without as much as an eyebrow being raised. Some theorised that a matriarchal society was only one step up the evolutionary ladder from the sexual chaos of promiscuity. The Minang is the largest surviving matriarchal society in the world. There are few such opportunities to ask the question: what would women be like if they were brought up to believe they were entitled to priority in education, support in pursuing their ambitions and economic power? And does the ownership and control of property really make women leaders?

And what will be the fate of the matrilineal culture as industrialisation pulls it out of its isolation in the mountains and sends daughters like Yurnilawati into international careers?

From 1815 to 1825 the Minang fought a war against the conservative Muslim teachers who wanted to overthrow the *adat* in favour of their own view on the role of women. Islam remained, and is practised seriously in the region, but it did not defeat the *adat*. When a truce was finally called the matrilineal line remained. Islamic rules specify that a son must gain a larger share than a daughter of a father's property. But there are no rules governing female property. Islam did not state that a mother could not bestow her wealth upon her daughters, simply because it had not imagined that a mother would have property or authority of her own.

The road to Bukittinggi leads right up into the clouds, the moist, cool mist dividing the quiet mountain kingdom from the hot noisy coast. The domain of the matriarchs is clearly marked, the roofs of their traditional homes curving upwards like elves' shoes, smaller cottages clustered around, sitting low on the ground in deference to the main house.

The *adat* states that the big house is ruled by a woman. Her husband will come to live with her upon invitation, her sons should move to the *surao*, of village dormitories before puberty. Each daughter will be granted a space of her own in the main house and she, too, can invite a husband in. There are up to nine rooms, arranged around a common meeting space, each woman referred to as a 'pillar', the strength holding up the roof.

The ownership of the land goes back to the time of legend when the first Malay seafarers found their way down the rivers from the east coast of the island of Sumatra and began cutting back the towering rainforest by hand, and settled down to plant rice.

Where the matriarchal line begins no-one has ever discovered. Right across South-East Asia there are records of pre-colonial matriarchal societies and some influences remain in Thailand, the Philippines and even Vietnam. But, socially, religiously and politically women have lost much of their power in the region.

Nineteenth-century European evolutionists assumed the matrilineal family was universally the most ancient form of social organisation, which would be inevitably replaced by patriarchal society, writes Dr Joke Van Reenen in her study of the Minang. 'The highest stage of evolution was marked by the development of the conjugal family, consisting of husband, wife and children, with the husband as the head.'

Anthropologist J.J. Bachofen wrote in 1861 that matriarchy was the origin of the human family, believing it to be preceded by a state of promiscuity. Bachofen's evidence was taken mainly from Greek mythology and he argued that the matrilineal system could be traced back to the invention of agriculture by women and the passing down of land from mothers to daughters. A whole series of religious and cultural practices emerged centring on the Earth Goddess, which reigned for some time, until men revolted and established a male-based power structure.

The Minang men, explains Dr Wahidar Khaidir, who grew up in a rural village near Bukittinggi, in the early part of this century, were like 'dust on the tree trunks; one gust of wind and they would be gone. Women live in the house and when they get married the men come to them. If the family is important the girl can pick just about anyone she wants to father her children,' she says. 'The most important thing is to have a baby girl and then after that the fate of the husband depends on the wife, whether or not she still needs him.'

There are 'several standards' of husbands, she explains. Those irresponsible ones can be pragmatically handed back to their mothers or sisters. 'If you don't need your husband anymore, just don't open the door, because the man does not have the key to the house,' she says, eyes twinkling. 'In a traditional house there is a ladder to get in, if the husband comes home he waits downstairs politely coughing to be noticed, if no-one opens the door then he will just go back to his mother's house.'

If a girl is not born, she says, no-one looks for blame. Instead the man can leave and both can try again with a different partner.

Did she, herself, believe she was special just because she was a girl? 'Oh, yes, of course,' she says. 'When a boy is young he is physically and emotionally pampered, making him dependent on women; girls on the other hand are given a lot of responsibility and told "these are your properties, take care of them and learn well, otherwise people will cheat you".'

Modern-day Minang culture is really an adaptation of the original *adat*, says Dewi Fortuna Anwar, Dr Wahidar's daughter, a prominent academic herself. 'Anything that clearly violated the teachings of Islam within the customary laws would be done away with, but Islam didn't specifically rule against a female lineage, so that remained in force.' In some cases in which a Minang man later 'acquired' property, like motor bikes or cars, then they can be passed down to sons, according to Islamic law.

'But, in practice, *adat* is stronger in terms of social behaviour and is very, very strong in West Sumatra. Even when a family leaves the clan area and moves to Jakarta away from the *adat* the brothers will make sure that the sister is given the parents' home,' she says, even though Jakarta is dominated by the patriarchal Javanese culture.

'In the clan a husband is an honoured guest in his wife's home. Women are used to taking responsibility, they are used to managing their own properties and doing the sums. Even if a husband works on his wife's land he cannot assume management of the land as, say, a European husband might manage an heiress's fortune. My father, for example, could not become involved in my mother's land.' Dewi is the oldest daughter and the heiress herself. Although she followed her mother's academic career as far as London she was sent back to the clan lands for ten years during her childhood to learn the *adat*.

'I had to take care of my lineage responsibilities. My mother was doing her Masters degree in the United States at the time. Children are considered communal property and not just the property of the parents.'

Her own daughter, the next in line, has just returned to her parents in Jakarta after four years in the village.

Her mother had been sent away for a higher education to the island of Java, her first encounter with girls whose idea of attending university was to snare a decent husband. But Dr Wahidar continued to plan her own career and, later, chose her own husband, a man who shared the Minang culture. Her academic career took her to the United States and Europe.

In the West, she encountered strange notions of subservient Asian women, she says, laughing. 'It is much nicer to have your own money. I was amazed that my friends in the West had to ask their husbands for household money, in the West they treated women like slaves,' she smiles.

Yurnilawati is 29 years old. 'Almost thirty,' she corrects me, laughing. She is about to leave Indonesia for a posting in Washington as a correspondent for a major national paper. Her previous position was as the Indonesian producer for an American TV network. Of all her siblings she is the only one to have achieved a university education.

She is still single, well beyond the magic age of 25

when an Indonesian girl slips over the crest and slides down the other side into spinsterhood.

'My parents met each other at the wedding site,' she says, wide-eyed, 'I used to ask my mother how she could have married him?, just like that. She told me that she had asked around and had heard that her future husband was a nice man. Nowadays I am so impressed because they love each other so much, when I see them looking romantic I say "come on you old guys".'

Arranged marriages are not entirely a thing of the past, particularly in small towns and villages. 'People started approaching my father when I was about 23. Sometimes my Dad would tell me that if I didn't have enough time to find a man or I was too shy then he would find someone for me. There is so much pressure on me because I am the only girl and if I don't get married and have a girl then the clan line will end.'

By the time she was 25 the issue of marriage was 'very hot', she says. A distant cousin rang to tell her: '"Yurnilawati, we do not have a history of old maids in our family, so find a man and get married", she told me,' she laughs.

But, everything that had happened in her life so far had taught her not to stop now. As a young girl, she said, her father would encourage her to read and discuss politics and religion. At the dinner table it was the only daughter leaning forward on her elbows in heated debate with her father about the latest happenings in the world. He spent much of his limited cash on expensive subscriptions to foreign magazines so that her world view would be stretched way beyond the dusty streets of her home town.

'I think,' she says, and pauses, searching for the right word. 'I think my friends in the town, who were not Minang, thought I was really weird. I wasn't interested in buying lipsticks or getting married, I was ambitious, so if there was something I wanted to do I would do it.'

When she wanted to leave the family home to go to university on Java her father was reluctant, but finally relented. He also funelled the family resources into paying Yurnilawati's way.

'It was a kind of joke in the town that the parents who sent their daughters to university were just wasting their time because the girls got married and came back pregnant. My father asked me to study hard and not to humiliate him by wasting my time on boys. He asked me not to get a boyfriend until I had my degree. When I was younger he had talked to me about sex. Of course, he never said the talk was about sex because Minang people talk in parables, we never say things like that so directly. He told me a woman was like a glass, once it is broken it can never be repaired. I, of course, disagreed with him straight away and said I had learnt in school about glue, so you could glue it back together again.'

'"But it will never be the same" he answered. He said as a woman in Indonesian society I had to respect myself and be smart.'

Yurnilawati graduated at the top of the class and won one of a handful of full scholarships to a post-graduate journalism course in Jakarta. At the same time she perfected her English and took her first job on an English language paper. She has never moved back home to her town.

'My parents would be so happy if I married a Minang man, but actually it would be okay if I married any man, so long as he was a Muslim. In this society it is hard to go anywhere not married and without a boyfriend, people think "What is the matter with you?", she says with feigned concern. 'But, I don't care. In my job if I meet high ranking Government officials, for example, they tell me I am too picky. Really I would love to marry and settle, but every time I want to establish a serious relationship with an Indonesian man he says I am too independent, too smart. These are educated men, not village men, and this scares me.'

'I tried, but my boyfriend told me that if we got married I would have to stay home. Even my father said he didn't want me to stay home, he said he sent me to school to use my education, not to become a housewife.'

Her female friends, too, pulled her aside and said: 'Yurni, please compromise'. 'No,' she replied, 'I can't'. All along she kept with her the story about the broken glass, which allows me to ask a question in a similarly indirect way. Her answer is short and clear.

'Yes, I believe in that story, because in this society a woman has to show that she respects herself, sexual freedom does not give her freedom, the woman is always the victim.'

'If you compare the Javanese culture and the Hindu and Buddhist areas with the Minang they are much more patrilineal. Books from Java talk very specifically about the responsibilities and position of women in relationship to men,' says Dewi. 'If you are a gentleman, you have to have a horse and a wife. A wife is like a chattel. The local Javanese *adat* was very male oriented so Islam overlaid it and reinforced it. In Java it is usually believed that a male should be favoured in access to education if the family is poor because he will have to earn a living and support a family. In Minang culture the logic is reversed. In a lot of Minang families the girl is favoured so the women become teachers or nurses or even doctors and the men become farmers. It is not uncommon for a woman to marry a less qualified man.'

In Indonesia the Minang people make up only a tiny pocket within the vast population of 200 million. Yet, six of the Ministers in the national Government are Minang, as are a handful of members of the House of Representatives and a number of prominent business women.

'Power,' says Dewi, 'is directly related to economic control'.

Her mother agrees. 'Money, is everything, in a way. It is your honour and your pride. In Islam we say it is better to give than to ask, so if you don't have to ask that is very important for your status.'

Yurnilawati says she was always dreaming of travelling. She is telling her story to me in Jakarta, in the last few days of her wait for the working visa to the United States.

'My grandmother was a kind of independent woman, she was always travelling around looking for something new and buying up more rice fields. When she was sick recently she told my Mum to have all the properties put in her name and that means whether they like it or not it will all be mine. And when my Mum is getting old I will have to go home and see the house and properties, they are scattered all over the place. It will all be for me, there is no other choice,' she says, emphasising the 'no'.

And so the story turns full circle, back to the 'almost 30' single woman.

Actually, this is not just an interview. Yurnilawati is a close friend, the only one of all my female friends in the region whom I have interviewed for this book. And so I know the next chapter in the saga, but I want her permission to ask the next question on tape.

'Okay,' she says. 'Well, actually, I have found a very nice man and we want to get married and have children. And I would want to bring my daughters home to the clan lands. But,' she says, laughing self-consciously, 'this is a very difficult thing for my society and for me and my parents. They told me I could marry anyone so long as he is a Muslim. But, my boyfriend is American and he is a Christian. So this is a very tense situation for us. They even told me that if they had two daughters, well, maybe it would be okay, but not for the only daughter. So I brought him to my parents and presented him and they thought he was a very nice man, except that he was not a Muslim. So they would not accept him.'

And then she is crying. So I switch off the tape.

I have chosen this story to introduce my book because the case of the Minang women is the closest I have ever come to a real, living example of how life might be for women if they were brought up believing they were entitled to both support and power. Their expectations and ambitions, clearly, would be different.

This example is not, however, about the way most women in the Asia region view themselves. Prevailing cultural attitudes are not overwhelmingly positive. Although much of Asia is made up of young, independent nations born following World War II, with Constitutions which enshrine the equality of the sexes, history and culture hangs heavily across their lives.

I was first approached to write this book because, as a foreign correspondent in the region for much of the last decade, I had individually researched some of these issues for newspaper articles. My initial response to the publisher's inquiry was that it was impossible to write a book on 'Women in Asia'. That title was so broad, and swept so blithely across millenniums of separate histories in the world's most densely populated region, that no-one could pretend to even begin to tell the story of Asia's women.

This was not a trifling topic: this was the story of

half of the population of the Asia region: half of two-thirds of the world's population. But, still I continued to debate the issue in my head, privately admitting that I was attracted to the challenge.

To make matters more complicated this was the fastest growing region in the world, in the grip of spectacular social change. Asian-style industrialisation was transforming societies in a single generation from subsistence rice farmers to armies of industrial workers, from feudal politicians to corporate business managers. Even the currency crisis which began last year cannot change the direction of that transformation, or turn back the demographic realignments.

And even more than men it was the lives of women that were changing, as polygamy was outlawed, as factories opened up millions upon millions of jobs outside the village structure, as contraception became widely available or compulsory in Government family planningn programs.

But then I realised that was the point, wasn't it?

For the first time in the history of the world these stories could all be told at the same time, even by women who lived side by side in the same families. It was possible to interview a grandmother who endured the misery of being the daughter of a polygamous marriage and a young professional who had chosen a life in business and dispensed with the marriage altogether.

I also believed that the book would provide me with an opportunity to tackle some of the entrenched cliches. Images of Asian women in Western literature and film have been predominantly of submissive Oriental beauties, manipulative Asian sex goddesses, or victims of the sex industry. Western newspapers have been filled with stories of 'mail-order brides' and 'child prostitutes'.

And then, there have been the Prime Ministers and Presidents. How was it that Benazir Bhutto could become the first female leader of a modern Islamic nation in a country which enslaves its daughters to its men? That was a particularly pertinent question for me as I had once stood on a dusty road, swarming with men who were following the Bhutto campaign trail and had thrown my query hopefully out into the crowd.

'Would you vote for a woman?' I asked.

'Vote for a woman? I would vote for Bhutto's dog, so I would vote for his daughter,' came one reply.

Benazir was a Bhutto first, the daughter of Pakistan's martyred founding Prime Minister Zulfikar Ali Bhutto, and a woman second. As was Cory Aquino, former President of the Philippines and widow of assassinated opposition leader, Benigno Ninoy Aquino.

In Sri Lanka and Bangladesh similar stories of survivors were emerging. In Dacca two widows lead the competing political factions and in Colombo another political widow was elected to lead. There, for Chandrika Kumaratunga, the election itself was grimly familiar. Her own mother had become the first female Prime Minister in the modern world three decades earlier following the assassination of her father.

And in Burma it is a woman, Aung San Suu Kyi, who is leading the perilous battle against the military dictatorship, spurred on by a responsibility she feels to honour her late father, Burma's independence hero, Aung San.

Right across the region women occupy positions of extraordinary power and excruciating powerlessness. This is a region of enormous social and economic disparity and the process of rapid economic growth is unevenly spread.

In South-West Asia, the same region which has thrown up so many female Prime Ministers, mothers still seek to abort female foetuses or kill girls at birth. In South-East Asia women control vast business empires in societies still grappling with the routine patronage of prostitutes by married men.

And in China, spurred on by the one-child policy, the Communist Party state has failed to protect baby girls from female infanticide despite strict laws on equality. The economic boom of the past five years or so, though, has created a new role for women as status symbols for the new class of entrepreneurial men—that of stay-at-home wives. At the same time the boom in the south and the opening of the border with Hong Kong has revived the practice of polygamy as factory owners and managers set up second wives alongside their new businesses.

In Singapore the Government has been grappling with a new phenomenon, that of the single Asian woman. One generation of spectacular economic growth has produced an affluent society with both professional and educational opportunities for women. Yet, a large percentage of the nation's most qualified women are choosing never to marry: the rules of personal relationships have failed to change rapidly enough to match the expectations which have grown with their professional status. A similar trend is also being noted in Hong Kong, Bangkok and Jakarta.

But, at the same time, mushrooming factories are creating millions of new jobs for women: in dangerous, poorly paid positions. Hundreds of women have died in factory fires in the region, simply because they were locked in by their bosses and could not escape.

The road to power for women in Asia is a fascinating one. Rarely is it a story of ideological struggle defined by Western concepts of feminism, athough all the countries I visited have their own women's movement fighting to protect their rights. More often than not it is a story of pragmatism and fate. For the daughters of the rural farmers of Thailand prostitution is not often a moral issue, but a practical means to an end in the face of limited choices. For the Western women's movement the position of Benazir Bhutto in a nation with one of the world's lowest female literacy rates may have appeared extremely contradictory: but along the dusty streets of Pakistan it did not.

The research for this book really began when I first moved to Asia in 1986, as correspondent for the *Sydney Morning Herald*. That was when I began to listen. After three years based in the Philippines I moved to Bangkok from where I covered seventeen countries in South-East and South-West Asia. Trips in between took me as far north as Korea. After a three-year stint as a foreign editor in Sydney I am again based in the region, living in Jakarta.

When I decided on the format for this book I realised the only valid approach would be to go back to many of the countries I have worked in and to listen even harder. There were many interviews collected for this book which I have not included, simply because of space and length considerations, but they helped to shape the overall form.

The research process was slower than I had planned. On most of my trips, my own daughters tugged at my skirt. 'Are all brown people poor, Mummy? I'm brown aren't I,' one daughter noted, recently aware of her own Eurasian face.

In northern Vietnam, my own mother balanced precariously on the edge of the hot, sticky seat of a cyclo, my youngest baby daughter on her lap, as we crept through the peak hour crush in Hanoi on the way to an interview. My mother had taken a break from her own professional life to give me a hand.

That I was able to complete the research at all was thanks to a community attitude towards children in the region, which does not relegate responsibility to the nuclear family, but offers aunts, cousins and friends. The gap between rich and poor also meant I could afford childcare wherever I went.

I have deliberately not included Japan because the process of industrialisation there began well ahead of the rest of the region and so my goal of capturing a snapshot of the lives of women during a period of unprecedented historical change would not be valid.

For a less sound reason, from a research point of view, I have to admit that China is underrepresented. I have never been based in China and due to the restrictions imposed by the Government on journalists travelling there I decided to forsake an official Government view of the correct position of women for a quick dash across the border, claiming my occupation as 'housewife'.

India, too, is glaringly absent. The honest reason is practical. I stood for two days in the queue at the Indian High Commission in Colombo waiting for a visa and was defeated by the bureaucracy, the original book deadline already long gone. India is another book on its own, I assured myself, as I reluctantly cancelled my ticket rather than extend my wait.

I have attempted to include both empowering and depressing tales of women, because they both represent the truth of women's lives. There are positive and negative stories in all countries; some of the positive, I believe, lie disguised beneath social norms of public deference to husbands and fathers.

The book intends to highlight issues, not to draw either positive or negative conclusions. It does not seek to convey my judgement on the lives of the women who have been so generous in giving me their time and their trust, but reflects their own assessments of where they stand and how happy they are in that position. It also intends to discuss both public and private power and powerlessness, how roles within family units are as important as roles within Parliaments.

There is, of course, no such thing as an Asian woman. So this is the story of many Asian women. Perhaps, though, what they all have in common is inevitable, far-reaching social change. Dr Marwar Daud, a member of Parliament in Indonesia and communications technology specialist, put it most eloquently. 'Gossip, they used to say women gossiped, that is talk of no value because they had to rely on the men to bring the news back to the village. But, nowadays, with television and jobs outside of their own and travel and education women no longer gossip. They discuss. So, of course, life is changing.'

Louise Williams
Jakarta, March 1998

The maid and
the washing machine

The dispute began over the washing machine. The wife told the maid she was not permitted to use it and stood by watching as she tackled the piles of dirty clothes by hand. The husband told the maid that he wished she was not so tired. The more he worried the more work his wife found for the maid in the small Hong Kong apartment.

'I slept on the floor because there was no other space. I got up before dawn and worked until late at night. I just had to do everything the wife told me. I had to make sure the house was spotless because if I made a mistake they would say, "Well, what did you do all day?" I didn't answer back, I just kept silent and waited for Sunday, my day off,' says Anna, a pert, smiling Filipina domestic helper.

'The husband was kind and understanding. The wife wanted to get rid of me because she was jealous of his sympathy,' she says.

In the end it seems the wife won. The husband was forced to transfer Anna to the home of his brother, and hire a less appealing maid in her place. This is not an unusual story, Anna explains. The husbands often chase the maids. It is not necessary to elaborate. Her very Catholic sense of propriety ensures that much is left unsaid, although little is left misunderstood.

THE MAID AND THE WASHING MACHINE

Stories such as Anna's commonly begin in the Philippines where hundreds of thousands of hopeful young women are videotaped by recruitment agencies every year for offer in wealthier neighbouring countries like Hong Kong and Singapore. 'The plain ones always get the jobs first,' says Anna, because it is the wives who choose the maids.

Anna is a qualified high school teacher. But, from the age of eleven she began to formulate a different plan to escape the economic shackles of a government salary in a poverty-stricken nation. Her parents were proud of her achievements, especially when she left her village on the island of Mindoro for a primary school in the capital, Manila. There she lived a frugal life and religiously saved her money. When she had enough for the agency fee she joined the queue to get out of the Philippines. It was purely a pragmatic decision—part of a long term strategy. She would sacrifice her twenties to cleaning the toilets of Hong Kong's middle class. She would save every single dollar she could and return to the Philippines with enough capital to start a small business. As a teacher in the Philippines she would remain enslaved to a subsistence income, she says. In Hong Kong as a maid she could earn at least twice as much as her graduate colleagues back home.

When Anna arrived in Hong Kong five years ago, at the age of 23, she had no idea what was expected of her in her new job. So, she says, on her first day she went to the markets in the morning too scared to admit she could not cook the Chinese food that was expected on the table for lunch. She wandered hopefully amidst the unfamiliar smells, the concrete floor of the market awash with the pungent runoff from the fish stalls, the sellers snapping loudly at their customers in the determined battle over prices.

'I just waited until I saw some other Filipina maids and I asked them what to buy and what to cook. That's how I learnt. I just waited in the market and asked questions.' At night, she says, she cried. 'I really wanted to become a doctor but my parents couldn't afford the university fees, so I became a teacher. But I knew I would end up a maid. At first I didn't tell my parents because they knew what it meant for my life.'

On Sundays, the tens of thousands of maids in Hong Kong meet in the public squares near the ferry pier at Central, the pavements and parks swamped by their picnics. Most come from the Philippines but smaller groups from Indonesia, Sri Lanka and even Pakistan huddle together—seeking solace in their common memories and ambitions. Their chosen meeting place lies in the shadows of Hong Kong's corporate success. The massive Hong Kong Bank skyscraper towers overhead and velvet carpeted boutiques front the side lanes where the bargain bazaars and the barrows still hawk their wares.

Everything—every piece of second-hand clothing handed down by an employer, every old pot thrown away by the affluent residents of Hong Kong, every bargain picked up at a factory fire sale—is part of the plan. An economic network begins here on the pavements on Sundays and extends right back to the rice farming villages in the Philippines where even old, outdated clothes can be sold or traded because poverty does not permit the luxury of choice.

In Hong Kong there are laws to regulate the maids' lives. For some they provide protection from unscrupulous employers seeking cheaper household help than the legal salary dictates. For others they pose new problems. Officially, Anna is currently a non-person and for that she is grateful. When her last family left Hong Kong ahead of schedule she begged them not to report that her contract had ended, giving her the few more months on her visa to look for casual work before being sent back to the Philippines to rejoin an agency queue and pay another placement fee.

She is immaculately dressed but, right now, she has no home. Her explanation is vague but it seems that late at night she sneaks into the maid's quarters of an apartment where a relative works and is up, dressed and out again before dawn. This grabbing mentality is not greed. It is obligation. Women in the Philippines accept a great deal of financial responsibility regardless of the macho posturing of their men. Every maid has a goal. Some want to build their parents a concrete house, others want to educate their children or siblings.

Anna's easy smile does not mask her determination. 'I buy nothing for myself, I don't need any new clothes anyway. I save everything I can.' For her thirties she is planning to pick up where she left off and continue what she sees as the natural progression of her life. She wants to go home financially secure, get married and have children. Only requests for help from her family have chipped away at her nest egg. But, she concedes, 30 is already old in a country of teenage brides. Just one more contract, she thinks. Another two years and she will be clear and ready to leave. Anyway, Hong Kong will soon be closing down with the change-over from the British to the mainland Chinese in June 1997 (when this interview was conducted Hong Kong was in its last colonial days) so there is a sense of urgency in the pursuit of her goal. Under the Chinese, she says, the maids are unsure of their fate.

It is difficult to establish the source of her drive. Yes, she has disappointed her parents by surrendering the status of her profession to the pursuit of profit. And yes, she is untiringly efficient and cheerful but unable effectively to conceal her underlying sadness. Perhaps she believes the success she hankers for in the Philippines must be as great as the disappointments she has endured. Only then would she be able to demonstrate the wisdom of her choice.

The landing in the bell tower is rotten but the steps and the handrail are still firm, pulling us up over the mounds of bat droppings and through the trap door into the light. The Spanish-style church was built in 1732 and stands now much as it must have stood then: iron bars across empty windows, large plain blocks of stone, worn flaggings leading up to the altar where so many candles have been burnt in hope and thanks. In the plaza outside, a large, neat, quiet park, the carved stone chairs of the Spanish friars remain—chairs designed for sitting, contemplatively, in the weak rays of European sunshine. No-one ever sits in the sun in the tropics.

From the church tower we can see the coast in the distance, beyond the vast tracts of coconut palms and rice fields, the houses swallowed up by the vibrant green. It rained last night and the night before and the night before that. Not just steady rain, really pouring rain, the kind of tropical downpour in which the black storm clouds suddenly descend to meet the rice fields in a collision of lightning and thunder, drenching every inch of the land and all in its path. In the morning, though, there is nothing left but an odd cloud climbing high into the heavens, tinged with just a touch of grey, the beginning of tonight's storm.

The town of Leon is spotless, the neat patches of land along the road carefully cultivated with attractive rows of tomatoes. Only the odd vehicle disturbs the lumbering water buffalos, the whiff of exhaust strangely suffocating in the sweet air of the foothills.

The road from the 'city'—really a modest provincial town—cuts through the rice fields like a long, straight ribbon. When it reaches the base of the mountains at Leon it twists and climbs a little before running out of energy and dropping away into a wide, shallow river, generously scattered with steady stepping stones leading to the walking paths ahead.

Before the Spanish came to impose Catholicism upon the people of this island, the Gods lived in the mountains, hurling fire from their heights when they were displeased, and were worshipped by the farmers for the good harvests they could ensure. Island folklore was dominated by tales of female power. The Spanish chronicles are filled with frustrated attempts to stamp out indigenous animistic religions, their greatest defenders the female priestesses who took up arms against the foreign invaders.

The pre-colonial history of these islands of the Visayas was a story of sexual equality. Girls and boys were educated together and shared equally in inherited property. Daughters could comfortably succeed their fathers as tribal leaders if they were the first born. Women kept their names and their property upon marriage, were free to choose the number of children they wanted and retained the right to initiate a divorce.

But, wrote Maria Cecilia Locsin-Nava, in her review of the impact of colonisation on the position of women in the Visayas (Third Conference on West Visayan History and Culture, UP, 1992), the feisty priestesses eventually gave way to a new ideal: the 'fragile, helpless image of heroines of the Spanish period—virginal before marriage, prolific after and long-suffering to the very end'.

To Aunty Sel, as she is locally known, this quiet lush town is as claustrophobic as the Spanish double standard. For several years she worked here as a science teacher, leading her students on long, rambling hikes through the hills in her own personal attempt to make the best of her lot. Aunty Sel was born in a village down the road back to the city. She grew up in a small house dominated by the practical sense of equality of rural tradition, not the fawning, restrictive values of the Spanish Catholic hierarchy. The girls and boys worked together in the rice fields, that was just how it was.

Now in her mid-40s, Aunty Sel is 'still single'. The word 'still' is commonly used in a society which considers marriage the norm, a kind of public statement of hope for the victims of spinsterhood. Her *baranguay*, as villages in the Philippines are known, is just a collection of pocket-sized parcels of land worked by hand by men and women with dark brown skin and plain, faded clothes. There are no phones and just the odd car like the giant black Buick—wide bench seats, tattered upholstery and a slow, bouncing rhythm—we have borrowed. Apparently it is passed around from family to family on occasions that warrant such luxuries.

At the 'wet' market, the courtyard of stalls filled with small piles of vegetables and the nauseating odour of fermented shrimps, the young men lie in wait with their tricycles. These small motor cycles, shouldering tiny seats for at least five, are much less grand than their names might suggest. We opt for the 'Aircraft Carrier' and putt-putt down the road, our driver's eyes concealed by a pair of cheap, imitation Ray Ban 'Aviators', his biceps shown off to their best advantage by his muscle-Tee.

There is something inconsistent, though, about this village. In between the thatched huts patched with damp sacking and the puddles of mud where the ducks forage for leftover scraps lie neat concrete homes behind high metal fences. That is how you can tell, explains Aunty Sel. You can tell the families whose daughters have gone abroad to work as maids by their possessions. First it is a television set and then a brick house. Nothing fancy, but a brick house nonetheless, perhaps with a small tiled bathroom. Some families leave the raised thatch rooms of the past standing alongside, together with the old charcoal fire and the hand pumps, more for the sense of comfort, of familiarity, than out of a desire to show off.

'The first thing I did was to deliberately put myself down and treat the husband and wife as my superiors. When they came home I would tell them I understood how tired they must be and offer them a drink,' says Aunty Sel of the lessons learnt in more than a decade as a maid in both Singapore and Hong Kong. 'I tried to show them that I viewed them as my superiors. As a servant you have to stay very low,' she explains.

'Of course, I was already tired because I'd done all the jobs but I just tried to imagine I was not tired and I thought of the lesson from the Bible which says that one who humbles oneself will be lifted up,' she laughs.

Some maids, she says, behave like this: invisible, efficient, obedient. But many bring with them the pride of their professions: teachers, nurses, English literature graduates. 'Then they have trouble. When they fill in their professions on their way into Hong Kong they write "graduate nurse". But, they are not graduate nurses here, they are just maids,' she says. As a strict Catholic Aunty Sel sees no shame in humbling herself for the sake of harmony on the job.

'You don't really believe you are inferior do you?' I ask, looking across the bare wooden table, the farm dogs snapping around my heels, the humming tropical scene framed like a postcard in the open window. 'Well, of course not,' she says, eyes sparkling with amusement.

You just have to know how to play the game.

Aunty Sel lived for six years in Hong Kong. Before that she went to Singapore after doing a string of jobs, including that of a babysitter and cook in Manila, to earn the money she needed to get out. 'I didn't mind being a domestic, I just wanted to have a job. But, I thought if I am going to be a domestic and not a teacher why not do the same job for more money outside the Philippines and, at the same time, I could see other places. Filipinos can't afford to be tourists, so as a domestic I could see other parts of the world.'

Aunty Sel took her first overseas job in Singapore. 'Do you know what?' she says incredulously. 'In Singapore, if possible, they don't want you to sleep. You start work sometimes at 4 a.m. because you have to take care of the baby and while the baby is sleeping you have to do the washing and after that come the heavy jobs like the cleaning. When the parents come home they inspect everything, even the baby, and even then they want to see you working.' At that point, she says, she almost gave up. 'What is money after all, I thought, if you have to work like this.'

It is not surprising that the hanging of Flor Contemplaçion in Singapore, a Filipina maid convicted of murdering another maid and her young Chinese charge, provoked such outrage in the Philippines. More than 40 000 people attended Flor's funeral when her body was returned to Manila. The Singapore government said she had confessed to the crimes she was charged with, but the Philippines government claimed she had no legal representation and may have confessed in panic because she believed she would automatically receive a lighter sentence. Almost as sensational was the later case of a 15-year-old Filipina girl sentenced to death in the Middle East after killing her employer, who had raped her. That sentence was overturned after diplomatic intervention.

In the villages that offer up their daughters as maids there was another version of the Flor tragedy. The story went something like this: the Chinese child was an epileptic and the dead maid, Delia Maga, had left the child in the bath where the child had a seizure and drowned. On finding the child dead, Maga's enraged employer killed Maga and when Flor knocked on the door minutes later to visit, he attacked her as well and then accused her of the killings. There was not, nor has there subsequently been, any evidence to support this version, but it was widely believed.

The Philippines media, in a frenzy of national humiliation and rage, claimed Flor had been harassed, tortured and raped and had been electrocuted to force her to confess. The climax of the tragedy was captured in the dramatic image of Flor's grieving husband beside her open casket, splashed across the front page of a leading Manila daily. The only problem was, according to the Philippine Centre for Investigative Journalism, that the picture was posed. The grieving husband had not been quietly and dutifully awaiting his wife's return but—it seems—enjoying her earnings instead. 'What so many of the Flor stories did not explore was how the steady flow of migrant workers out of the Philippines is tearing apart the fabric of the Filipino family,' the Centre concluded in its study of the case.

Of the 500 000 women who leave the Philippines every year, the majority are seeking work as domestic helpers. 'It is ironic that hundreds of thousands of Filipinas minister to the personal comfort and convenience of foreign employers the world over while leaving their own children and families to fend for themselves,' noted one of a collection of essays entitled *Filipino Women Overseas Contract Workers, At What Cost?*, published in 1992.

It is difficult to raise such personal issues in many Asian cultures. Do husbands really wait faithfully on the sidelines? How frequently are young women raped or coerced into relationships by their employers? How are the sexual needs of women fulfilled, isolated as they are for many years from their families?

There is enough anecdotal evidence to suggest that, under these circumstances, fidelity in marriage does not often survive. Men in the villages drink and court women, and some women in the big cities have affairs or, sometimes, join a lesbian network. But these issues are rarely discussed in the first person, face to face. Unlike western societies, which have gradually become accustomed to such navel gazing, few Asian societies have abandoned the public concept of 'face' in favour of such private truths.

Aunty Sel lasted only three years in Singapore and went home to try for the somewhat kinder climate of Hong Kong. In the process, she says, she became a recruiting agent herself before landing her pick of the Hong Kong jobs. 'I was trying to convince some of my friends that if they wanted to get married then they had better stay home with their husbands and not look for a job as a maid overseas. Men are men and a man can't wait three years. It's like a sad movie, a big cry,' she explains. 'I think that men and women are quite different. For the men their life is too easy just depending on the wife, some of them leave the children with the in-laws and just enjoy their lives. When the wife gets back there is nothing, all the money has been spent, sometimes he uses it for drinking and gambling and looking for other women, and there is nothing to show for her work.'

But, she says, she also blames the women for taking all the responsibility on their shoulders and 'spoiling their husbands'. 'The women get very upset so I tell them to stay in the village and let him look for work instead.'

Aunty Sel says she has already forgotten her past sweethearts and settled into spinsterhood. 'Yes, it is a kind of freedom. Nobody tells you what to do or what to think, you can go anywhere you like,' she says, efficiently brushing the topic aside.

She lives alone in the village in the home she built for her parents with her earnings because her parents are now dead, her siblings have left, and there is no-one else to come home to her house. But, she says, all wiry and energetic, 'I might just take one more contract and see a little more of the world.'

Splitting the bamboo

Mrs Corazon Aquino, former President of the Philippines, is speaking so effusively about her martyred husband that she seems to have forgotten the original question was actually about herself. For all her married life Cory Aquino, the shy traditional wife of the Philippines opposition leader Benigno Ninoy Aquino, prepared herself for his victory over the then dictator President Ferdinand Marcos and for her eventual role as First Lady by his side.

When Ninoy was cut down on the tarmac of Manila airport in a hail of assassin's bullets in 1983 Cory was 'just a plain housewife', tending to her five children in political exile in Boston. When she brought her family back to the Philippines and found herself leading the extraordinary mass uprising against soldiers loyal to Marcos, she was still a plain housewife. And when she became the country's first female President in 1986, one of only three female world leaders at the time, she had filled in her occupation on the Presidential nomination form in just the same way.

Cory was a mother and widow first, a firm believer in the Catholic church and the value of family lunches on Sunday. She was modest and polite and lacking in the political ambition to go beyond a single six-year term. She was a shining example of womanly goodness in a society that still enthusiastically honours the Latino conventions of machismo left behind by its Spanish colonisers.

Even in the fear and chaos that swept Manila in the numerous attempts by rightist military factions to topple her Government, Cory was busy organising deliveries of food for the personnel trapped inside the Presidential Palace. Yet it was she, not the politicians jostling for influence around her, who was President and Commander-in-Chief of the fractious Philippines armed forces during the crucial transition from dictatorship to democracy. And behind the public symbols of female subservience in the Philippines lies a very different story of the real power of political wives and daughters.

'If my husband hadn't been killed, I would not have been anything. I would have remained a plain housewife,' Cory has insisted on so many occasions. 'My husband was only 23 when he was elected to Congress. I called him a walking encyclopedia. He was very articulate, he was a speed reader, he really absorbed what he read and related it to others. I guess that was what gave me an inferiority complex.'

In the early years of her marriage Cory admits she struggled—a daughter of the élite, overwhelmed by the hardships of life in the small rural town her husband represented in Congress. She retreated indoors, soon to become a house-bound addict of television soap operas. That her own life was to become a drama even more compelling to the rest of the world was something she could not even imagine.

President Marcos took the first step in altering her fate when he addressed the nation in 1972 to announce the imposition of martial law. Ninoy was the first political prisoner on the arrest list.

The political struggle between Marcos and Ninoy was not a simple battle between the forces of dictatorship and the forces of democracy. It was, in fact, something more personal. So intertwined were the lives of the families of the Philippines élite that Ninoy had once dated Imelda Roumaldez (Marcos), who later gained considerable personal power and wealth through her marriage to President Marcos. But Cory, born a little further up the social ladder than the parvenu Imelda, was altogether more refined and humble and while the political battle was played out between the two men it was often said that Imelda, the jealous social climber, had pitted herself against Cory and was rumoured to have personally approved Ninoy's eventual assassination.

Today, ten years after she assumed the Presidency, Cory is poised, calm and very much in command. (This interview was in 1996.) That she so handsomely fulfilled the traditional role of a politician's wife did not reflect a nature equipped only to follow. More accurately, perhaps, it reflected her determination to succeed in whatever role fate offered her.

'They say life begins at 40,' she says with the wisdom of reflection. 'My husband and I were 39 when he was arrested and we both celebrated our fortieth birthdays while he was in prison. I often look back at those seven years and seven months as our greatest learning experience. Before martial law I always believed my husband could do anything and everything. It was devastating that he was no longer available to me and that he no longer had the powers that I had become used to.'

For an entire year Cory did not see Ninoy, and was forced to accept that she could do some things herself. When the Marcos government introduced weekly conjugal visits she began what she calls her 'undergraduate course in politics', her husband being her private tutor. 'But even then,' she says, 'I didn't think of entering politics myself'.

President Marcos eventually allowed Ninoy to flee to the United States, but the Opposition leader was never comfortable with the safety of political exile and decided to return. He knew the risk he was taking and asked Cory and the children to stay behind in Boston. Cory was at home in their Boston bungalow when the call came through. Her husband's blood was already drying on the tarmac of Manila Airport where he had been shot as he stepped off the plane. The police silhouette drawn around the fallen body would become the symbol of the struggle against Marcos. In many ways that chilling scene, forever frozen in Philippine political history, was Ninoy's most powerful stroke.

Martyrdom has considerable social currency in the Philippines. The legacy of Spanish colonialism is a real life melodrama built around honour and shame. In both the impotent drunken posturing of groups of young men seeking to establish their authority over their own thatch huts, and the real military and gang violence that controls so many people's lives, machismo appears to rule supreme. The pious, grieving widow Cory held considerable social appeal.

'At a memorial service for my husband in Boston an American academic said, "Cory, you might as well start thinking about running for President." I thought, Yes, yes, these people are just trying to be nice to me.'

But, the pressure continued. To every question Cory would reply in the same way: 'I am just a plain housewife, I will continue supporting the Opposition. What do I know about becoming a President?'

It was not false modesty. Cory did not covet power as did the increasingly flamboyant and extravagant Imelda Marcos who wielded her influence at her husband's side. In fact, she says, she felt she had already fulfilled her personal quota for suffering, and that she could now retreat into the safety and anonymity of private life. But in October 1985, having returned to the Philippines, Cory received a letter that made her very, very angry.

A former classmate of Ninoy's, now safely settled in the United States with his family, wrote:

> I can appreciate what you have gone through but what if you refuse to accept the challenge and Marcos wins the next election? Will it not bother your conscience that there was a chance to do something and you didn't even try?

'I was really mad that he was lecturing me from thousands of miles away but he was right, it did bother my conscience. It was a kind of self-discovery. Until then I had only thought it was my husband who would be President.'

So Cory went home to challenge her husband's most bitter enemy. 'When I told my eldest daughter about my decision she said, "Oh mum, haven't we suffered enough?"

'Of the five children only the youngest was excited and perhaps she didn't fully understand the trial that awaited us.'

In some ways it was an extraordinary decision. Cory had chosen to step into a struggle defined by symbols of machismo and hinging very much on the tens of thousands of soldiers of the powerful armed forces. But what that analysis fails to acknowledge is the power women in the Philippines have always held behind the scenes. While it is true that few public decision-making positions have been held by women, the power of the family, rather than the individual, has long granted wives and daughters considerable private influence.

According to the pre-Christian Filipino myth of creation, men and women were created by the splitting of bamboo into two equal parts, a mythology that does not shackle women to a concept of physical or

intellectual weakness or inferiority. The two parts of
the bamboo were called *malakas* (strong) and *maganda*
(beautiful) and, although the quality of strength was
originally assigned to the male, the status *malakas* can
apply equally to both men and women.

'The *malakas* concept implies one's closeness to the
powers that be. The brother of the President is *malakas*,
just as the wife of the President is *malakas*. Even
employees of the President are considered *malakas*,'
wrote academic Mina Roces in the *Asian Studies Review*.
'Power is not concentrated on the individual official
but perceived to be held in varying degrees by his
kinship group. It is through their kinship ties with male
politicians that women exercise their power.'

Thus Cory, all public displays of humility aside, was
the daughter of a powerful family of *hacienderos* (big
land owners). It was not culturally inappropriate for
her to inherit her husband's considerable political
power on his death.

The apparently contradictory role of women in the
Philippines is explained by Dr Albina Fernandez in this
way:

> In pagan times it was the women who were the priest-
> esses, it was the women who could heal and it was the
> women who mediated between the natural and the super-
> natural. The priestesses were the focal point of the
> religion and were quite powerful.

On 27 April 1521, Spanish explorer Ferdinand
Magellan was killed by a tribal chief when he landed
on the Philippines island of Mactan. About thirty years
later the Spanish returned in force to colonise the
islands and convert their inhabitants.

> When the Catholic friars arrived they could not under-
> stand the traditional bride price. In the Philippines the
> family of the man paid the family of the woman because
> her family lost so much of value in terms of her role on

the farm and her reproductive value. In the West families were just too eager to get rid of their daughters, especially in the middle class where women were confined to decorative roles dependent on their husband's wealth.

If we look at the early accounts of the Spanish chroniclers they say that the position of women here was rather high.

Women had the right to divorce their husbands, they had the right to property and they controlled the running of farms and the weaving of cloth to the extent that one foreign visitor advised traders to go into the kitchen to make a deal because it was the women who could really make it possible.

But, the Spanish friars considered the women of the Philippines of loose morals and set about re-educating them.

'It was the Spanish who invented machismo here.' But it was and is, argued Dr Fernandez, merely 'sexual Catholicism'. The Spanish succeeded in introducing the double standard, the concepts of the 'madonna' and 'whore', the good and bad woman as defined by her personal morality. The most significant impact was on personal relationships. Prior to Spanish colonialism a married woman could take a lover, in the same way as a man. She just needed to pay a little compensation to her husband and then everything was okay.

'Now if a man is cuckolded and he kills his wife in rage the law does not require him to be penalised,' says Dr Fernandez.

But, at the same time women have retained much of their economic power at every level of society. In the village it is the women who control the markets and in the families it is the women who run the budgets.

The raucous real life soap opera of love triangles and romantic intrigue rolls on in the villages and cities, in the cinemas and on the TV screens. But, the thwarted wife or girlfriend of the Philippines doesn't meekly accept her position, head bowed. With a wide swing of her arm she strikes back, publicly slapping the offending male across the face.

While Cory's popularity continued to grow, that of Imelda Marcos continued to slide.

Imelda liked to call herself the mother of the nation. But, in truth, she had broken all the rules. While Cory could stand one step back behind her husband in public Imelda could not bear to limit her power to the private domain.

Imelda Marcos held no official power. Yet, she managed to expand the office of the 'first lady' to the extent that her husband's rule was often referred to as a 'conjugal dictatorship'. In the 21 years that her husband held the Presidency she paraded her natural beauty and gushing hospitality from one political rally to another. She immersed herself in construction projects of extraordinarily voluminous proportions: building the country's longest bridge, the Coconut Palace entirely from coconut shells, the Film Centre, the Lung Centre and Kidney Centre, to name a few, at a time when the majority of the population was living in abject poverty.

Her own family began to benefit considerably from the economic favours her position facilitated and it is often said that the Romualdez clan built a greater business empire than even the Marcos family.

In 1975 Imelda became the Governor of Metro-Manila, her first official role. Later she was appointed the Minister for Human Settlement, chairwoman of numerous Government corporations and without any official diplomatic credentials she held talks with several US Presidents, as well as the leaders of China and the then Soviet Union. She is also reported to have signed a major loan agreement with the World Bank.

Ironically, many people blamed Imelda's insatiable desire for public power for her husband's demise. When his Government finally fell it was not the image of the dictator being whisked off into exile aboard an American helicopter that remained in people's minds, it was the hundreds of pairs of shoes that his greedy, scheming wife had left behind.

Long before her political contest with Marcos, Cory had actually recruited an unusual political ally: her Catholic God.

Like so many mothers in the Philippines it was Cory who safeguarded the family's spiritual future, and spoke often of her practice of deep prayer.

It is not surprising then that as the nuns and priests led the people out onto the streets to face the military's tanks and banks of soldiers, Cory was holed up in the provincial town of Cebu, seeking strength through religious retreat. Religion was not just a cynical political prop: the support of her church was a critical factor in her success. And the image of womanly goodness that the conservative Catholic church nurtured—that of a long suffering, ever loyal mother and wife—fitted Cory perfectly.

'In this country, at least men still treat women with respect and kindness, so that was an advantage,' she said. 'I always thank my religious faith; with faith comes courage and you just have to believe that if this is something you should do then just go ahead and do it regardless of the consequences. With each step it was like a new discovery of the new Cory. I could not have done it alone, there was an Almighty helping me along the way.'

It was a magnificent moment when the staff of the Electoral Commission began to walk out right across the country. The votes they were counting showed a landslide victory for Cory but the result the Marcos Government announced showed the opposite. Marcos was cheating crudely.

Cory had the formidable church network behind her. In the tense stand-off between pro-Cory civilians and the soldiers of the Marcos Government it was the nuns who stood in the front line—face to face with the machine guns and tanks—their only weapons bunches of flowers to place in the barrels of the guns.

When a powerful faction of the armed forces swapped sides to join the hundreds of thousands of anti-Marcos protesters occupying Manila's main high-way, Cory's victory was sealed. But the fact that she was not alone would later become a powerful criticism of her Presidency. She was surrounded by relatives and old friends who had worked hard in the campaign against Marcos and were now jostling to collect their dues: power and influence in the new Government. She was said to be weak and unable to make hard decisions.

In the middle of the bloodiest coup attempt against her by a right-wing military faction, Cory, Commander-in-Chief of the armed forces, was said to be cowering under her bed at the Presidential Palace. A local news-paper even ran the story on its front page.

'I knew there was a great danger and that I could be killed at any moment. But I knew how important it was for me not to leave Malacanang [the Palace], to stay on regardless. I had to be visible, to stay on the phones to the generals and the colonels, so that the military would see that I was not afraid. My two

41

daughters were with me at the time and one was really so upset and nervous she was crying so I said, "Well, just pray and whatever it is God will not abandon us, what we are doing is the right thing. We have no other choice."'

In retrospect Cory says, yes, she was scared 'but I did not show it'. And, she says, she was not under the bed. In a celebrated court case the shy, traditional wife sued the newspaper that doubted her strength.

Cory sees no need to pretend that she was just another leader, regardless of her sex. She was a female leader and that was significant. It was significant in the way people treated her and in what it meant for all the women of the Philippines, she says.

Once, during her Presidency, she was asked by a group of foreign journalists about the trials of being a woman and head of state. She answered, without a hint of embarrassment, that a male Commander-in-Chief of the armed forces could just hop out of bed and go straight out onto the streets during a military coup attempt. She, on the other hand, a woman in her fifties, had to stop to pay a little attention to her hair and make-up.

Cory would not call herself a feminist or a crusader. 'One of the advantages of being a woman is so many doors are open to you,' she says, smiling ruefully. 'There are not too many women heads of state so we are known all over the world. One of my assistants always joked about my face value. In my time there was just Margaret Thatcher, Benazir Bhutto and me, and so many men in suits. I remember at the bicentennial celebrations in Paris the TV presenters had trouble identifying so many heads of state but they all recognised me,' she laughs.

The hardest job, though, was being the Commander-in-Chief of the armed forces.

'It was quite a problem not just in terms of the

generals but right down to the enlisted men. They just looked at me and thought, how can we have a female commander? She is just a woman, what would she know?'

Her mechanism for coping, she says, was to introduce promotions strictly in line with seniority, bypassing all the behind-the-scenes power-broking that characterised a highly politicised and powerful armed forces. 'I got a lot of flak for my promotions, but I meant what I said and I stuck with my decisions.'

Cory was also widely criticised by women's groups, for her stand on contraception and abortion in such a poverty-stricken nation. She supported the position of the Catholic Church. Filipinas would just have to keep having lots of children in one-room shacks, even though they could barely afford to feed and clothe them. This is not an issue she is interested in debating, as though she had some kind of choice in the matter. It is just a matter of fact. But for her there are other kinds of choices about public power and the inevitability of change.

'I put a number of women in very sensitive Government positions and the fact that they performed well contributed to the standing of the rest of the female population. In my case, if my husband hadn't died I would not have carved out a separate career or profession for myself. But my daughters all have their own jobs so this is no longer true for their generation.'

At the port of Manila, where semi-trailers lugging containers squabble with overloaded cyclos for space on the road, and ferry passengers dragging overnight bags stream along the dirt verges, there sits an old, white Spanish building. Upstairs, within the cool, air-conditioned inner office, sits the Philippines' most popular Senator. Outside, the hopefuls seeking her patronage wait on the rows of sticky, vinyl chairs.

Senator Gloria Macapagal Arroyo was one of the competent women appointed to the bureaucracy by the then President Aquino. She held a doctorate in economics from Georgetown University but was little known for her own accomplishments.

'I was known as the daughter of a former President,' she says of her father, Diosdado Macapagal, who had risen from abject poverty in a rural village to lead the Philippines in 1961, but was ousted by President Marcos four years later. 'People used to say to me that if they had my genes they would be in politics. I used to laugh it off until I realised they were not joking.'

Senator Macapagal is both petite and attractive with the smooth skin and boundless energy of someone considerably younger than her 47 years (1996). She is also exceedingly smart. In the very first move of her political career Senator Macapagal flew to Hong Kong, Singapore and Italy to launch her campaign. Her targets were the hundreds of thousands of Filipinas who flee poverty at home to work as maids in wealthier economies, a constituency never before considered by traditional politicians. 'I went and listened to them and told them I would do my best,' she says.

Word filtered back to the villages. Every maid who sends money home enjoys status in dirt poor communities of thatch huts. That they trusted Gloria Macapagal earned her millions of votes. In the Senatorial elections of 1994 she won the highest number of votes ever recorded.

As a daughter of a President, she says, she grew up in a household where her father ruled supreme. Her mother, a doctor, gave up work to get married and devoted her intellectual energies to her children and her home. In line with the prevailing political culture, all family members were expected to assist in the father's political campaign. At home, the children were expected to comply with their mother's strict discipline and sense of family hierarchy. But although her father played the patriarchal role, says Senator Macapagal, he educated his two daughters just as he educated his two sons.

'When I went to school our biggest aim was to get married. If a woman became successful in a career we cheered her, but at that time we didn't think of following,' she said.

Senator Macapagal married well, and raised three children. She later lectured at university, the burden of her domestic responsibilities lightened by the privileges of her class. Like so many women of the élite she had family nannies and cooks and cleaners to help her fulfil her domestic role. When President Aquino came to power Gloria Macapagal became the Undersecretary of Trade and Industry, bringing to a tired and corrupt bureaucracy her late father's ideals and scruples. It was Cory's brother who later convinced her to run for the Senate.

'This culture of machismo, the idea of women as madonnas and whores, puts wives and mothers on pedestals so my sex was an advantage,' she says. 'That I was already known because of my family background also earned me a lot of support.'

But her main consideration was her husband. She said she could not say 'yes' until she had his enthusiastic support, not just his grudging permission. Politics is a family game and her husband, a prominent lawyer, would have to become the political 'wife', standing by her side night after night as their caravan took their political rallies to the provincial villages and towns.

Just as Cory Aquino despatched her five children to towns across the Philippines, so did Gloria

Macapagal. 'I was raised in a rather disciplined, hier-archical manner and I raised the children in the same way. I didn't ask them what they thought, I simply told them that they would be expected to help in the campaign.

'Some days I would have seven rallies in one prov-ince. I would finish one speech in one town and go to the next town. If I had any time in between I would go to the market or look for a fiesta so I could walk through and talk to as many people as I could. Because I was younger than most male politicians I could keep up a faster pace. Most of the time I could sleep only four or five hours a night.'

Her status as a wife and mother, she says, 'enhanced my political acceptability'. But she does not believe in just those roles. As a female politician, she sees herself as a crusader with a double burden, that of a politician and that of a feminist. And, naturally, she has her fair share of stories about trying to push women's issues in Parliament. Her efforts to introduce new legislation to protect battered wives were met with the predictable barbs: 'What about battered husbands?' her male colleagues quipped.

Now she is working on sexual harassment and access to credit for poor women. Yes, she says, in many ways Filipina women are strong and can boast of their matriarchal tribal history and economic independence. But there are many more problems to tackle. And, she says, as a woman politician it is her responsibility to represent women.

When her old school held their latest reunion, she was surprised to find that most of her friends had followed her into a new era, beyond the lives of Cory and Imelda. 'Almost all my friends had good jobs of their own now, even though we had aspired to mar-riage. The only one who wasn't working was the wife of a director of a bank who would have had high status in the past, but I think she felt a little uneasy amongst us,' she says.

In a penthouse in Manila's business district of Makati, Imelda Marcos, widow of the late dictator, now lives off the residual trickles of power of her once vast empire. In a decade her life has turned full circle. The Philippines is now a democracy so she was elected to Congress in a region that still remembers her husband's political favours. Her sense of melodrama has not faded, but her outlandish statements and wails of grief over her new-found poverty and impotency have little effect on a tired public audience.

The focus has shifted several blocks south to the home of socialite and charity queen, Rose Marie 'Baby' Arenas. 'Baby' was once a wife. Now she is a much more famous mistress.

According to local gossip, her youngest child was fathered by the current President of the Philippines, Fidel Ramos, despite having been registered under the name of her then husband. 'Baby' has since been divorced. Part of the evidence cited of the boy's parentage are the frequent 'private trips' made by President Ramos to Switzerland where the teenager is at boarding school.

But perhaps more important are 'Baby's' public activities. How is it that she so frequently appears by the President's side and hosts a 'Wednesday Club' at her home where politicians close to the President plot strategies? And, according to a newspaper series prepared by the Centre for Investigative Journalism, 'Baby' was using her access to Malacanang Palace to boost businesses, influence Government appointments and 'facilitate' duty-free shipments for friends.

The articles argued that her power was 'both real and perceived'. 'Baby's' defence that she was merely helping her friend President Ramos and not meddling in politics did not amount to a convincing denial. On her own admission she was involved in 'lobbying', to fulfil promises made when she led the fundraising efforts for President Ramos' campaign in 1992.

That President Ramos remains married while yet having a different First Lady by his side is not entirely inconsistent with the prevailing double standard of machismo. But the mistress is not necessarily a victim. She is merely sharing the *malakas* status with the official wife.

'In a country of underground kinship politics and underground political wheeling and dealing it may be argued that a woman who holds power behind the scenes is immensely powerful indeed,' writes Mina Roces.

'In some cases power held by the woman may even seem to have unlimited parameters since it is by its very nature unofficial and therefore its limits remain undefined.'

Cory Aquino is glowing with good health. As a private citizen she looks years younger than she did as a harassed President. Imelda Marcos' home is close to her family's office block. She is well aware that Imelda is back and lurking nearby.

'We live in a democracy and unfortunately even those who fought against us and denied us our freedom can now take advantage of the rights of living in a democracy. As far as forgiveness is concerned I have always said that someone must first ask you for forgiveness and show some repentance. I also believe in forgiveness with justice.'

There has been little justice for Cory. The death of her husband has never been officially traced back to either Ferdinand or Imelda Marcos.

'I believe all of us have to die and my husband said many times that if he could choose how he could die he would like to die for his country. My husband and I both considered it a privilege to offer one's life for one's country.'

Cory is polite and calm. Then, one of the small group around her asks how far she would be prepared to go in the future to prevent the return of dictatorship to the Philippines. Now, she is clearly annoyed.

'In the past I risked my life,' she says, bristling. 'What more do you want from me?'

I am not a prostitute

'In all honesty it was the money,' says Jade, a name of good fortune she has chosen for herself, in defiance of the reality of her life. Eight years ago Jade took a job as a hostess in Japan, learning to massage male egos in the interests of the bar owner's profits. A couple of months ago she was back in Tokyo in the Supreme Court taking a landmark paternity claim against her Japanese former boyfriend on behalf of her two-year-old son, the exorbitant cost of DNA testing having been raised by hundreds of Filipina hostesses and entertainers in Japan.

In the Philippines young women like Jade are known as Japayuki-sans. Technically, they are entertainers hired to grace the clubs frequented by the male corporate warriors of Japan's economic success. In the poor rural villages of the Philippines aspiring young teenage girls practise their song and dance routines in their bare feet, kicking up dust in the local plazas and belting out heavily accented renditions of soppy American pop songs alongside tinny ghetto-blasters.

The village girls have heard the tales of fantastic wealth and watched the Japayuki-sans return home weighed down with the televisions and VCRs of their material success. The power of the big Yen salaries dwarf the pathetic Filipino peso so they take their clumsy routines to Manila: all the qualifications they need for an entertainer's visa to Japan.

Technically, entertainers are not prostitutes. But in reality few have the show skills that once made the Filipino folk troupes famous right across Asia. An entertainer's role is to make the bar's male customers so comfortable that they will stay on into the night buying round after round of overpriced drinks. A song and dance might help but a coy smile at a drunken grope will probably be more effective. And to keep the customers coming back it won't be long before the bar owner will advise his entertainers to humour requests for further services after closing time.

Jade is sitting facing me across a formica table, tense and emotional. She was not a prostitute in Japan. She is not a prostitute now. She feels the need to clear this up right away. It was not that I had even asked her to be so specific. She is weighed down so heavily by her own perceptions of a judgemental society that it is difficult to separate the facts from her sense of shame.

'I thought it was so exciting,' she says of her decision to apply for a visa to Japan at the age of 25. Even then she was relatively old, so she lied about her age in the hope of stretching out the job as long as possible. Thirty is already too old in the entertainment business. At first she took a six-month visa at US$850 a month. US$500 for Jade, US$350 for the agent. A fortune in the Philippines, a pittance against the Yen. And she kept on going back: seven contracts in all over almost five years. 'I was on holidays from university. I come from a poor family and I had a friend who had a promoter acquaintance so she booked me for the entertainment division. I was planning to go back to college but, honestly, money is so addictive.'

The system was very efficient. The Japanese agent met Jade's first group of eighteen at the airport, took them to a big house, got them dressed up in tight, satin, mandarin-style suits and put them straight to work the same night. 'For a provincial lass it was all a bit "Wow!" The cabaret looked like such a nice place. We had to keep the men there for as long as possible. There were so many different characters to deal with. The older ones, though, loved to touch us and pat our bottoms. We were taught how to fend them off naturally. When they wanted to peek at our breasts we would lead them out onto the dance floor. They were mostly married men. They were mostly bored or tired.'

At first Jade did not tell her parents. When her father found out he was very angry. 'I guess he was ashamed of me. They are provincial folks. I was able to save and I sent my family money but my father gave it back and told me to keep it. Other people there in my village thought I was a prostitute.'

It is a familiar tale. Lured by easy money into lifelong disappointment. But, Jade's story has a nasty twist which explains the source of her deep-seated shame. In 1990 she met a single Japanese engineer in her bar. He was 37, ten years her senior. He pursued her doggedly, so she surrendered to his attentions. 'I was afraid to take him as my boyfriend. But he followed me even as far as my village in the Philippines where he proposed.'

Jade and her boyfriend went to the Japanese embassy in Manila but, somehow, he didn't have the appropriate documentation with him for the marriage to proceed. But in the eyes of her parents and her neighbours she was, at last, engaged to a respectable engineer. In retrospect she knew something was wrong when she became pregnant for the first time. He was angry and adamant. He did not want the baby, despite all the earlier romantic cooing about making a baby together. Jade aborted once, then again, then a third time.

This is a very sensitive topic. In the Philippines abortion is illegal. But it is not the laws of the state which dispense the punishment of guilt. It is the Catholic church which has taught women to endure motherhood, no matter how unsuitable their circumstances. Backyard abortions are available but they are dangerous and come laced with eternal damnation. It is difficult to assess exactly what we are talking about here. Eventually, I realise Jade is not talking about a clinical procedure but a potion—modern drugs or traditional medicines, I am not sure—which induces a miscarriage, especially with the help of a *heilot*, an old woman skilled in abdominal massage.

But Jade still wanted to have a baby and fell pregnant for a fourth time. Despite the booming warnings from the pulpit, pregnancies out of wedlock are common in the Philippines—perhaps because the use of contraceptives, too, carries with it the guilt of a religious breach. And again her boyfriend raged.

'I bought a lot of medicines, I tried so many drugs but my stomach just kept getting bigger and bigger. He had always told me that he wanted us to have a baby but by the time I was four months pregnant he was gone. I went to the Japanese Embassy but they said they only dealt with diplomatic matters. When I knew I really had been abandoned I told my parents. My parents just kept silent. I was so scared about having the baby. In the province people would scorn me and I was already almost 30 so I wouldn't find anyone to marry now. My friends had warned me, they thought I was a bit smarter than that.'

Jade went to seek help from a support group in Manila but when she was due to give birth her mother arrived to help her and offered to take the baby back to the village and raise him herself. 'I took it as the best thing. I can't feel any motherly feeling and, besides, he took his father's features. When I see my son, I see his father's face, it is so painful,' she says, through floods of silent tears.

For some time Jade believed that perhaps if she found her boyfriend her problems would be over. Then, late last year she did. He was living as he had always lived in Japan: married with three children, 18, 15 and 10. Not only did he deny knowing her, he denied fathering her son. How could an entertainer possibly make such an outrageous accusation? How could she, with all those men leering and breathing heavily against her neck, possibly know who the father was?

I have not asked, and will not ask Jade about the practice of *dohan*. Already she is hanging by a thread to her self-esteem, only her insistence on her fidelity to her Japanese boyfriend separating her from the moral abrogation of prostitution. *Dohan* is the name given to the compulsory meeting with customers outside the clubs, away from the protection of colleagues. Some clubs set up to 25 *dohans* a month and fine the entertainers for every meeting missed.

According to Philippine government statistics, more than 57 000 entertainers travelled to Japan in 1991 on official visas. At least as many went on tourist visas and sought jobs as entertainers illegally. This is despite the tales of horror which filter back: girls forced into prostitution, girls raped and, in several highly publicised cases, girls drugged and kidnapped or beaten to death. The trafficking in women in south-east Asia is—at least superficially—a simple story of poverty and wealth. Poor rural girls from the Philippines, Thailand and Taiwan make up the bulk of entertainers in Japan. But, each individual case is overlaid by the very specific filters of culture, history and Government policies. Poverty alone does not create prostitution.

The Filipinas are by far the biggest group, a fact

many women's groups blame on Government policies which encourage the export of 'entertainers' by providing an infrastructure to facilitate visas. A less tangible push factor is culture: after 400 years under Spanish colonial rule and another 50 under the Americans— '400 years in a convent and 50 years in Hollywood', they say—many Filipinos suffer from a lack of national identity and national pride. Instead they hanker after everything that is not theirs, spurred on by dated American soap operas and cheap local copies of *Lives of the Rich and Famous*.

' "Going abroad" means getting ahead and enhancing one's social status in the Philippines' context', wrote Professor Aurora Javate de Dios of the University of the Philippines. Ordinary Filipinos have a romanticised view of the outside world, whether it be Japan or Europe or the US, because 'going abroad' is often entwined with economic deliverance. Filipinas are primed by orientation and socialisation to take on the role of the 'sacrificial lamb'. Many women are, or are expected to become breadwinners for their families. Usually much thought has been given about going to Japan and the attendant dangers. Many women go anyway, hoping against hope that nothing untoward will happen to them.

Sex tourism from Japan to the Philippines exploded in the 1970s, when the height of the Japanese economic miracle coincided with martial law in the Philippines and a tumbling economic decline. 'Although the presence of the American military in Asia and the Vietnam War is usually viewed as the catalyst for massive prostitution in Asia, it was the tourist industry which acted as the stimulus for the sex industry in the 1970s and 1980s,' Professor Javate de Dios wrote.

The Japanese *yakuza*, or mafia, played a key role in establishing sex tours to the Philippines with the co-operation of the then President Ferdinand Marcos who announced the 'professionalisation' of some 300 000 'hospitality girls' in anticipation of massive Japanese arrivals.

In the late 1970s and early 1980s, company-sponsored sex tours to the Philippines were common. However, when the Casio company held a banquet in a major Manila hotel for 200 of its highest achieving salesmen and included 200 numbered hostesses with the after-dinner drinks, women's groups in both the Philippines and Japan launched a protest campaign. Widespread international publicity focusing on the Philippines' sex industry and the demise of the corrupt Marcos regime towards the mid-1980s eventually shifted the sex industry back to Japan, but failed to break the link with the Philippines.

According to Matsui Yayori, a prostitution system catering to the *samurai* or warrior class has existed in Japan since 1528. The *kuruwa* or prostitution areas were the designated place where the *Yugo*—later on known as the *geisha*—served the warriors.

'Men are supposed to maintain families and wives viewed by society as good women and enjoy sex with prostitutes, the bad women. Although prostitution has been legally banned since 1957 there is a flourishing prostitution industry euphemistically referred to as the "entertainment industry".'

Economic prosperity in Japan has opened up many new opportunities for Japanese women, offering employment in offices and factories and freeing many from the economic needs of their families. Few now are choosing to adopt the life of the *geisha* and most Japanese hostesses are approaching middle age. The labour shortage in the Japanese sex industry is being filled by young migrant girls from developing countries. The improved social mobility of Japanese women has led to an exodus from the rural areas to the cities, leaving many Japanese farmers complaining that they can no longer find wives. Shopping for a partner from a catalogue of Filipinas has become one solution: the so-called 'mail-order brides'.

Ms Yayori argues that trafficking in women to Japan has become more attractive to the *yakuza* than even the smuggling of guns or drugs. The leasing of women to Japanese clubs is highly profitable and, given the protection provided by the entertainer's visa, the risk of severe legal penalties does not apply.

I met Jade through a women's support group in Manila. There were some members of the group who opposed the meeting. I encountered the same hostility and opposition to my project in a number of other countries of the region. Why should I want to tell Jade's story? The line between voyeurism and the dissemination of useful information is very fine indeed. I can understand why some feminists do not want this story told. On one level it is the same story over and over again. This is the story which has created the myth of the 'Asian prostitute', a myth that affects the way Asian women are viewed all over the world. This myth is not the truth about Asian women. But it is a very small part of the truth. In every setting prostitution represents a different set of cultural, economic and social variables. Prostitution exists in some form in every society, both eastern and western.

There have been many efforts to deal with the sex industry from a moral standpoint. At the same time there have been, and continue to be, many efforts to strip back the layers of morality and empower prostitutes with the same rights as any other worker. But it is almost always true to say that the sex industry exists because of the imbalance of social or economic power between men and women, within the same society, or across national boundaries. Therefore, it does affect all women. Easy access to alternative sex partners for a husband erodes the power of a wife in a marriage, and is rarely balanced by similar sexual services being available for women.

The point of telling Jade's story is not to take a moral or political position. It is to ask her how she sees herself and to juxtapose her experiences against those of other women. The Philippines is culturally dominated by a religion which originated in the West. Thus Jade is heavily burdened by imported concepts of honour and shame. The same is not necessarily true for women in other parts of the region.

'It was not a good job and I am not proud of myself,' says Jade. She is not prepared, however, to walk away defeated. With the encouragement and financial assistance of hundreds of women who have made the same choices she is now seeking financial support for her son.

Several months ago she flew to Tokyo with her child. It was the first time they had been alone together since he was born. She was cranky and intolerant, she says, ashamedly. The visit was to begin the DNA tests required for the Supreme Court hearing of her paternity case, at a cost of about US$30 000. She has no doubts about the results. It seems that the drawn out legal battle is as much about her own reputation, and her fidelity to an unreliable man, as it is about her son. But, it seems, her boyfriend is equally confident that he courted an unreliable woman. He has responded to her claims by saying, 'Prove it in court'.

'As far as my reputation in my village goes, yes, it matters a lot. Even until now the people there don't know my son is illegitimate.'

Upstairs from the canteen is a work room where a

support group retrains former hostesses in dressmak-
ing—a couple of racks of neat batik suits and shelves
filled with batik letter holders are on display. The pay
for such work is only about US$5 a day. 'We do not
tell the girls not to go back to Japan. We just try to
provide an alternative,' says one of the support group's
members. She says about 10 000 children have now
been born from relationships between Filipina entertainers and Japanese men. Few are born into stable
marriages.

'Most problems begin when the couples start to
have babies. In the beginning it is usually very sweet
and there are success stories for the first few years but
after five or six years the relationships start to break
down.'

Myrna has been sitting so quietly listening to Jade that
I have assumed she has come to support her. But she
is part of the sewing circle, getting up at 3 a.m. every
day to travel to Manila from her village in a southern
province.

The road that runs past the building is a grim,
concrete lunar landscape—endless crawling queues of
belching traffic pushing up against the pavements,
pedestrians picking their way through the chaos with
clean folded handkerchiefs held ineffectively across
their faces against the billowing fumes.

This is a six-week retraining programme and travelling is already taking its toll. But Myrna has two
daughters at home and cannot afford to stay overnight
in Manila. Myrna is 28. When she was 16 years old
she went to Japan as the bride of a 40-year-old seaman.
She gave birth to two daughters but eventually fled

the cultural isolation of her mother-in-law's home where she endured months on end of loneliness while her husband was at sea.

For a while her husband visited her in the Philippines and provided her with everything she wanted. But then he met another 17-year-old in another Philippines port. Myrna was already old.

'I was jealous and I was angry with him when he visited. Seven years ago he stopped coming. He has other children in another city now and stopped sending money. I was 16 years old when I met him and still a schoolgirl. I didn't really think it was okay to get married but my father was already dead and my family was poor.'

Myrna has since spent almost two years in Saudi Arabia as a domestic helper, an experience she did not enjoy. And she is not too keen on the sewing either. Later when the support worker has left I ask her about her future plans. 'I am trying to save money to go back to Japan as an entertainer,' she says. Jade nods. Maybe this time Myrna will be lucky.

A tale of four
mothers

Of the seven daughters born of her father's four wives
Lily was the ugliest. At least that is what she says.

'I had a chip on my shoulder. My grandmother
always said to me "You are so ugly no-one will ever
want you." That was the influence she gave me, that
I was useless and ugly,' she explains. It is a point she
will come back to again as we sit sipping coffee in the
sedate lounge of the Mandarin Hotel, a solid, historic
building of sandstone blocks overlooking the busy
harbour, while she recounts the story of her life within
one of Hong Kong's richest and most powerful Chinese
families.

Hers was a family of very rich men. Men who
collected charming, beautiful women, like the trophies
of their financial success, at a time when the teeming
Hong Kong waterfront was lined with the squat, stone
warehouses of trade.

Biologically, Lily's grandmother was wife number
three out of nine, but the authority to mete out
sweeping criticism of the young Lily, olive-skinned and
thin, was the privilege of grandmother number one.
For the principal Chinese wife, at least, there was
authority within the walls of the family home with
which to compensate oneself for the fading of beauty
with age.

Lily's grandfather had made his first million by the age of 18 as a *comprador* for a powerful British company in Hong Kong, a job description invented for a 'chief native servant' of a European business house in Chinese territory. At that time, she says, there was a saying that a man should take another wife for each new million, just to show the rest of the world that he had made it. So Lily had nine grandmothers, living in nine solid, stone mansions.

Her father was not the number one heir, but the son of wife number three. Although he did not have his own private butler sent with him to university in England, he was indulged nonetheless. With his English education came his own aeroplane, his name emblazoned on the tail, for hops across to Europe.

When it came time for him to enter into his own string of marriages the family of his first true love, a girl of lesser financial status, fearfully sent her away to China to escape his privilege and pride. But he merely flew himself over and brought her back. She was Lily's mother.

So being ugly was not insignificant in this family of beautiful women. In retrospect, she says, it was probably the key to her decision to break the rules, determined to prove her grandmother wrong. At the age of 60, immaculately attired and quietly spoken, Lily clearly has never been ugly. But it doesn't really matter now that it wasn't ever true.

'My grandfather was not an educated man, but he learned very quickly,' she says. What he learned first was the English language, which, at the turn of the century in Hong Kong, made him an invaluable link between the native Chinese population and the powerful British trading companies. Initially, the company traded in sugar, she thinks, but she doesn't know much about this period. By the time she was born her grandfather didn't seem to work at all. 'He was so wealthy, he didn't have to do any more business.'

We have agreed to leave her grandfather's name out of the story and to change her own name. He was a very famous man. This story is not really about him, however, although it was he who shaped the fortunes of his many descendants. But later on we will introduce another famous family name: that of Lily's daughter, the great-granddaughter of the patriarch.

'Every Sunday we would go to visit him and almost every year we would have a new grandmother. We visited him with whomever he was with at the time. The wives didn't live together, they each had a big house, a mansion. But, the family often had get-togethers for birthdays or feasts and they were all there with all the children and there was no jealousy. At that time, it was a kind of honour to be a rich man's wife. His responsibility was to see that everyone was properly taken care of.

'The number one wife was always the most important, though. She was the manager of wives, she controlled everything. When the wives were together they all had to kowtow to the number one, then the number three had to give respect to the number two and the number four to the number three, to bring them tea or do whatever they demanded.

'But it was always the latest wife, who was the youngest and the most attractive, who had the power with the husband. They systematically got younger and, of course, they were all beautiful.'

Lily is counting on her hands, listing the wives and children. Not all the wives produced sons; some produced no children at all. After the first wife produced a son, she had no more children. The next wife to give birth was wife number three, who had two sons, one of whom was her father, and one daughter.

'Of course, I remember much more about my own immediate family. And I remember my father was my grandfather's favourite son, even though he wasn't the first son. When the number one wife's son went to Cambridge University my grandfather sent him his own butler. Of course, he was one of the first Chinese men to go to Cambridge. My father went to university in London and didn't have a butler. But, he learnt to fly and was given his own plane.

'He flew to Paris and around Europe. He was a handsome man, he was financially supported by my grandfather and, of course, he didn't have to work. Everyone knew he was a playboy and with all that money to throw around he was always surrounded by women.'

Lily's mother was middle-class. Another beautiful woman, she worked for Lane Crawford's, the elegant Hong Kong equivalent to Harrod's of London. Lily's father would wait outside for her to leave work almost every day.

'But my mother's family were against the courtship. They didn't like the idea of her marrying into this rich family. He was surrounded by women and they were concerned she would be challenged by them, that she would not be happy. When a woman gets married in Chinese society she becomes part of the man's family. When you join a family and you are not of the same class then you will not be treated with respect within that family. So her brothers decided to send her away to China. But my father went up in his plane and took her back. She was only about 18 years old at the time and he was not much older.'

Later, when she talked about the wedding, her mother told Lily: 'Yes, I was worried that my husband was a playboy, but I was young, he was so handsome and I was so completely in love.'

Of course, after the wedding, she could no longer work. So, she began having babies. 'The funny thing was the first one was a girl, then the second one was a girl, then the third is me, and the fourth one is also a girl. The grandparents were not very happy.'

With the arrival of the fourth granddaughter the grandparents made their move. Their son was obliged to take a second wife. Never mind whether you love the woman or not, if she gives you a son this is more important, they told him.

'I was told that my mother was very upset, she was trying and trying and trying. She had four girls in four years. This was very difficult for her.' But, she had no choice but to accept the decision. 'When you marry into a Chinese family the mother-in-law controls every-thing. At that time a daughter-in-law had no say, she just had to do what she was told.'

This was in the mansion of the third wife of the patriarch, the grandmother who found Lily wanting in beauty. But, unlike his father, who set each successive wife up in her own home, Lily's father moved wife number two in with his first family. 'I was very young but I remember my mother crying. The second wife lived with us, but each wife had her own floor, it was a very big house.'

Then, something very unfortunate happened. Both wives became pregnant at almost the same time. The second wife gave birth first. The child was a son, so a big party was held in recognition of his status as the heir. Lily's mother just cried. Later she too gave birth to her first son, too late.

'She accepted that she had to have a son, she wanted a son because then she could stop having children. But I remember my mother didn't like to cause problems, she never said no, she never answered back, she was a model daughter-in-law.'

Lily doesn't remember much about wife number two because she soon left the family. 'It was not unusual, she was a very beautiful woman and the marriage was more or less arranged to produce a son so if she had already done that, and the husband allowed her, then she could leave and remarry. She would also have been given some kind of financial incentive to leave.'

And what of the heir? 'Well, of course, she couldn't take the baby with her, because that was the idea: to produce a son. So she gave the boy to my mother to raise and he became our own, even now we are still close.' Thus, Lily's mother regained her status, at least for a while.

The regret of being born a member of a *jue fang* (terminated) family was not easily overcome. The girls of families without any sons were called 'the daughters of terminated male lines', and their parents were destined to become 'floating ghosts' after their death.

It was not just a case of securing a male heir to take care of life on earth, to take the family name and fortune into the next generation and to look after a widowed mother and unmarried sisters. In traditional Chinese culture a son is responsible for his parents' death rituals and for continuing the proper annual rituals of ancestor worship. Without these rituals a parent's ghost will just float around, trapped forever in a spiritual void.

Families without sons could adopt a boy or coax a son-in-law from a lower social stratum into the family to take the woman's family name. But often adopted sons did not take proper care of their new parents or unmarried sisters. Many a story is told in rural China of an adopted son who snatches his inheritance upon his new father's death but fails to carry out his ceremonial responsibilities. Alternatively, a daughter would take on the ceremonial responsibilities herself, calling herself a 'son and daughter combined'.

'Aside from shouldering the majority of domestic chores and death rituals the women had to endure the humiliation of being a member of a "terminated fang". A common swear word among the villagers meant "you will have no male successors"', writes anthropologist Eliza Chan of the University of Hong Kong.

The man known today as Confucius was born in 551BC into a family of the lower aristocracy of the Middle Zhou state of Lu, in the region of the Wei Valley which flows toward the east coast of central China. According to historical accounts, this was a time of incredible violence and turmoil. The primary source of power for the individual states was warfare waged in the name of ancestral spirits.

'Thus a noble was above all a warrior and sacrificer, a man who took life in order to feed the spirits who gave him power', according to Gina Barnes' account in *China, Korea and Japan: The Rise of Civilisation in East Asia*.

'Warfare, hunting and sacrifice, activities symbolically linked through the ceremonial exchange and consumption of meat, reached their culmination in the offering up of living beings at the altars.'

Within the walled city of the Lu state Confucius grew up to become a minor court official whose self-defined mission in life was to teach moderation and harmony in the face of the overwhelming conflict that racked the Wei river valley. At the age of 60 he left his native state and carried his ideas into neighbouring walled cities, searching for a means of wrenching back control and returning his land to the moral, 'golden age' of the Zhou king who founded his empire some 500 years earlier.

His concept of good government was based on an analogy with the family and was both authoritarian and hierarchical: children honour parents, wives obey husbands, husbands serve lords and lords serve their ancestors. He also believed that human nature was basically good and the practice of loyalty, reciprocity, filial and fraternal affection and duty within these rules would lead to the natural emergence of moral leaders who could restore social order. Without such morality, Confucius believed, a ruler had lost the 'Mandate of Heaven' and could be overthrown:

> Man is the representative of Heaven and is supreme over all things. Woman yields obedience to the instructions of man and helps to carry out his principles. On this account she can determine nothing of herself and is subject to the three obediences. When she is young she must obey her father and elder brother, when married she must obey her husband, and when widowed she must obey her son.

As a form of government his teachings held sway for more than two millennia, in varying degrees, across what are now China, Korea and Japan.

His influence was perhaps even more strongly felt in families in this vast tract of East Asia. With such emphasis on ancestral worship and the continuation of the male line, the status of a wife immediately rose with the birth of a son, and her failure to so produce was grounds for a divorce, as was her jealousy of any additional wives or even her talkativeness. The low status of women led to many restrictions on their lives and a belief that education would be wasted on them, backed up by the Confucian saying that 'a woman without talents is virtuous'.

During the Tang Dynasty (618–907AD) the fashion of footbinding was copied from the court and spread from the upper to the lower classes and from north to south China to a point where bound feet, or 'golden lotuses', became a distinct advantage over natural 'duck feet'.

'The tiny feet became a love fetish. Men were said to be sexually aroused by playing with them and women with bound feet were said to have tighter vaginas', wrote Dr Linda Koo, a medical anthropologist of the University of Hong Kong. One of her interviewees recalls the agonies she underwent as a child:

I was afflicted with the pain of footbinding when I was seven years old. I was an active child who liked to jump about, but from then on my optimistic nature vanished. I was told a girl had to suffer twice, from ear piercing and foot binding. I wept and hid in a neighbour's home, but mother found me, scolded me and dragged me home.

My mother washed and placed alum on my feet and cut the toe nails. She then bent my toes towards the plantar with binding cloth ten feet long and two inches wide. She finished the binding and ordered me to walk, but when I did the pain was unbearable.

After several months, all but the big toe were pressed against the inner surface. Whenever I ate fish or meat my feet would swell and the pus would drip. If I mistakenly punctured a sore it gushed like a stream. Beatings and curses were my lot for covertly loosening the wrappings. Every two weeks I changed to new shoes, each one to two-tenths of an inch smaller than the previous ones.

I had been binding for one month when my younger sister started; when no one was around we would weep together. In summer my feet smelled offensively because of pus and blood, in winter my feet felt cold because of lack of circulation. Four of the toes were curled in like so many dead caterpillars; no outsider would ever have believed they belonged to a human being. It took two years to achieve the three-inch (foot) model.

According to Dr Koo, footbinding reinforced male domination over women. 'Women with small feet could not do most jobs outside the home and thus were unable to achieve economic independence from men. Because walking was painful and difficult, female chastity could be reinforced. This intent was summarised in the Sung Dynasty saying: "Why must the foot be bound? To prevent barbarous running around".'

At times of economic hardship the raising of daughters became a luxury many families could not afford. Daughters were sold by fathers, wives were even sold by husbands. Girls too young to be marketed were killed, said Dr Koo.

Female infanticide, wrote Sherly Wuddunn in *China Wakes* was:

> . . . simply one of the long list of things that people should not do, such as leaping over food served on the floor; stepping over a person lying on a floor mat; weeping; spitting; or urinating when facing north (the direction of the emperor); spitting at a shooting star or pointing at a rainbow. If you committed these sins, the Arbiter of Human Destiny would shave three or three hundred days off your life. The text does not indicate that infanticide is any worse than, for example, urinating when facing north.

Foot binding was officially outlawed by imperial decree in 1902 in mainland China and had virtually died out by 1949 when the Communist revolution swept the country. The new Communist government also dissolved hundreds of thousands of polygamous marriages and ushered in a whole range of reforms intended to restore the status of women.

A TALE OF FOUR MOTHERS

Chairman Mao Tse Tung said women could hold up half the sky, cutting down the Confucian edict that man was the representative of Heaven on earth. Women were brought into all occupations but remained a notable minority in the country's political leadership.

In Hong Kong, ruled by Britain and the forces of the free market, women made similarly slow progress in the field of political power. Up until the 1960s, the failure to produce a son remained ample justification for the acquisition of a second wife or the rejection of a first. The *Marriage Reform Ordinance* took 17 years to pass and it was not until 1970 that monogamy was made the only form of legal marriage in Hong Kong.

But the weight of history is heavy indeed. Since the 1980s in mainland China, Confucianism has haunted tens of millions of women since the introduction of the one-child policy, aimed at controlling the massive 1.2 billion population. With only one chance to produce a male heir, abandonment and female infanticide are well documented. Compulsory abortion, even in very advanced pregnancies, for mothers attempting subsequent births have also been widely publicised.

Birth statistics show that in 1953 there were 104.9 newborn boys for every 100 girls, a fairly natural ratio. But, after the 1982 family planning crackdown the statistics begin to veer into the abnormal. By 1992 a government-sponsored survey showed 118.5 boys for every 100 girls. If the norm is taken to be 105.5/100 then 13 per cent of all Chinese baby girls, or 1.7 million, go missing each year. Probably only a small percentage are drowned in the buckets of water kept at the side of the birthing bed in case the child is female. Many more are abandoned or adopted out informally through networks of relatives.

Still more, nowadays, are probably never born. Ultrasound technology has given us the ability to look inside the womb and determine the sex of a baby with a reasonable degree of accuracy. Thus couples can seek to determine the sex of a child before birth and abort what they believe to be a female foetus. The practice is not limited to China. Similar social pressures exist in India, without limits on family size, and even in the highly developed nation of South Korea couples are choosing selective abortion to avoid enduring multiple pregnancies in the high pressure urban environment of the newly industrialised nation.

'We are getting into some very serious long term social problems with female infanticide. In China alone there are some 50 million bachelors hanging around without the possibility of marriage because there are not enough women,' says Christine, a politician, and daughter of Lily.

I have chosen to use only first names because although Lily was willing to talk about her life openly, she did not feel she could make the same decision for her extended family who are part of the same story.

'We didn't have a family life. We only saw our father on Sundays and our parents were always out of town travelling or having parties. My grandmother was a fanatic for Chinese opera which she used to hold in the house and invite hundreds of people,' says Lily.

'We had a nanny each and the nanny used to take us everywhere. We saw our mother more than our father, but she was always busy organising functions and parties. My parents had their own bedrooms and when the second wife came in I wasn't aware of father going between the two.'

That all changed with wife number three. During the Second World War, Lily's father fled Hong Kong for India. The house was seized by the Japanese occupying forces and the family moved to the basement, nannies and all. Because Lily's mother could speak English she was given a job teaching Japanese officers in exchange for rice. 'I remember mother used to disguise herself when she went out to teach as an old, ugly woman. We didn't understand, we just laughed at her.'

When the war ended and her father returned Lily's mother began to cry again. He brought back with him another son and a third wife who quickly gave birth to a second son and a daughter. Later, a fourth wife was brought into the house. 'She was very young, barely any older than us,' says Lily.

'The number three and the number four were always fighting. They were asking, "Why does he spend so much time with you?" Then the children had to fight too, because they had to take sides.

'My mother stayed away from it. We children knew it was hurting my mother but we couldn't do anything. I remember when I was nineteen years old I said if my husband has another wife I will walk out, I will not tolerate that. Growing up in a family like that, with so many grandmothers and mothers, you realise your love is all sort of scattered, you don't feel you are getting anything whole. Why should I scatter my love away? I thought.'

This is a subject that should not be discussed outside the family, least of all with a stranger. That was just how it was, says Lily. 'We were not supposed to say anything about the family.'

In the beginning, Lily's mother was the wife who would go out with her father. She was presentable, educated and fluent in English. But, later, when the others arrived, she just kept to herself in her home. 'A principal wife is always a principal wife, she doesn't have the option to leave.'

It was a fabulous wedding, a Chinese and Western extravaganza worthy of the careful attention of the best social writers around the world. Lily, the ugly duckling, was the first grandchild of the patriarch to marry. Of course, she and her husband barely knew the guests. It was her grandfather's grand show.

'All of a sudden my husband had appeared. I met him at a party and he said he fell in love with me at first sight and that made me feel pretty good. My grandmother was happy I had finally got someone to take me.'

Lily was just out of school, her husband was twelve years older. He was from a similarly wealthy family. It was a suitable match. Their first child was a girl, Christine.

'Yes, I was hoping for a boy. There are many old wives' tales and my *amahs* (maids) would give me special drinks during the pregnancy saying this is good for you because you must have a boy. But I was pleased with a girl and my husband was quite pleased. For the first few years my marriage was okay, but I got bored and the initial spark faded, with maids doing every-thing for me. At that time young, married women did not work. But then there was an opportunity for a receptionist at Lane Crawford so I just grabbed it.'

From there Lily was recruited by Elizabeth Arden and sent to London to train as their Hong Kong agent, leaving her husband and daughter behind for nine months.

'I just felt there was more a woman could do than stay home. Because of the influence my grandmother had on me that I was ugly and useless it was a reaction, to prove that I was not. In a way, not being beautiful was liberating, I didn't think of myself as an ornamental wife.'

Lily returned home and continued to work. Her marriage ground on, both partners returning home to an ever increasing silence.

'We had no fights, but there was no communication. After work Christine's father did nothing but sit down and play mahjong. I heard he had girlfriends outside. I was attracted to others but our society wouldn't allow me to have a boyfriend. One day we just agreed that we could not go on like this.'

It was the first divorce in the family, a scandal which reached even the American newspapers.

'I was an outcast, it was a loss of face for the family. By that time I was not so close to my grandfather but the younger aunts and uncles looked at me and said, "There she goes." It was difficult to take in at the beginning.'

So, Lily, now a single, working mother, moved to a two-bedroom apartment, refusing to take a cent from her husband and having already disqualified herself from the financial support of her own family by insisting on the divorce. 'I worked, I progressed, I was comfortable and happy. I encouraged Christine to be independent and I made sure she was well educated,' she says.

Much later, Lily, herself, remarried

It is only a short walk from the gracious calm of the Mandarin Hotel to Christine's office. Inside, she moves quickly and talks fast, her delivery as busy with ideas as her life.

No two people tell the same story in the same way, so Christine has another perspective to offer.

'I have talked quite extensively to my mother—she said she was miserable and that in her thirties she contemplated suicide. For my mother I think it was the fact that my father was a man of the world. In the evenings he would go off with his friends to what they called clubs and play mahjong there. They had hostesses, of course, it was a man's island and my mother found that very difficult to cope with. My parents were probably the first generation with the opportunity to take the legal route to separation.'

Christine was one of a small group of female politicians pushing at the edges, before China reclaimed Hong Kong, which managed to push through new sex discrimination legislation. Education and work opportunities have gradually increased the pool of independent Chinese women in Hong Kong and the traditional family structures of sons and daughters-in-law living in the patriarchal home has become impractical in Hong Kong's tiny high-rise apartments. It seems odd, then, that Hong Kong is suffering from an increase in female suicides.

'My own mother put all her eggs in one basket right from the very beginning and focused on my brother,' says Dr Koo, a professional of Christine's generation.

'I think it was merely a pragmatic decision on her part, even though she came from an educated family, for the mother to put in the effort for the child that would be her social security for the rest of her life. It is through a son that a woman becomes a matriarch. "I will spoil you to death, but you owe me. When you get married, will you give me a diamond ring as well?" she would ask. An older woman has a lot of power through her son. And, psychologically, we know that when people play out a subordinate role, the junior or the daughter-in-law, they often learn both parts and when they assume the senior position they perpetuate the system.'

'Now, society is in transition,' she says. 'There are many women who were dominated as daughters-in-law whose children now live independently, so they do not get to play the mother-in-law role.

'My mother is always complaining about this. Older women are not getting what they expected in terms of status, they have indulged their children and sacrificed their lives for them and now they are not getting their reward.' This, she says, explains the high suicide rate among older women, most of whom choose to jump from the high-rise residential towers.

'Traditionally, it was the young daughters-in-law who were abused by their new families who would suicide. Classically, it was the ultimate revenge against the mother-in-law. They would jump in the well saying "My ghost will haunt you forever."

'Now it is the older women who are sending their ghosts to haunt their children.'

The mistress village

Ching is lolling about in the beauty parlour waiting for the afternoon to pass, her thick, black hair caught up in a clip, her carved porcelain face bare and fresh. The beauty parlour is more of a tiled corridor really, lined with a cramped row of chairs and mirrors, a couple of out-dated hairdryers hanging like beehives off rickety metal stands. Tacky posters of blonde women in G-strings with fake orange tans have been taped, provocatively, diagonally across the dull, cream tiles. Out the back a facial steamer competes ineffectively with the sickly mid-summer humidity which suffocates the booming cities of China's south.

Ching is not in need of the services of the painted, giggling beauticians. She is outstandingly lovely. Her pale, serene face is her fortune, her status and her future. She sits cross-legged and confident in the moist, vinyl swivel chair talking about herself, the pretenders of the parlour hovering hopefully in her glow.

Ching is married. Most of the thousands of girls who totter on high heels along these muddy streets are not. Ching does not live with her husband, nor does she know when to expect him in her studio apartment upstairs. And so she waits. He likes her to wait, so she does not work or study or stray too far. In Shanghai she was at university studying accounting when they met—she a 19-year-old beauty trapped in Communist China, he a visiting kitchen hand from Hong Kong, empowered by his passport and his pay packet.

So she came to Heung Biling Village, on the outskirts of Shenzen, the southern boom city of China's open economic policy. Over the border in Hong Kong the name 'mistress village' is more commonly used and for most of the tens of thousands of Hong Kong businessmen and workers who make the regular pilgrimage across the border, this is exactly what it is.

The ancient walled village of dank, dark hovels, the original rural settlement, now lies trapped in an industrial moonscape. Around the narrow cobbled paths rise white condominium towers filled with studio apartments rented from Hong Kong; the streets are lined with dress shops and karaoke bars.

At lunchtime the 'mistress village' is just coming to life. The girls are emerging into the hazy light, blinking, from another night spent out dancing in search of their Hong Kong man. The street outside the parlour is filthy with the mud and rubble of the surrounding construction sites. A pair of girls dressed in black, their features masked by thick pancake make-up, pick their way down the hill, linked by the elbows atop shaky stiletto heels. In Communist China they are an outrageous sight—fishnet stockings, black leather shorts grabbing at the crotch. One of the girls is sporting a clear plastic pocket stuffed full of Hong Kong notes on her left rear cheek. Literally showing off her money.

Ching is paid 10 000 Chinese yuan (approximately US$1200) a month to wait. The average wage is about 700 yuan in a region considered to be China's richest. She is a success. Now, she says, she is free. 'At the beginning,' she says, 'I didn't want to go all the way. He was ten years older than me. But I was told that if I had a Hong Kong husband I would get a better life. My parents were very upset. My family, especially my aunties, were very ashamed because we lived together before we got married. Many people were trying to break us apart and were saying that I just wanted a Hong Kong man for the money, but really it is genuine.'

Three times, she says, her Hong Kong man smuggled her across the border and three times she was caught and deported. It is not clear why her wedding ring does not give her the right to residency in Hong Kong. She explains vaguely about the long queue to enter Hong Kong legally. Too long, she says. And so she settled here, halfway up the mistress village hill.

'My husband just comes when he is free so he prefers I am not working so I am always available. I don't need to work, he provides everything. I just go around, watch television, gossip. In the beginning we used to talk on the phone every day, now I don't know when he is coming.'

China is not an open society. Across the border in Hong Kong, the 'mistress village' is widely discussed and various efforts are being made to prevent a return to the days when the power and wealth of Chinese men was measured by the number of their wives. Polygamy is illegal in both Hong Kong and mainland China but many believe the economic disparity across the open border has created an ideal atmosphere for cross-border concubines.

My search for Ching had begun in Hong Kong with a failed attempt to secure a Chinese tourist visa. My passport, so full of stamps for strange and unattractive destinations, was not that of a tourist, the Consulate had so wisely concluded, but more likely that of a western journalist. My application was rejected. So, on a hunch I took the swish MTR line to the Canton railway with another woman journalist from Hong Kong and an interpreter, both of whom had the proper stamp in place. I brazenly joined the long queues at the Hong Kong side and managed to get out of Hong Kong without a visa to get into China. I just followed the crowds across the bridge to the Chinese side, peering out intently at the high walls and barbed wire and down at the red muddy water below in case this was all I was going to see. And then there it was, the 'On Arrival' visa counter. All I needed was money.

The men behind the desk barely looked up to check my photograph, so overwhelmed were they by the streams of people pouring across the bridge looking for profit. Then we waited. For several hours we waited patiently in the dull corridor lined with blue painted planking behind the sign that said 'Foreigners'. A tall American-Chinese businessman was very curious indeed why a couple of women were going to China, this way, on foot, hot and sweaty, waiting and waiting. 'To shop,' we said. 'Yes, housewives,' we said. 'Oh,' he replied, explaining that the extraordinarily long queue must be part of the new Chinese security measures put in place to prevent the entry of journalists on tourist visas since the recent arrest of human rights activist Harry Wu.

We inched past the duty-free shop. A frightening feeling, being trapped in such a crowd moving so slowly. I sought refuge at the counter surveying the cigarettes and biscuits. When another immigration booth suddenly opened my friend disappeared in the stampede so I elbowed my way rudely through, finally finding our new businessman companion holding a small space open near the front.

Would we like to have lunch at the Shangri-La Hotel? he asked. 'Oh, so sorry,' we say. Our Chinese friend, the interpreter, in another queue for the Chinese from Hong Kong, is taking us to a village for lunch. Friends of hers. 'Oh, mistress village,' he laughs at the name. 'What on earth are you going to do there?'

THE MISTRESS VILLAGE

At the station we fought with the crowds in the taxi queue, unsure whether the driver knew where we wanted to go. At the entrance to the old walled city we tumbled out and went shopping. The local super-market was small and neat. We picked out a few items. By the way, we let the interpreter ask, do you know any Hong Kong 'wives'. No, no. Not here, said the salesgirl. So we strolled the streets, most conspicuously. The clothes on display were cut for the low lights of the nightclubs. The girls weaving their way down the narrow pathways were overdressed and very young, to the last one virtually crippled by high heels. The open drains were blocked with rubbish. We were in the right place. We wandered upstairs to a beauty parlour. No luck. A pretty girl did not want to talk. Finally we sank into the chairs of a small beauty shop just across the path from the local administration office: a group of grim-faced young men were looking at us, peering out at the shop's pane glass window. They were the only group of men we had seen. At first the shop was empty, except for the surprised but hospitable owner.

One by one the girls from the pathways filled the chairs. Giggling and demure, chatting, mainly to each other. The need for an interpreter destroyed the spon-taneity of everything but a smile. Then, a young, fair-skinned girl in a flowing floral skirt gambled like a fawn towards the door and returned with a fistful of lollipops. She passed them around. Her legs slung around the back of the swivel chair swinging, she laughed like a child.

Miss Wong, Miss Cho, Miss Chan, Miss Tan, Miss Wu, Miss Lam. Nineteen, 21, 18, 18, 22, 23. From all over, not from here. These girls are educated. Their parents occupy positions on the middle rungs of the hierarchical ladder of the state. They are pragmatists, not prostitutes. They were yawning at lunchtime. They had been dancing from midnight to dawn, they confessed, giggling. A night out is expensive, 100 to 200 yuan a head.

Miss Lam, in sheer, wide black pants slit up the side, said she has a Hong Kong boyfriend. 'But, I do not like to call him,' she said, 'or ask for money.' Or say too much. Why did you come here? 'Because there are a lot more chances,' she said.

'I came here to have fun for a few years and earn some money,' said another. The girls said they work, but at what they can't say. They said they have lots of friends from Hong Kong whom they meet in the bars. They said their parents were worried but now Chinese girls have much more freedom that their mothers ever had.

The young, pale fawn signalled that she had to go. The girls wanted to have photos taken, giggling, arms around us, arms around each other. The wet concrete floor awash underfoot, a plastic basin of leaves for lunch soaking in the hair-washing trough. Photos accomplished, the fawn donned her tiny backpack and bounced off on cork platform shoes, skirt swinging.

We continued our shopping expedition, carefully rubbing the synthetic fabric of outlandish black and gold filament creations before walking on.

The interpreter, a Cantonese woman from Hong Kong, was labouring across a vast cultural and linguistic divide. The girls here were not local, and spoke Mandarin, being equipped with only a smattering of Cantonese small talk for the Hong Kong men. Sometimes the conversation lurched through two translations, a notebook necessary to jot down the Chinese characters and check their meaning. In China it is unusual to engage in such personal conversations, especially with foreigners wandering the streets of suburban Shenzen.

We met another girl outside a grocery shop. She stopped and smiled but then made a long-distance call from a public phone to her Hong Kong man. And left. No, no, he told her not to talk.

At the beauty parlour next door Ching is only willing to talk in such a public setting because she is wearing a ring. Last year, she tells us proudly, only 33 marriages were registered here between Hong Kong men and mainland Chinese women, despite the thousands upon thousands of liaisons which support the studio flats. Does Ching know that so many of the Hong Kong men have wives at home? 'Usually, we do not talk so personally,' she says. 'Some girls don't know whether he has a wife or not, so they just ignore the situation. And some girls just don't care as long as he pays; they are getting their freedom.'

Do not underestimate the importance of face, the interpreter explains. Appearances and power are more important than what is left unsaid. The question, the interpreter says, has already been answered, in case we missed the subtlety of Ching's reply. And in China, it is most unusual to live as a housewife. Officially men and women in China are equal, and required to fulfil positions provided by the state.

Following the Communist victory of 1949 the Party outlawed prostitution, child marriages, the use of concubines and the sale of brides. Women's associations were formed throughout the country and neighbourhood committees began knocking on doors to intervene in domestic disputes involving violence against women. From a mere 600 000 women in the industrial labour force in 1949 the number soared to 50 million by the early 1990s, meaning that 82 per cent of employable women in the cities held jobs.

The Party encouraged the education of girls for the first time in China's history. Women and men worked side by side in industry and together they tilled the fields. But in the late 1980s, as China swung its doors open and embraced the new free market economics on which it was pinning the survival of Communist rule, academics began to report a new shift in the status of women. For all their newly-acquired education and employment status the new woman of China of the 1990s was a housewife. Men, newly liberated from the confines of central economic planning, began to make money in business. Business success re-kindled the desire for a wife who stayed at home: women re-appeared as status symbols, a stay-at-home wife being evidence of one's personal wealth.

The new influence of rampant consumerism that accompanied the opening up of the Chinese economy brought with it contradictory western images of com-mercialised sexuality. Sheryl Wudunn, in *China Wakes*, writes:

> The obstacle (to women) was not just the strength of traditional beliefs but the market itself. The market economy raised living standards for women along with men, but also led to the return of the male-dominated Chinese society—coupled with the sexist features of Western society. Advertisers quickly discovered the best way to market their products was by airing commercials showing lovely young women, preferably wearing as little as possible.
>
> To promote the sales of weapons abroad, the army began publishing a calendar with a pin-up each month of a buxom young woman clutching a gun. In 1994, for example, Miss February wears a bikini top and a red skirt slit to the waist, accompanied by an AK–47 assault rifle. Miss November wears a strapless formal (dress), high heels, red gloves and carries a submachine gun.

According to Wudunn, during the 1980s, pornography and prostitution began to spread rapidly through China and bosses began to hire pretty, young women as playthings or ornaments. She also documents a number of cases of the *nouveau riche* businessmen of the open market procuring mistresses from the workplace.

Had she not followed her fortune, Ching says she would be working in a government unit as an accountant.

'My parents, for example, are given work in the city where they live and they don't have much choice about it. If I hadn't come here I would be allocated a job too. My husband,' Ching says, 'is my first priority.' But, she says, she is regretful she didn't finish her university degree. Recently she told her husband she was bored and asked his permission to study computing in Shenzen.

'He said "No." He is a bit scared that I will get better educated than him and I feel it is my duty to respect him and I do not want to do anything against him,' she says with little spirit. 'When I was young love came first. Now I am a bit regretful. Actually, I loved the student life,' she says. Resigned, wise, rich, respected. Now 24 years old.

On the massive concrete pedestrian overpasses which stretch from the Shangri-La Hotel to the Shenzen train station the child beggars of the new capitalist China bite like young summer flies. Swatted, they withdraw momentarily, but keep on bouncing back. So we take refuge in a cavernous emporium, all glass cases and shop fronts, mainly empty, the hawkers more comfortable with a space on the floor and a couple of giant raffia bags of stock.

Here, in the middle of a suffocating summer, are quilts for sale. Hundreds of beautiful handmade patchwork quilts made by women workers, branded for a country cottage craft store in New York, the 'Made in China' label very small and unobtrusive.

We buy more than we can comfortably carry at less than US$20 a piece, the nylon rope handles of the parcels cutting into our palms as we struggle up the escalators and into another interminable queue.

At Chinese Customs the officers are very impressed and want to have a good look at the quilts. Yes, a bargain, they nod and let us pass.

Her father's face

Mary Li was born with her father's round face. That was her problem. 'You see, my father had two wives,' she explains. 'My mother was the first wife and she had one daughter, me, and one son. But my father's family wanted more sons, so they got him a second wife.' That was when the trouble started, when she was still a little girl.

'My mother did not accept such an arrangement. All day long she would scold the second wife. All day long the second wife would argue back. A couple of years after the 1949 revolution my father went away to Hong Kong, maybe to get away from all the conflict, and left his two wives behind in China to fight with each other,' she says.

In the house her two mothers shared, Mary would look up, a child's round face seeking approval. But all her natural mother would see was her father's image. And so her mother would harangue her, too. Constantly. 'You are just like your father, just as bad as him,' she told her, day in and day out.

Eventually, Mary and her mother and brother followed her father to Hong Kong where her parents resumed their miserable union. Her second mother, though, did not come. She had failed to fall pregnant at all, let alone bear the required sons, so she was divorced when the Communists outlawed polygamy. Later, Mary says, she remarried and had children of her own. But her own mother had no more children. Her father, it seems, had so many affairs that he was no longer fertile. The explanation is incomplete, but it is safe to assume that Mary is referring to a debilitating sexually transmitted disease.

What all this has to do with Mary's own marriage is slowly becoming apparent. How Mary came to be here, talking quietly and confidentially in the playroom of a social welfare organisation, set up to deal with the myriad of social problems simmering within the faceless walls of Hong Kong's high-rise residential towers.

Like most Hong Kong housewives, Mary presides over a small, two-bedroom flat of maybe 400 square feet, high in a numbered tower at the end of the bus line which links the last subway station with downtown Hong Kong. Along the road which winds down the coast towards the New Territories hundreds upon hundreds of similar towers rise, the heartland of the middle class. The hills which fall into the brilliant blue sea are bald and brown. The water is choppy with activity, the island lying just offshore, where the new Hong Kong airport is being built, is a raw gash of red earth.

There are attempts at variation. Different colours, different widths and breadths, mid-air bridges hanging precariously between twin towers. But, the effect is pretty much the same. Isolated boxes, one on top of another. It is not so surprising that Hong Kong has a suicide problem—mainly middle-aged women, jumping from their tower cages. Less directly, that story has something to do with Mary's marriage as well.

As a child Mary did not judge her father. Polygamy was just a way of life. He was a 'big enough' man, a businessman, to afford two wives as well as a string of affairs, so that was what he did. But Mary was very unhappy so she wanted to escape her mother's blame and take her father's face away with her.

She laughs nervously at her youthful logic. With the benefit of hindsight and the wisdom of middle age, it was silly enough, she says. 'I married at twenty. I chose a husband myself and didn't even think about the concept of marriage. I just wanted to get away from an unhappy family.'

After the birth of her first child, a son, she gave up her work as an embroidery worker and, several years later, had another child, a daughter. Her two children are now grown up and what happened in between, within the walls of her high-rise box, she kept secret for all those years.

'I did not want my daughter to have the same experience as I did so I decided not to practise my mother's habit of always talking badly about my husband. I wanted the family to be as normal as possible.' But two years ago, when she first came to the social welfare office for help, she made a major tactical move in the private psychological battle which has consumed her life. 'I gave up the marriage in my mind almost two years ago. I stopped having sex with my husband as a way to emotionally remove myself. In my mind it is finished.'

Mary came for help because her husband was, and is, constantly unfaithful. His business takes him regularly across the border into China, so now he has a mainland Chinese wife, one of a string of additional partners along the way.

The translation of the welfare group's name requests Hong Kong's housewives: 'Let us be your marriage supportive group'. But this is not a marriage counselling organisation in which both parties seek help to find a manageable compromise. It is a network of confidential meetings for wives, still living with polygamy more than two decades after multiple marriages were finally outlawed in Hong Kong. For the handful of female legislators who have fought so hard to overturn inheritance and marriage laws which favour husbands and sons, this new phenomenon, fuelled by the opening of the southern border with China, represents the return of the concubine.

'Many, many women in Hong Kong have husbands who now go to work in China at least once a week or live in China and come back once or twice a month,' says group coordinator, Pauline Kwok. 'For many generations Chinese men have had mistresses and concubines and they think it is a good thing to demonstrate that their status is very high. The husbands are usually between 30 and 50 years old and so they still hold these ideas. When they go to China they are not known and there are many women who come to the south from the poorer provinces looking for Hong Kong men.'

'This is,' she says, giggling with embarrassment, 'the quickest and most convenient way for the Chinese girls to make a profit. There is a lot of competition amongst the women in China for a Hong Kong man so they won't even consider whether he has a wife or even another mistress.'

Legislator Christine Loh says: 'For many women who have had few opportunities to do different things the husband and family are the most important part of their lives, so even if the family has had problems they have not had any choice but to stay married. The cross-border mistresses issue with China is bringing up a lot of fear that we are, in fact, returning to the past.'

On the Hong Kong side of the border the issue is an emotional minefield. Even Ms Kwok's organisation is feeling its way forward warily, already criticised as 'family wreckers' for supporting women like Mary. Divorce is viewed by many Hong Kong women as a very public failure in life.

'Marriage is the most important goal for many women here so they have to start to think about their lives in a completely different way,' says Ms Kwok. 'They have a very dependent attitude. They have to learn to believe that happiness is built by themselves and not their husbands. We have women coming in here whose husbands blame them, tell them they are getting old and ugly. The husbands tell their wives that they can't control them.'

In some cases, she says, husbands have asked their wives to jump off the apartment building. When women come here for therapy their husband's affairs are already well established so it is difficult actually to do anything practical. 'And many women themselves think: "Okay, okay, my father and my grandfather had mistresses and my mother and grandmother put up with it." In many cases, if it is just a sexual, casual thing they tolerate it as part of the marriage. But once a woman knows that her husband has another steady partner, then she will become very frustrated. Some women will start speaking out and quarrelling very bitterly with their husbands.'

It seems extraordinarily intrusive to ask Mary for the details of her husband's infidelity, given the social context we have been discussing, but Mary is on a roll. She has been practising for two years within the safe confines of the support group so she seems more than willing to acknowledge the truth about her marriage. I am not, however, prepared for her answer.

'When we got married I loved my husband but of course things change. After seven years, the seven-year-itch, I already thought my husband was having casual sex but then I got the evidence.' Which I take to mean that she followed the other women. No, she explains. She had to take herself to the doctor who told her she had contracted a venereal disease. 'My husband thinks it is normal for a man to behave like this and a woman to tolerate it. He thinks that so long as his financial obligation to the family is fulfilled then that is enough.'

Mary said she did not accept the situation but kept quiet and stayed married because they had no property and two young children. She did not even consider looking for support outside her apartment: her own parents would have no sympathy for her and her husband's family would support him on the issue.

But, even then, she began to formulate a long term plan. Bit by bit the family saved and she convinced her husband to buy an apartment in her name. For her part she fulfilled her obligations to cook and clean and support the children. Sometimes her husband came home, sometimes he didn't. When he did, she says, he insisted on her fulfilling her conjugal obligations as well. She became ill again with an STD but kept quiet, encouraging her own daughter to delay marriage and seek out a career. She walked from the apartment to the shopping centre, from the apartment to the clothes line—fuming. It was the most recent bout of STD that gave her the courage to join the support group. 'In my childhood I already had a strong sense of injustice. Then I became aware of other women in my situation and some even worse off with young children whose husbands have left and who are still waiting for them to return.'

At 45 it is difficult to imagine life alone, freed from the driving resentment her marriage has given her. Her husband, she says, travels regularly to China where he has another wife. She has not tried to follow him. For a couple more years, she says, she will cook and clean until her young adult children have left home and the mortgage payments are complete. Then she will file for a divorce and have her husband removed from her apartment.

For herself she is unable even to imagine any hobbies that might occupy her time with her family gone. She would like to go into business with a couple of friends but has no work experience. Stout, middle-aged, neat, an open-wide face, short hair, a simple gold chain and watch, an imitation leather handbag clutched on her lap, Mary dissolves into embarrassed tears.

'It is not socially acceptable to be divorced. Even if a woman becomes financially independent, it is not the same as being psychologically independent,' Ms Kwok repeats.

Of her options for a partner in the future Mary can only laugh at her prospects. But, yes, she says, she would like a boyfriend. 'But my husband would kill me,' she says, an expression which is not always used figuratively in a society in which the concept of possession is acutely honed.

The execution of
Nguyen Thi Chien

Clearly, there is an important part of her story missing. Even in her own words she was born into the lowest ranks of a stratified society, condemned at the age of five to scavenging in the open market like a feral animal, the sole survivor of a family destroyed by starvation. At the age of seven she was 'rescued' to become a house slave to a petty village official, beaten at will and banned from seeking an education. And then, as a young woman, she took the place of a buffalo and dragged a plough through the rice fields at night: a mere beast of burden in much of her society's eyes.

Yet Nguyen Thi Chien rose to occupy a position of considerable fame and respect, to win a Government pension and deserve an ample Government house.

At first she is not telling. The rest of her story is harrowing enough: how she came to lead a platoon of women guerrillas in the war against the French in Vietnam, equipped—in the beginning—with only seven landmines and imitation wooden guns; how she lived in tunnels underground, only the closeness of the earth walls more suffocating than the stale, humid air; and how she hid beneath the waterlilies in the ponds dumped around her village by the torrential wet season rains, a hollow tube of bamboo allowing her to breathe.

The questions are not easily put, so around and around we talk, politely, compassionately. Her eyes well with emotion, not bravado. And then, in the end, she volunteers the missing link herself. Quietly, carefully, tearfully. Hers is the story of an exceptional judgement.

As she stood, tied to a bamboo stake, an execution squad lining up her heart in its sights, Nguyen Thi Chien decided it would be the third, not the first, volley that would hit. For days she had been tortured, but she had refused to confess. She was, of course, a Communist guerrilla leader of considerable local note, the guardian of crucial information about the campaign against the French and their local Vietnamese allies.

Only when death had become inevitable would she reveal her hand. And so it would not be at the first round that she would shout the slogan she had prepared, thus allowing herself an honourable death. The first bullets, she judged, would be fired into the air in the hope that she would scream for mercy and offer up her comrades in exchange for a reprieve. The second would be fired to maim, not kill, still leaving just a slim chance that she could escape to plot her revenge. And so it would be on the third round that she would shout: 'Long Live the Indochinese Communist Party'.

Indeed, after one round, fired to miss, the execution squad cut her down. But they did not make good their taunt and throw her tied to the stake into the river so that the fish might eat her flesh. Instead, they took her back again to the prison, for one more try. And then, finally, when her body was crawling with insects drawn to the urine and faeces that dripped down her legs, her limbs were paralysed and her consciousness could no longer be retrieved from the blackness by their buckets of cold water, Nguyen Thi Chien was tossed away.

It is summer in Hanoi. Outside the simple wooden house the war is long over. The Communist victory of two decades ago delivered the reins of government to the guerrillas and their cadre, but the free-wheeling forces of capitalism have returned to rule the hot, noisy streets.

This is the decade of open-market Communism, that curious anachronism of the 1990s that blends absolute political power with consumer choice in the handful of Communist Party ruled nations which survived the collapse of the Soviet Union.

The experiment with Marxist economic theory is over. The inefficient state-owned enterprises are dying a natural death in the face of foreign investment and local private business initiatives. The dull, functional products of the old Soviet-style factories are gone from all but the shelves of the cavernous government emporium. In the street markets and behind the new, shiny pane-glass display windows of renovated shops the Coca-Cola cans are stacked high.

Outside the Hanoi hotels wiry, brown cyclo drivers hover, offering their hot vinyl seats to tourists, more in the name of nostalgia than efficiency. The smooth, quiet streams of bicycles that once flowed along Hanoi's shady avenues of tatty colonial mansions are gradually being forced off the road. Now, from beneath the graceful arches of trees billow the fumes and the racket of the tens of thousands of motor bikes and cars of the capitalist economy.

But inside the wooden house, behind the shutters hung by the French to hold back the heavy summer air, the war will never end. Half a century is such a long time in the recent history of Vietnam, one war

97

sliding into another, dragging with it so much misery and pain.

There was the first war against the French colonial regime, then the Japanese occupation during the Second World War, and then the next war against the French, followed by the war against the Americans. And when the Communists finally won independence in 1975 there was the war against famine, the border battle against the Chinese and then the Vietnamese invasion of Kampuchea and the war against Pol Pot.

For the small group of former soldiers gathered at the headquarters of the War Veterans Association, the Coca-Cola cans and the old American sit-coms now beaming in on satellite TV are merely cosmetic changes. It is the slogans of the revolution and the deprivations of the armed struggle that forever will define their lives.

Nguyen Thi Chien is now 65 years old. Her grey hair is tied in a neat bun, the medals of her courage are displayed prominently across her chest and the rank on the shoulder of her heavy khaki uniform is that of a lieutenant-colonel in the regular army. She was born into a family of landless peasants in the Red River Delta, the so-called cradle of the Communist revolution in the north of the country. Here the frequent floods pushed the people to the brink of starvation and the taxes levied by the French often forced them over the edge.

I had assumed that a few simple questions about her family background would provide an easy opening for her story. In my ignorance I have failed to factor in the crucial filters of self-perception, such as shame and pride. So within minutes I have it. Just the facts. A mother and four siblings dead from hunger, a father absent, having fled the French tax collector to die later in a distant French-owned mine (in Vietnam).

'At five I was wandering alone in the market and one very kind lady who sold cheap food sometimes gave me something to eat. I lived like this until I was seven years old,' she says baldly, through a translator. But does she remember how she felt, a feral child, good enough only to graduate from the market to a life as a domestic slave?

'There was just no way out for me, that was all. I went to work for the head of the village in the feudal system. I had to get water from a very deep well and sometimes the earthenware pots broke and I was beaten very brutally,' she says. 'I was small and weak and could barely carry such heavy loads.'

Was she angry? I ask. A question which has no answer for a young girl who believed only that she had no choice. And so the question is ignored and the story continues, only the barest outline of her childhood discernible as she races ahead to the time when her identity began to form.

She was, she says, an orphan, with no relatives still alive. She was nothing, she says, as though this will explain why she has so little to say. At the bottom of the heap, she expected no more than a very hard life and the possibility of survival. Nguyen Thi Chien was born into a strictly ordered society built around a static hierarchy. The legacy of a millennium of Confucianism was particularly cruel to a young girl with no male relatives from whom she could borrow her social status until her own marriage.

As we talk she measures her own worth using the same set of rules: in her own eyes Nguyen Thi Chien is still foraging under the market stalls.

It would be safe to assume that for many years Thi

Chien suffered a great deal, and suffered without choice. Then, when the ideas of the 'revolution' reached her village in the late 1940s she found herself with her first option in life. It was, too, a path of great suffering but, she says, an obvious path to choose. Of course. It is redundant to point out that she had absolutely nothing to lose.

It was in 1949 that French troops reached the Red Delta as they reoccupied Vietnam after the end of the Second World War. At first Thi Chien disappeared into the arms of the propaganda teams, spreading the word of the revolution by day, catching fish and snails in the rice fields by night. She learnt to read and write, a privilege denied her by her former boss in line with the Confucian belief that women are difficult to educate and so must be bound, ignorant and obedient, to the men of their families for the rest of their lives.

In the small cluster of thatch huts that stood alongside the rice fields lived another young woman: robbed of her social status by the death of her husband from starvation. Thi Chien went to live with the widow and together these two nobodies, without husbands or sons of their own to serve and protect, made the decision to fight, to become comrades-at-arms. Naturally, she says, it was something of a joke around the village when Thi Chien formed an all-women's platoon, to fight alongside two platoons of men.

'There was an old saying in Vietnam that when the enemy arrived even the women could stand up and fight. But there was a very strong belief—said half as a joke and half truth—that women had very weak arms and legs and could barely hold a rifle.'

The small group of war veterans, all men except for Thi Chien, shift to the edges of the sticky vinyl couches. The cacophony of noise from the street outside fades as the story draws the listeners in. 'No guns,' they say in turn in English, repeating the translation.

Her platoon had a formidable enemy but no guns, just seven mines and some pieces of wood, carved with much optimism into gun-like shapes.

Here, it would be tempting to hark back to the words of the leader of the Vietnamese revolution, Ho Chi Minh: 'Those who have guns can shoot the enemy, those who have knives can fight with knives and those who have only bamboo can fight with bamboo sticks'.

But Thi Chien is looking much further back in history. The story she would like to relate is that of the Trung sisters, legendary warriors who led an uprising against the Han (Chinese) occupation of her own Red River Delta almost two millennia ago.

The story goes that in the year 34AD, the delta was invaded by the Han people from the north who installed a tyrannical governor, a man of great cruelty who spared not even the most senior Vietnamese officials. In the mountains lived two sisters, daughters of a Vietnamese military governor. The eldest, Trung Trac, and her husband Thi Sach were plotting an uprising but the conspiracy was discovered and Thi Sach was executed. So the younger sister, Trung Nhi, took her dead brother-in-law's place at Trung Trac's side and together they fomented an insurrection so powerful that the Chinese were driven from the land.

One of the sisters' most crafty generals was an aristocrat, Lady Le Chan, and so the powerful vision of three women, leading their men into battle atop the gilded seats of their elephants, tumbles forward through the generations, a national source of pride and strength. The victorious Trung sisters, the translator says, were later crowned 'kings'.

Written accounts of the Trung sisters' lives, which have been published in English, use the word 'queen', so it remains unclear whether the people bestowed upon the sisters the status of honorary men, or whether they basked in their glory as women. Thi

Chien is not merely talking about historical role models, though, she is talking about tactics. What she really thought about her all-female platoon was not that their limbs were weak or their courage lacking. 'In reality we had to know how to fight with our brains,' she says. 'One lady platoon was really equal to two platoons of men.'

For the women, she explains, had three roles, not just one. They worked the land by night so that the village could eat, they dragged the injured out of battle and tended their wounds and they fought alongside the men on the frontline.

From the Trung sisters and a long line of Vietnamese heroes who had fought the Chinese for almost 4000 years Thi Chien learnt about weapons.

'We had very few mines so we had to create a way to kill more of the enemy by putting broken ceramic pots and glass around them. We also built bamboo traps filled with sharp bamboo spikes and camouflaged them carefully and let the enemy chase us until they fell in. And it is very interesting to tell you,' she says, 'about how we bent down the tops of many, many bamboo plants and when they flipped back up we cleared away many, many enemy.' This method is not made clear to me, but the rest of the group nods intently, adding a few words in French and English.

'Why do we have to do this? If you compare the Vietnamese side with the French or the American artillery and infantry it is very rudimentary, and the battle is very unequal. That is why we were taught by the old people the ancient methods used by our ancestors to kill,' she explains.

Life in the jungle, she says, was 'very exciting'. Again, the exact nuance is uncertain, her apparent exuberance perhaps magnified by the translator's choice of words. Very quickly Thi Chien's platoon snatched the rifles they needed from the enemy soldiers trapped in their bamboo pits. By night they ruled the village, by day they melted back into the jungle when the French forces rose to begin their patrols.

'At first the women were frightened. At night, when the enemy fired, the bullets made a line in the dark and a terrible sound,' she says, making the 'ping, pinging' noise herself. 'But later we got used to it.'

It is difficult to convey the claustrophobia of life in the underground tunnels of the Vietnamese resistance. The Cuu Chi tunnels outside Ho Chi Minh city, formerly Saigon, have been enlarged for Western tourists and opened for inspection. Even with their larger doorways the sensation of walking bent double down a dark underground passageway is one of panic and suffocation. But it is without the embroidery of emotion that Thi Chien describes her daily life: hiding in ponds using a bamboo snorkel, crawling into the underground earth network, surviving for months on end on green bananas, sweet potato and unboiled water. 'Yes,' she says, matter-of-factly, 'it was a very, very hard life, a very, very terrible life. But there was no way out.'

She nods when I ask her about killing. Did she kill anyone herself? Does she believe that women feel any differently about killing than men? The answer is very long, but not complete. Hate, revenge and honour. A magnificent motivation. The enemy, the Vietnamese 'henchmen' of the French, stand accused of killing innocent women and children. As a warrior she must avenge their honour.

'Many times,' she says, 'we lectured the enemies we had captured. We goaded them as cowards, we told them to go back to their families and lead an innocent life. Many, many times we gave them lessons and set them free but they could not change their nature. We told them that if they continued to commit crimes the bullets would not spare them and they would have to leave their families. We had no jail to put them in, and no food to feed them even if we had.'

At which point our host from the Veterans' Association motions for me to wind the discussion up.

'In one battle 21 of my comrades were killed,' she says, 'and many, many houses were burnt.'

'It was because of their great hatred that they killed,' says the translator by way of summing up. And so I do not insist on attempting to unearth feelings that I cannot possibly understand, nor risk implying a moral judgement from the safety of my own peacetime existence.

I swing right away from the friction and return instead to the question of women and just how difficult one's personal life must have been in such trying conditions. The tension breaks and she laughs. The concentration of the men listening, though, remains steady.

'One family in the village wanted to ask for my hand in marriage but I was so busy with the fighting. It was an exciting life, and so I had no time to take up a love affair,' she says, smiling.

In the wars against the French and the Americans, an estimated 10 per cent of combatants of the Viet Minh, or Viet Cong as they were more commonly known, were women. Women were widely used in sensitive positions such as intelligence gathering, carrying information through road blocks set up by conventional foreign armies and transporting, mostly on foot, huge quantities of arms and supplies. They were called the 'long-haired soldiers', and although most began combat careers in local village militia a small number, such as Nguyen Thi Chien, gained ranking positions in the regular North Vietnamese army.

The legend of the Trung sisters is often quoted by both men and women as evidence of a Vietnamese tradition of female warriors. Other anthropologists have gone further back to the roots of a Vietnamese matriarchal culture. Archaeological finds point to the widespread worship of mother images in primitive Vietnamese society, and in isolated villages oral histories tell of surviving practices such as the sharing of the pain of childbirth. In northern and central Vietnam it was common for a father to lie in bed and mime the pains of childbirth to lessen the ordeal of his wife or for him to climb up onto the roof of the house during labour to equal the risk his wife was running in delivering the baby.

But, any truth can be plucked from history. It is true that the Trung sisters led a courageous and splendid assault against the Chinese invaders. But it is also true they drowned themselves in the face of defeat several years later. It is true that the doctrine of Communism gave Vietnamese women equality. But, it is also true that the centuries of Confucianism, which came with the Chinese, weighed heavily on the society on both sides of the ideological divide. The mobilisation of women by the Communist forces was, wrote one prominent anthropologist, 'a completely new idea to most militants whose attitudes were strongly influenced by feudal prejudices. There were, therefore, quite a number who found it difficult to accept that women had been given a role to play of national importance.'

From the eleventh to the nineteenth century, Confucianism formed the basis of the Vietnamese legal system. As such, the doors of both public and private schools were closed to women and a network of male relatives—fathers, uncles, brothers and later husbands—brought up girls very strictly from a young age.

The Rule of the Three Obediences deprived women of legal rights for their entire lives: young girls had to obey their fathers, wives had to obey their husbands and widows had to obey their sons. Successive dynasties issued codes of conduct for women. The Gia Long code of the nineteenth century listed seven reasons why a man may repudiate his wife, ranging from failure to bear a son and properly serve his parents to a propensity to gossip. A woman had no right to reject her husband and could be punished by 100 strokes of the cane and then put up for sale if she tried to run away from the family home. The penalty for adultery on the part of a woman was strangulation.

'Mothers-in-law were traditionally cruel to their daughters-in-law over whom they had absolute power. Ill-treated all their own lives by their husbands' families, they carried out their revenge on their daughters-in-law who would wield power in much the same fashion when their turn came around,' writes Le Thi Nham Tuyet, a Senior.

As both child marriage and polygamy were permitted, rich men frequently took multiple wives, a process sometimes started by parents during their son's childhood. Poor families would sell off their grown daughters to be married to a rich little boy, effectively furnishing his family with a domestic slave to be cast aside when he came of age and took another wife. Nyugen Thi Chien is a woman for whom war meant social mobility. But for millions more, bound by the weight of history to their traditional obedience to men, war meant widowhood and much silent suffering.

The tape has been turned over and replaced many times. The light, if not the fierce heat of the day, is fading. I have heard much about pride and the revolution. But, I would like to ask one more question, if I may. 'Were you ever captured?' I ask, knowing the answer already from my own research.

In English I ask the translator whether the question is inappropriate, offering him an opportunity to ignore it altogether. He does not answer and so Thi Chien begins.

'I was assigned to a group of cadres who were having a meeting in the area and there was only one route out using an open road.' She was, she says, walking about 200 metres ahead, a simply dressed, long-haired young farm girl, when she encountered the French side. 'I have come back from the market,' she shouted to imaginary relatives in the huts nearby. Her comrades heard the sign and turned back. But the enemy troops knew of the girl commander, tales told by the 'running dogs' of the enemy earlier set free by the guerrillas.

'They tortured me with electricity. My whole body was shaking and then I would lose consciousness and they would pour water over me. I just said yes, that sometimes I had carried out activities for the resistance but that I knew nothing of their organisation or of other members. It was very, very painful. Then, the enemy got out the hot iron and all I could think about was that I was an orphan who used to be brutally beaten so I tried to endure,' she said. At that moment she is again a cowering child.

There is, she says, no discrimination in torture. It is as bad for a woman as it is for a man. Thi Chien explains, almost apologetically, that 'one's urine and manure automatically come out'. And still she manages to talk on. After the execution squad cut her down and tortured her again she was so badly injured, unconscious and paralysed, that they thought she was dead. So her body was released to the cemetery and it was there the militia of a nearby village found her and dragged her back into the jungle to nurse her back to health.

'Did she think she would survive?' I ask. At which point she finally breaks down. 'No,' she says through tears, 'I felt I had no hope at all, but I wanted to die in a very honourable way.'

I feel that I should apologise and my attempts are acknowledged with a nod. Our group is exhausted. There are many more questions to ask but a reluctance to go on. So I ask Nguyen Thi Chien not to respond to my questions but to tell me what she would like to say. 'I am very proud that although I am an orphan, that I have no mother or father, I have taken a very honourable post in the society,' she begins, and talks on and on in thanks to those who were not rescued.

In 1953 Nguyen Thi Chien was awarded the title of Hero and taken into the regular army, moving from her guerrilla base to a stronghold in the north. There she married and raised a daughter as she rose through the ranks as an officer. (But, torture does discriminate. Often, it is worse for women prisoners. Later, I am told that her daughter was adopted, the torture having left her unable to bear children.)

'I think you must know,' she says, 'about the carpet bombing by the American B-52s, every day and every night. I think you must know that even though we have won the wound will never heal.'

It is not necessary to ask whether she has been disappointed by the poverty of her nation at peace. It would be impolite in the extreme to try to take away any of her pride. So, instead, we step outside into a blazing dusk of a Hanoi summer evening.

A heroine

Thai Thi Thinh had waited more than half her life. When the medal, officially naming her a heroine of two long-finished wars, was finally pinned on her chest she was already 85 years old and had, she says, no more tears left to shed.

It was in 1946 that her husband took her hand and placed it in the palm of their eldest son. He had brought the family to the safety of a rural village but was returning to the city and the war, leaving his teenage son in charge as head of the household. Wait for me, he told his wife. And so she did.

For nine years she waited without news in the safe hills of northern Vietnam. She sent two sons off to the front and all that came back to the village were the letters informing her of their deaths. The war against the French ended. She moved to the Communist held capital of the north, Hanoi. The war against the Americans began. Her fifth child, who had played at her side during her lonely vigil in the mountains, had grown up and was ready to leave. Another letter bearing bad news returned to take his place. And still, she has had no news of the man she called her 'darling', just the last report of him, an army doctor, riding his bicycle towards the shelling almost half a century ago, and her own vivid recollection of the touch of his hand.

A HEROINE

Thai Thi moves slowly and carefully, fussing over the tea and bottled water she has laid out on the small table in the single room she now shares with her surviving daughter and son-in-law. By day she stays home alone in the damp, crumbly Hanoi flat. A large dog tugs angrily at his chain, patrolling the doorway, filling the room with the odour of his sweat. She has cried so much, she says, that she has run out of tears. It is not that she is hard, relating her story dry-eyed, but her ample grief has already been expended.

In honour of the visit she dons a fresh dark brown tunic with small pearl buttons, her medal already in place. Her eyes have turned milky, her vision is fading, so she is trapped inside unable to watch television or make out the words in the newspaper. She is small and very thin, like a tiny bird. Her thinning hair is pulled back, her face a leathery sea of lines.

She fiddles self-consciously with her medal. It is the honour of a 'heroine mother', belated acknow-ledgement of the incredible losses suffered in two wars, mainly husbands and sons lost to millions of women. She slowly takes out the photos of the ceremony and explains the pictures of Government officials hanging on her walls. Finally, she says, she can feel that some of her suffering has been shared.

Thai Thi was born in central Vietnam. Her father was a corvee labourer for the French, travelling at call around Indochina building roads. Her mother had no choice but to follow him, bringing their six children along. Life, she says, 'was so difficult. There was not enough money to buy clothes, not enough money to buy food or to build a house.'

As a girl she went to school only up until primary level. 'I am so sorry,' she says, through the interpreter, 'but at that time girls and boys in society were not equal. They [girls] did not need to learn any more because then they would not follow their father and

husband. The job of a daughter was to help her mother
do the housework, the cooking and the knitting, so
that is what I did,' she laughs, her eyes almost disappearing into the folds of her face.

At the age of seventeen Thai Thi fell in love. But
her darling was still a student so even when they
married two years later she stayed at home with her
parents while he continued his medical studies. It was
the practice, she explains, for the bride to go to live
with her husband's parents. But they were farmers and
her family were labourers. She did not know how to
farm so they did not ask her to come.

Was it difficult, I ask, seeing your husband only
once a week, living apart? 'No,' she answers pragmatically. Her husband's family sent sacks of rice from the
farm so life was no longer difficult. It has not occurred
to her that the question was actually about her own
feelings.

At the age of nineteen she gave birth to her first
child. Of course, everyone would like to have a boy,
she says, and she did. Her husband was a medical
student and a modern man so he turned away the
superstitious gifts of meat and sugar and eggs in favour
of a clean bed and told her that she need not hide
herself inside for 30 days after the birth, as tradition
dictated.

Three years later her husband qualified and took a
teaching position in Hanoi. Thai Thi, now with two
sons, realised her dream of a family home and travelled
by train to join him. 'I would like to mention that
when we were living together in the medical college of
Hanoi a doctor held a high position in society and I
was happy and respected,' she says.

Her life as a wife and mother of stature was short
lived. During the Japanese occupation of Vietnam,
Thai Thi was again relegated to life in the countryside
with only a wooden bed, a woven mat and a torch to

her name. Four more children were born, two of them
dying very young. From their camp near the Chinese
border her husband was training for a life in the
resistance forces. But even then life was not so difficult
for her. 'There is an old Vietnamese saying which goes
that a goat which gives birth to an elephant will find
enough grass to provide for that elephant,' she
explains, before rising again to check on her guard dog.

But when the war against the Japanese ended and
the French returned to Vietnam Thai Thi was very
angry. Her family had just settled back down in Hanoi,
her husband in charge of a medical faculty when Ho
Chi Minh ordered the evacuation of the city so that
the French would find only soldiers in the houses when
they came.

'So my husband took us out again to another
peaceful place. I deeply remember the last minute
when we said goodbye. I always thought he would
come back and I sent many, many letters to the
resistance and each time they told me that he was lost
and that they were still trying to find him.'

With the other wives Thai Thi picked tea, baked
cakes to sell, grew vegetables, taught the children to
read in the shade of the trees and waited.

'Many, many times the wives of other doctors came
to ask me to come back to the city but I refused
because I had promised my husband that I would wait,
so I could not leave.'

When her oldest son went to join the resistance he
also asked her to wait, and to relieve him of his
responsibility for his siblings.

'I did not try to stop him. At that time there was
a saying in the school: put down the pen and pick up
the gun. I was proud but told him not to let himself
get surrounded.' Then, inevitably, her second son told
her he was leaving to join his brother.

Thai Thi does not know exactly what her sons' roles

were in the war, except that the eldest boy became a bomb disposal expert. But she does know that they both fought on the side of the Communists in the legendary victory against the French at Dien Bien Phu, the critical turning point in the war against the French. In July 1954, the year of that victory, she received two letters in a single week, one for each son.

'At first I thought it must be a mistake. My first son had died in January but I received the news only then. I thought they were telling me twice. A week earlier I had received a letter from my second son. He was on his way home, he was already near, eager to tell his family about the campaign at Dien Bien Phu. But, it was not a mistake and he never returned.' Later she would learn that he had been killed after the signing of the Geneva Agreement of 1954 that divided Vietnam into north and south and was supposed to bring peace to the country.

She did not try to stop her third son leaving when the war against the Americans escalated. And he too died in the rainy season of 1973, two years before the end of the war, when his eight years of luck on the battlefield ran out. The place where her husband had asked her to wait was no longer safe so the family moved about, stopping here and there for a day or two at a time, the land destroyed by bombing runs.

Thai Thi's name means rich and prosperous, the kind of name commonly given to a baby by the very poor in an attempt to defy her certain fate. And, comparatively speaking, Thai Thi now enjoys a luxurious life, even in her single-room flat, with bars for windows and shutters in place of glass. A frost-free fridge sits shiny and new beside the hard wooden beds and the television shares the family altar alongside the medals and old family photos.

Earlier that day the editor of a local women's magazine had explained life this way. 'It is so easy to

have an official policy saying women are equal in
society but in fact it is not true. Generally speaking
neither men nor women in Vietnam want women to
be equal. The biggest dream for a man is power, the
biggest dream for a woman is to have a happy family.'
And the loss of that family is also the greatest loss,
she said.

So Thai Thi is still waiting for her husband. Tradition, she explains, dictates that a funeral must be held
so that the dead person's spirit will be able to find its
way home. Her husband's spirit is still lost, she says,
wandering aimlessly, frightened.

'It is such a shame not to have a grave where I
could go to burn joss sticks so he would know that I
am thinking of him.'

The rear legs
of the elephant

A Thai woman is like the rear legs of an elephant, always following in the footsteps of the front feet, says Thanpuying (Lady) Lersakdi Sampatisiri, one of Thailand's most powerful businesswomen. Yet, when her own father died she took over his business empire, which included much of Bangkok's bus and canal boat network, and rose to become the first female Minister in a Thai Government.

'Of course,' she says, 'a powerful woman is expected to behave differently from a man in the same position. It is not possible to bang on tables over a deal or socialise in the men's only hostess clubs. But, the shy, smiling, public face of that Thai woman is widely misunderstood outside Asia.

'The graceful deference is not an expression of subservience or powerlessness, but a means of negotiating a path through a male dominated social structure. Sometimes we feel we want to shout and talk back, but, being women, we keep quiet and walk away to do something better—and that is our revenge.'

Nowhere is the apparent contradiction between the Western perception of the agreeable 'Oriental woman' and the reality of their effectiveness more stark than in business. Right across Asia female entrepreneurs control vast business holdings within societies that openly favour sons in the distribution of lifetime opportunities and passing of wealth from one generation to another. So strong are family ties in Thai culture, for example, that in the absence of—or even incompetence of—sons it is frequently daughters who are asked to take control, rather than male professional managers from outside the clan. But this is only part of the reason why women have achieved so much as entrepreneurs. Paradoxically, the inferior social standing of women may have actually contributed to their success.

Traditionally, women were discriminated against in access to education and in entry into the prestigious ranks of government service or the armed forces. At home in the villages with the children they set up small lunch stalls or established a handicraft network and gained control of the local markets as well as the family finances. Often they started up small businesses out of necessity, forced to supplement low Government wages or military salaries.

'Women have always been in business,' says Thanpuying Lersakdi. 'In the beginning they were at home selling vegetables or if they could cook well then they could sell their food. When men see the result they appreciate it and women take a more and more active role in the family in earning money and in making decisions. But the nature of Thai women is never to tell a man, "This is my right." Thai women never complain.'

The elegant lobby of the Hilton at Nai Lert Park ripples with recognition as she walks in, slowly, to take her seat in the lounge overlooking the cool green of its famous garden. This is Thanpuying Lersakdi's hotel. Now close to 70, she lives next door in the house built by her father, some of his wonderful garden given over to her hotel enterprise. Here it is still possible to imagine the Bangkok of her youth, the wide tree-lined

streets set alongside *khlongs* (canals) bobbing with gar-
ishly decorated long boats, the golden temples, their
yellow streamers flying in the breeze, gracing the sky-
line. Even this modern hotel cuts only a smooth
low-rise arch through the gardens, refusing to join the
canyons of high-rise towers of Bangkok's recent economic success.

Her father sent her to Japan to study in the 1930s,
considering that it was there that economic power
would be centred in his daughter's generation. She had
to be content, though, to attend a college as Japanese
universities did not accept women at that time. When
she returned her father sent her to work for the Office
of Civil Servants Commission, to find out how the
Government worked. 'I was an only child,' she says,
by way of explanation. There was no male heir.

'My father read all kinds of books available at the
time. If the text was in English he would sit there with
a dictionary looking up words he did not understand.
He advised me to have an eagerness to learn. He also
liked to socialise with foreigners with whom he could
exchange knowledge and cultural ideas. All these gave
him business initiatives such as the ice factory—the
first in Thailand—which he ran himself without hiring
any foreigners.'

After three years in the Government service her
father said, 'Okay, that's enough'. Then she returned
to what she described as doing nothing. 'I sat by my
father's side all morning in the office, then I invited
my friends for lunch and was free to go out and have
fun all afternoon.' It was a life of privilege, rather than
family duty, within Thailand's small economic élite.
But the obligations were always there lurking in the
background. When her father suddenly died when she
was 27 years old she found herself at the helm of his
empire. His white buses dominated the city's transport
routes, his ferries plied the canals and his ice factories

supplied tens of thousands of Thais before refrigeration was widely available.

'My mother was a traditional Thai lady who was not inclined to go out. I had to assure mother that I would take charge and not let the businesses dwindle. I decided to start straight away. I talked to all the old staff, asking them to carry on working and help keep Nai Lert's [her father's] name famous. I told them frankly that I had never worked in private business and I asked them to help me with what to do so the company would survive.'

Every morning, she recalled, the general manager would stand ceremoniously in front of her father and report to him on the state of the business, then formally hand over the previous day's earnings, wrapped in paper, to the chief accountant. She also remembered her father saying that any business enterprise needed at least one investment that returned cash on a daily basis, like the ice factory. Putting all the money in long-term investments was dangerous. So the first thing she did was to convince the managers to stay and ensure they enjoyed considerable status and respect, even from herself. But in a way her father had already secured the transition. He had offered shares in the business some time earlier to long-standing employees, so they already had an incentive to keep the company going. These were conservative times for Thai women, so when Thanpuying Lersakdi took over she became the first and only female in the company.

The ice factory was the most profitable part of the enterprise but, more and more, Thanpuying shifted her emphasis to transport, seeing the coming of refrigeration. Normally, it would have been a sound business strategy, following very much along the lines of the lessons her father had taught her. But in 1975 her carefully planned expansion was swept away overnight in the chaos of Thai politics. The buses were nationalised leaving Thanpuying Lersakdi with only 30 or so of her former 4000 employees.

'I went to see all my bus drivers at 2 a.m. to talk to them personally. I said to myself, stay calm, keep still, but I wondered how I could go on living in this country.'

Later, when the Government was facing a transport strike, Thanpuying Lersakdi was asked to swallow her pride a second time and intervene. 'I agreed to go to see the drivers, the white buses had never been on strike, we always served the people. They were no longer mine but when I talked to the drivers they went back to work.'

It was at this time, she says, that her belief in the quiet ways of Thai women was seriously challenged. Had she been a man she believes she would have been able to push her way past the secretaries screening visitors for the new Government. She says she would have thumped her fist on their desks and refused to comply with the nationalisation order. Instead, she was merely turned away at the gate.

Clearly, she is angry but her smooth, measured tones do not waver. She sips a glass of water and continues, sitting pertly on the edge of the lounge, her assistant hovering nearby just in case she needs to check the English translation of a word or two (she does not).

'I was determined not to spend the Government's compensation money so I had to use my own. I also wanted the business back but I had to get it with clean hands.'

So, immediately, the Nai Lert company vacated their city offices and put them up for rent. The company moved into the back of the family home and literally started again.

'We had to think of what we could do next, the buses had been very profitable. But, I still had a couple of buses left and some loyal employees so we began a school bus service to two private schools. When that stabilised I decided to build townhouses on some of our land, sell them and the rest of our land and leave Thailand.'

But the cycle of politics turns quickly in Thailand and power is as easily lost as it was won. In 1979, Thanpuying Lersakdi found herself being offered the job of Minister of Transport in a new Government. 'I had to think about it for a long time. Finally, I agreed because I am a Thai and I think that when opportunities allow, we should serve the country.'

She served for one year and her decisions still mark the country. It was Thanpuying Lersakdi who convinced the Government to open an international airport on the island of Phuket, allowing for a major boom in resort and tourism development. It was also her recommendation that opened up road links in the remote north and kept the existing rail link running, allowing the spectacular growth in tourism income to spread across the country. But she never did get her buses back.

'In Parliament,' she says, 'the handful of women Members of Parliament would conspire in whispers but they would never tell their male colleagues how to vote. Thai women do not tell men what to do,' she repeats. 'Whatever we did we tried to do well because we were afraid the men would look at us and say that women were no good.'

As the first Thai woman to serve as a Minister she was certainly noticed. A British TV crew, she says, came to Bangkok to interview her. But, when the segment went to air it was juxtaposed with shots of skimpily-clad bar girls gyrating in front of Western sex tourists just a couple of kilometres away in the red light districts. The point was hardly subtle. How could such contradictory roles, such apparent power and such apparent powerlessness, exist side by side?

Naturally, she had thought the interview was going to be about her. In retrospect she smiles, able to see the funny side. She says she even keeps in touch with the journalists responsible and meets them for lunch when they come to town—no hard feelings.

Actually, I had been wondering how to break into the calm flow of her life story with a question such as this. It would have been impolite of me to do so, and I appreciate the initiative coming from her. I was based in Thailand for three years as a foreign correspondent and I learnt very quickly that the most effective approach is not normally the most direct. I also learnt that this is a country of deep national pride, so it was not my right, as a foreigner, to fly in, eager to impose my own moral judgement of what I see on my first walk down the street.

'In Thailand women are the same. They are kind and gentle, they are good mothers. But with this kind of publicity [about the sex industry] people see a different kind of Thai woman, their lives are different because they have to earn a living in this way. When I see them I know that they have had no other chances, so I would ask people not to destroy them with their judgements. People cannot choose their fate.'

Today, her extended family are having lunch together as they often do. With her two daughters and their husbands and children by her side she is clearly the matriarch. Proper deference is shown as she steers the conversation. Her voice remains calm and measured, the waitresses gliding around the table with a feast of Chinese delicacies, her choice from her hotel's many cuisines.

She has said little about her family life but this too is her privilege, not my right to inquire. As she built her business she raised her two daughters, bringing them in early to the decisions, teaching them to respect the managers her father left behind, even in their old age. 'It was my eldest daughter who suggested we build the hotel in the grounds, but we couldn't build a hotel without any knowledge so we went to Hawaii to look at hotels.'

Despite having made the business decision to invite the Hilton chain to manage the hotel, Thanpuying Lersakdi kept control of the hotel's character, building the modern facilities around the graceful lines of traditional Thai architecture, filling the wide, open lobbies with rich Thai fabrics and distinctive furniture as well as fish ponds strewn with lilies. Now much of the responsibility for the running of the hotel and the rest of the group's business interests has been divided between her two daughters. 'Thailand is becoming more and more open for women. Now a woman can even become a Governor. Perhaps,' she says, 'my granddaughter's generation may learn to shout.'

The Kingdom of Siam, as it was known, was an absolute monarchy until 1932. Power resided in the palaces and outside their walls the peasants were little more than feudal serfs.

Social patterns that still strongly influence the position of Thai women today were set by the ruling kings, according to academic Dr Juree Wijitwatakarn. A Thai man was permitted up to four wives: a Royal wife chosen by the king; a major wife chosen by the family; a minor wife chosen by himself; and a slave wife, literally purchased out of slavery for similar use in his own home.

In both the noble and the common class the position

of a woman was defined only by the role of her male relations. In the predominant Buddhist religion, the belief that attainment of merit in this life determined one's position in the next was central. Many poor mothers would coddle their sons in the hope that they would gain merit on their behalf for the next life by entering the Buddhist monkhood. Outside the temples, social status could be won on entry into the civil service or the armed forces. The heritage this system left behind, Dr Juree argues, is the continuation of the practice of taking 'minor wives'—despite modern laws which no longer permit polygamy—the widespread acceptance of multiple partners for men in line with their status and wealth, the patronage of brothels by married men and priority for boys in education.

But on a practical level common men were frequently conscripted as male labourers for road building or as foot soldiers, leaving their women alone in the rural areas to fend for themselves with the result that they were forced to become traders or small-time businesswomen to provide for their families in the absence of their husbands.

'Business or trading did not require a formal education and could be launched as modestly as setting up a stall outside the home, enabling mothers to continue to fulfil their child-rearing responsibilities uninterrupted,' says Thanpuying Somsri Chareon Ratchapark, whose own business empire includes a five-star hotel and office and apartment blocks. 'In the past the greatest prestige and power came from being in the military or working for the Government in Thailand. Business people were looked down on by the political élite, so it was actually okay for women to go into business. It is a similar story across south-east Asia.'

The census of 1947 found three times as many women as men registered as business owners or managers and a regional study in the 1980s found 56 per cent of Thai businesses headed by women. In the Philippines, women headed 51 per cent of business, in Burma 47 per cent and in Cambodia 46 per cent—all countries with similar female domination in traditional markets.

'Women can carry the family business, they already have the name and the reputation,' says Khunying Chanut Piyaoui, whose landmark Dusit Thani Hotel stands only kilometres away from the Bangkok Hilton. 'When I was working alone it was like digging the earth with my bare hands,' she says of her struggle to build the Dusit Thani empire, now a chain of more than 50 luxury hotels of distinctive Thai character both in Thailand and overseas.

To be fair, Khunying Chanut was born with some money, but not a business empire to inherit. Her mother ran a small rice mill outside Bangkok, her father had a small saw mill in the city. 'It is the tradition of Thai women to become entrepreneurs. I would like to say that Thai women have been participating in business for a long, long time. Thai men who have the education or are well-to-do want to become Government officials and the Thai women are always helping earn the money because the pay is not high.'

So it was not particularly unusual that her mother lived in the countryside, a full day's journey away, and that the children lived with their father and went to school in Bangkok. 'At that time many people still believed that women should stay home but in my family my parents were very happy as soon as they saw us pick up our books and leave for school.'

Actually, she says, laughing, she had few ambitions as a girl. When Bangkok was bombed during the Second World War she was sent to the countryside to her mother, her education put on hold. 'When I came back my classmates were already in university and I was so far behind I would not be accepted. I then thought that one way to catch up would be to go to the United States even though I didn't know anything about it.'

Khunying Chanut convinced her mother to put up the money and left for New York alone to try to gain entry into Colombia University. She failed, being unable to speak English well enough, and was sent instead to an English school for foreign students, where she lived very frugally on her parents' small allowance. But after completing English school she again returned to Bangkok without any further qualifications.

'I felt ashamed about that; my peer group were still in university and I had no more chances to get in. I was about the age to marry then, but I didn't want to marry so I borrowed some money from my mother— because I didn't even know how to borrow from a bank—and started a small hotel, an idea I had come up with in the United States.

'I called it the Princess, after her Royal Highness. It had only 60 rooms but I made sure that each room had a modern bathroom attached, every room had a telephone and that we had a generator because Bangkok was often without power for a long time after the war. I didn't know the business so I had to work there myself every day and every night. Sometimes I was in the telephone office, sometimes I was helping the engineer to start the generator or helping in the front office.'

For Thai people, she says, the name *rong ram*, meaning 'hotel', had a different connotation, that of an entertainment establishment for men. 'So my hotel was a bit strange for them. Every time we had a complaint we fixed it straight away, we apologised to the people and made them feel okay,' she says.

Her time in the United States was not really wasted. The Princess won the contract for the PANAM flight crews laying-up in Bangkok. They got talking with Khunying Chanut. They brought in magazines with lots of ideas about promoting Thailand as a tourist destination. Khunying Chanut managed to arrange the lighting of two nearby temples, the beginning of the famous spectacle of Bangkok's temples at night, and, wanting to provide the crew with something more than a tiny lobby to relax in, she built the first swimming pool in Bangkok, even the cleaning equipment being flown in by the PANAM crew. 'Then I decided to travel to Europe and the United States. I had very little money but I tried to stay in the really good hotels, like the George V in Paris, for one night before moving to a cheaper hotel.'

She says she was far too shy to introduce herself as a fellow hotelier and initiate a chat about the business. 'No-one would have heard of my little hotel.' So she crept around the corridors sneaking a look at as much as possible in her precious 24 hours. 'I realised I had made many mistakes, the location was wrong for a start, it was merely a place for people to stay overnight. So I started dreaming of putting up a really grand hotel, a landmark for Bangkok. I was just dreaming really.'

Then, Khunying Chanut got married and had three children, while still running the Princess Hotel. 'My husband—he is a Thai man and a Thai man is always like that—when we got married expected his wife to take care of him and the house, and when he had people come over for dinner he expected his wife to be there. I did try to fulfil this role.'

126

It was about this time that Khunying Chanut met the head of the Oberoi Group of hotels from India.

'If I said to him I don't have the money but I would like to have a big hotel, he would just chase me away, wouldn't he. How can you want a big hotel without any money? So I talked to him and I said if I could come up with the land then maybe he could arrange for some financiers to put up a hotel. I could pay by instalments and eventually buy the hotel back from them. He was very encouraging so I went out to look for a site and when I had four of the best to choose from I asked the man from Oberoi to make the final decision.'

Khunying Chanut entered into a complicated financial deal to build a 500-room hotel and office block across the road from Bangkok's famous Lumpini Park, right in the middle of the emerging business district. At the last minute, though, she pulled out, not being able to accept that she would be unable to select materials and guide the design.

'I went to the architect and asked him to reconsider his fee and to work for me directly. Then I registered the company and I went out and asked the public to invest. At this time [the late 1960s] Thailand didn't even have a stock exchange. The first time I sold shareholding I raised only 40 million baht (US$1.6 million), much of which was used just for the foundation. Then I increased the public stake to 80 million then 120 million. I borrowed from the Japanese banks, then the US banks, then the German banks to buy the steel bars and the boilers and the kitchen equipment.

'But the price was still too high so I had to become the general contractor myself. We had ten to fourteen contractors working at the one time, piling, or pouring concrete or putting up walls. I met with them every morning and we shared three meals a day discussing progress. At night I used to do the accounts, I didn't have enough money, I had to keep every payment on time because if I didn't the whole project would collapse like a domino effect.'

It was then that Khunying Chanut moved her three children into the top floor of the office block next door and began to live on site. 'In the evening I would go and see them and put them to bed, then come back down to work some more. My husband didn't want a divorce, but I begged him, and I forced him. If I could not participate in my responsibilities in the marriage I would prefer to walk out and to take full responsibility for the children. I had already reached this level in my work and there were two roads to walk. I had actually already taken the [business] road before I was married so it was impossible for me to fulfil the expectations of marriage,' she says.

This is not a topic she would like to dwell on. Nor does it seem necessary to enquire whether her husband might have been able to support her on the site. That was not an option.

'We did it very quietly,' she says of the divorce. 'I wasn't lonely because my work kept me busy during the day. I had many bosses, the banks, the Government [regulations], the shareholders, I had to be concerned about them all.'

Khunying Chanut wanted to establish a truly Thai hotel at a time when the international chains were making an inroad into the Thai market. Many advised her against using a Thai name from a language barely recognisable outside the country. But she insisted, and settled for Dusit Thani. *Dusit* means 'heaven' and *Thani* means 'the granting of power to the people', the expression used by the last absolute monarch, King Rama VI, when he relinquished his political power over the Thai people in 1932.

'I realised we had many good things in our culture and I wanted to present these to hotel guests. This is why in my hotels the waitresses will not stand up when they serve you, they will kneel down graciously, because it is impolite in Thai culture for them to take a position leaning over you.'

The hotel opened on time and Khunying Chanut's concept of Thai culture and hospitality was an enormous success, setting the standard for a major boom in tourism in the 1980s. Now she has shares in 50 hotels worldwide and the Dusit Thani name sits atop hotels in Indonesia and Malaysia as well as the United States and Europe. 'I wanted to expand to present Thai hospitality to other parts of the world.'

Of her role as a businesswoman she says, 'It is still easier to be a man. No matter if we are tired we still have responsibility for our children, we have to give honour to our relatives, we have to behave correctly. For me, the most important thing in my life was my children. I sometimes had to work day and night so that when they had their holidays from school I would take a holiday as well. I cut their hair, I bought their clothes, because if I let someone else do that I would be neglecting them. And when they grew up I brought them with me to work.' Now, her three children are managers at Dusit Thani.

In Asia there has been no mainstream feminist revolution to parallel social changes in the West. A major study of businesswomen by the Asian Institute of Management (AIM) found that deeply ingrained expectations on women to put their family first persisted despite legislative changes which have given women greater equality in law and the very visible successes of women in business.

The portrait that emerged of the average south-east Asian female entrepreneur was significantly different from the image of the corporate feminist of the West. A woman who controls large amounts of capital in south-east Asia is typically in her early forties with three children and has been married for almost 20 years.

In all the interviews I conducted there was an often unspoken assumption about family. That was that a successful woman would not be arguing with her husband over who did the dishes after a hard day at the office. A successful woman was backed by domestic help and sometimes a network of poorer relatives. It is not an insignificant point. In south-east Asia, the unequal distribution of wealth means that poor women work in the households of richer women, freeing up one class while locking another into the powerlessness of their cultural heritage. But the domestic helper, too, may be supporting her own family back in the village, and have even poorer relatives to fill in there.

While cheap female help remains available, even by bringing in poorer women from Sri Lanka or the Philippines to richer countries, the issue remains one of the redistribution of domestic drudgery among women. It is not one of challenging men to change their perceptions of their roles. In the AIM survey the majority of female entrepreneurs singled out domestic help, not the shifting of any of their domestic responsibility to their husbands, as a major contribution to their professional success. That reason alone may explain why women in Asia's economic élite appear to achieve much more senior status than their western counterparts.

Clearly, the economic take-off of the past two to three decades has opened up immense opportunities for business expansion as well as opportunities for women, simply because there are many more jobs available to both men and women.

Khun Supalak is of the next generation, 39 years old (in 1996) and executive Vice-President of a retailing empire with 10 000 employees. Two days after graduating in pharmacy she opened the first shopping mall for her family company and has since opened one shopping complex a year, complete with water parks, ice skating rinks and bowling alleys. Currently, she has three 20-million-dollar developments in the pipeline and such a heavy schedule of appointments she is constantly on the move. The growth of her business is directly linked to Thailand's growing consumer spending power.

'It is tough to be a woman boss. There were lots of people watching to see if I could do it. I had to act strong and stay out late at meetings, not act picky like a housewife or shy like a traditional Thai woman.'

In reality, she says, she is a very simple person who likes to wear shorts and wander around on the weekend eating ice cream cones. But her position requires something more conservative so she is careful to present a more modest image when attending business functions. She laughs at the thought of herself, unmarried and escorted by one of her managers, at dinner with a guest list of businessmen and their wives. 'It happens all the time.'

Khun Supalak believes the prominence of women in business in Thailand does not reflect any significant changes in the expectations of men. She travels regularly to Japan for business where she has noted that economic independence for women has allowed them to choose not to marry and take on the dual housekeeper/business role. In Thailand, where economic growth is much younger, there has been little such change.

'There is no pressure here on men to be faithful. I

would like to get married but I am already in such a position of [economic] power that I would have to marry someone of equal standing.

'But, for a rich man it is normal to have many wives [mistresses]: the more successful the man the more likely he is to have a second wife. I couldn't take that,' she says, laughing, but obviously deadly serious.

The night bus
to Bangkok

Wanphen thinks she is lucky. Twenty or so years ago
fate landed her on the night bus to Bangkok. The chilly
mist was already settling over the terraced rice paddies
of Thailand's far north where her family huddled
around a lantern inside their single-roomed thatch hut.
It would have been easier to wait until morning, as so
many girls did, and walk away from her quiet, rural
life with the optimism of morning sunshine stroking
her long, black hair. She can't remember why she took
the night bus, but it was probably the most important
decision she ever made in her life.

It was just luck that she arrived in Bangkok in the
daylight. The bus terminal was grubby with the trash
of groggy new arrivals, the air thick and hot with
fumes, the bitumen splattered with oil and dirty puddles from overnight rain. The din of the traffic was
just incredible to her country ears.

The day bus from her home in Chiang Mai arrived,
of course, at night, in the dark. Then, the pimps were
out and prowling, waiting for the young country girls
to spill down the bus steps, their legs stiff, their eyes
glazed and blinking into the harsh neon lights.

'I had heard people talk. They said that if you were
lucky you could get a job in Bangkok and earn money
for your parents. If you were unlucky you would be

picked up and sold into prostitution. I was really lucky that day. I could have just as easily come in at night and been sold off,' she says, laughing.

Actually, as Wanphen's story unfolds it becomes clear she was not just walking, but running, away from her life in the north. A few years earlier she had made her first trip to Bangkok at the age of fifteen, the eldest of three daughters of poor rice farmers. Her parents, she says, wanted her to go, but the final decision was hers. 'At first it was quite exciting when I saw the big buildings and all the coloured lights. In my place we only had lanterns, no electricity.'

Her aunt was waiting for her at the bus terminal, the first time. She would live with her aunt and work in a factory. She would never see any of the money she earned. It would be shared, she thought, between her aunt and her parents.

'My father used to tell me to look at the other families whose daughters had gone to Bangkok, they had big cement houses, they didn't have problems any more, just because of the money the girls sent back. He used to suggest I go and do the same sort of work, he never actually told me to go to be a prostitute but I said that if these girls were doing anything good then they wouldn't get rich so fast,' she says. 'My mother opposed him and I felt strongly that I didn't want to fall into this trap.'

Wanphen's aunt found her a job in a factory making aluminium pots. She was supposed to work with another young girl, in a kind of industrial pair, in the section where the molten metal was poured into moulds. 'My partner would hardly ever work, she was always wandering off into another part of the factory. So finally I asked her what she was doing and she looked at me and said, "Don't you know how dangerous this job is?".

134

'Apparently, the pots sometimes flipped off the moulds, and took off your face.'

It is almost a funny story, the way she tells it, at her own expense, tripping along through the ordinariness of her average life. It is difficult to convince people who are not famous or rich or eccentric or bizarre that they hold in their memories fascinating lives.

Wanphen is one of millions. Now approaching 40, she was part of the exodus of young women from rural Thailand that began with the rapid expansion of industry beginning in the 1970s, a migration pattern that is still continuing. She lives a very average life in a slum house in the vast, teeming expanse of humanity called Klong Toey, a kind of higgledy-piggledy jumble of shanties running down to the fetid docks of Bangkok.

Klong Toey is a world of its own within the city, only the edges of its rich, dense life peeping out onto the choking twelve-lane highway of the city proper that cuts around its edges. So it is not possible to ask about turning points and ambitions and dreams. Most people's lives just happen, the sum total of a random set of circumstances. Or, if you prefer, what the Thais call fate. It is better just to listen, chronologically, and wait to discover what will come tumbling out.

Initially, Wanphen didn't even live with her aunt, but slept in a dormitory at the factory, a plain room with four beds. 'I was young, we just slept wherever we could, I didn't think about it much really. But I remember thinking the city was so noisy. Even at night there were lights still on and people still talking and driving around. In the countryside we had to sleep by 8 p.m. at the latest because oil for the lamps cost money. I ended up thinking that maybe people in Bangkok didn't sleep at all.'

Wanphen kept working until her aunt told her to

stop. She doesn't know what she was paid, she never saw even a single baht. She didn't really know where the factory was, she just waited for her aunt to pick her up. Then, she was put to work in her aunt's home. The interpreter is struggling for the correct translation. It was not a wood house, no, not real wood. Finally, we agree on the word 'fibreboard'—cheap, thin panels of compressed pulp tailings knocked together into a shack. Which was fine in Wanphen's eyes. Klong Toey was one step away from poverty. The walls of the shack were not bare. Instead, they were hung with cheap souvenirs, trophies of the emerging consumer power of the new urban working class. Here, in the slums, lay opportunity and chance.

In the narrow alleys of Klong Toey the thin drug addicts grabbed at the naive young country girl from the silent, cool hills of the north. Underfoot the rubbish fermented in the heat, the smell rising like a thick wave of nausea on first venturing in. But then the smell simply disappeared, edited out of conscious thought by the mind, just as the constant hum of the traffic in a city can be unheard. 'I was scared at first because I had never seen drug addiction before. They [the addicts] would just grab you, trying to get your purse or money.'

In her aunt's slum house she lived with her aunt, her aunt's cousin and a child. For a while her aunt had been paid to look after the child; then the money stopped coming but the child stayed, no-one ever came to pick her up. Another child appeared at the house and the aunt got paid again. Wanphen looked after the child without any questions. 'I just wanted my parents to have a better life.' Remembering back to her childhood she says, 'Yes, there were many times when we were really, really hungry.'

But after three years her aunt sent her back to Chiang Mai again where she joined her sister as a domestic helper, washing, cooking, cleaning and babysitting in the home of an American couple. 'The work was just about the same but I could see my parents once a month instead of once a year, so that was better,' she says. She enjoyed her job, she enjoyed being with her sister. But, after a year or two, she can't remember exactly when, she discovered why she had been sent home. She was nearly twenty years old and a young man from a village near her parents was waiting to marry her.

This seemed fine for all concerned. He was in agreement, her parents were in agreement and his parents were in agreement. The young man had a little money, more than her family, so they were actually very keen. 'But I didn't like him. He had taken my sister out many times but when it came time to ask for a wife he asked for me. He was not a good man.'

Fortunately, she lived in the home where she worked, so she could get a head start, she says. 'I went to my employers and told them the truth. I asked for my month's wages and 200 baht extra, which was 500 baht in all (about A$25). I told them that when my father came to collect my salary at the end of the month to say that I had gone. Yes, of course,' she says, 'my parents were very, very angry when they found out. Even now the parents of that man do not talk to my father.'

So, this is how she came to be on that night bus, with no aunt at the terminal to meet her. She had left town with a friend whose entire family had moved to Bangkok, thinking her friend would know where to find her aunt's house. But her friend could only find her own home—the city was so big and hot and the air was so choking it made the two girls dizzy. When they got to the friend's house her father simply turned Wanphen around and dumped her back at the bus terminal.

With part of her money she got into a taxi. Another stroke of luck: the driver knew where to find Klong Toey. (In truth, it was a landmark most of Bangkok would know.) She was not sent back home. There were no telephones and Chiang Mai was very far away, so the scandal would take some time to reach the city. And by then, it would have lost some of its sting.

This time Wanphen went to work in a factory which made sweet syrup. Another lucky break, so she says. Her tasks were rotated. The worst was the job of dumping the empty bottles into hot water for the dishwasher. She had to work so fast it was difficult to check whether the bottles were cracked. So she nicked her hands on the broken edges, over and over again, until they dripped with blood and stung with pain.

Wanphen and her aunt woke up very early every morning and gave food to the shaven-headed, orange-robed monks who wandered through the alleys at dawn. She might have gone to the temple herself with a garland of sickly-sweet, white buds and an offering of fruit but this was a daunting, dwarfing city and she still didn't know her way around.

Like the majority of Thais, Wanphen was raised a Buddhist, infused with the obligation of giving to the monks and the temples in exchange for merit. Buddhism can serve as a static social force. Its primary teaching is that merit gained in this life—by correct behaviour, self-discipline and material sacrifice—will determine one's fortune in the next. That logic in reverse provides people with ample opportunity to explain their misfortune in this life in terms of a poor effort in the past.

'Sure, I thought about it. I wondered why people lived in big houses and had good educations and why me and my parents had no possessions at all,' she says. To which the translator adds: 'And she has no answers for these questions.'

While she was working at the syrup factory Wanphen met her husband, a worker on the Klong Toey docks, and they moved into their own slum house, just down the alley from her aunt. When she began to feel the first discomfort of morning sickness she left the factory. It was a year or so later that she went back, hoping to rely on her aunt to take care of her young son. 'I was a good worker so they took me back, there was no problem.'

But, she had a different problem. Her aunt, it seemed, was not reliable enough to take care of her baby. On the days her aunt failed to show up she could not go to work. 'The sister of my husband said, why don't you take a sewing course so you can work at home. My husband was ten years older than me and he was worried about me being in the workforce, by that I mean he was a bit jealous that I was outside the house meeting other people.'

Wanphen was eventually forced to trade the factory for piece work. For one baht per garment (about 5 cents) she put together shirts and pants from pre-cut pieces. 'I had a toddler to look after, I had the ironing and washing and the cooking to do so the money would depend on how much time I could find to sew every day.

My husband would help in taking care of the baby just a little bit, like holding him sometimes,' she says. But the domestic chores? 'Well, of course, he wouldn't help. That is women's work,' she says, quickly dismissing the question.

'I thought if I had another child quickly and had to look after two children at the same time as well as work, I would probably die, so I used birth control. My second son was born ten years later when I was about 30.'

Wanphen says her husband used to go out at night with his friends almost all the time. 'He didn't know how hard it was for me, he just thought if he gave me part of his salary his responsibility ended there. Initially, I didn't know that he went out to the brothels.' There is a very brief pause while Wanphen and the translator talk, an apparent agreement reached that what is to be said next need not be avoided because of any false sense of shame.

Wanphen found out about the brothels when she contracted VD. 'My husband always denied it, he said it was caused by the seafood I ate. My doctor told me that was impossible, that I got it from my husband because of what he was up to.' Again, she was lucky. She had contracted VD before the real killer of Thai wives—AIDS—began its rapid spread from the brothels.

Wanphen vaguely thought of leaving her husband. 'But after I had the second baby I thought of another solution. I refused to sleep with him and we have slept separately ever since.'

Wanphen has not really changed jobs. But one day she met some friends who were sewing only trousers for 20 baht a dozen, just a little less per piece but a more straightforward job than a rack of rotating fashions. It was easier because I didn't have to think so much, she says. In a blur of trouser seams the next five years of her memory gallops by, in the time it takes to raise our coffee cups for a sip. She stops only to mention that the price has increased to 28 baht a dozen for completed pants.

Then, one day, in March 1991, she thought of leaving Klong Toey. It was a truly terrible day, a very unlucky day. The sun was obscured behind a vile, black cloud of toxic smoke. There are no high-rise towers in the slums to obscure the view so the cloud rose like a monster into the vast empty sky above the shanties, framed by the dull, concrete arches of the expressway overpass.

As was usual around the Klong Toey slums, chem-
icals were stored with little care. When a factory
caught fire its entire toxic cargo went up in flames,
choking the slum dwellers, burning and peeling their
skin, poisoning their drinking water and then seeping
into their bodies with their every breath, the hidden
pockets of their lungs seared by poisonous fumes.

'I looked out at the smoke and thought "I should
leave." But then I realised I wouldn't know where to
go, this is my home now. I have my job and with that
there is some flexibility. I can make some money for
my parents. One of the most inconvenient things about
my life is the traffic, it is so hard to go anywhere. I
get sick from the pollution, sometimes I can't breathe
and I have to take medicine. But in Chiang Mai I could
make only 300 baht a month, so here my life is better.
I can see rich people here, but I have nothing to do
with them so I don't compare. They have their life, I
have mine,' she says.

I ask, somewhat foolishly, whether she has ever
thought of finding another man. She laughs. 'Life is
boring enough with one man, why would I want
another?' she replies, eyes twinkling. The translator
explains her choice of words: 'boring' is the literal
translation; 'problematic' would be more accurate in
the context, she says.

For more than 400 years, from the fourteenth to the
eighteenth century, Thai women were legally bought
and sold. As young girls they were the assets of their
fathers, as wives they were the property of their husbands.

When, in 1782, the Royal Capital moved to what

is present-day Bangkok the status of women began to change. King Rama IV abolished the sale of wives, his successor abolished slavery and King Rama VI gave the first public endorsement for monogamy and introduced primary education for both girls and boys.

The actions of the kings were of enormous significance. The Royal Family in Thailand, even today, is a powerful institution outside political life, enjoying the deep reverence of the population and shaping society by example. It was of considerable significance that, in a later population programme, free vasectomies were offered on the King's Birthday, perhaps the most important day on the Thai calendar.

Before the absolute monarchy was abolished in 1932 Thai women already played a very important part in the national economy. Men of the common, rural class were routinely conscripted to work on royal construction programmes and were often away from their families for extended periods of time. Their wives were the economic backbone of the family, carrying out much of the agricultural work and controlling the local markets. Nationwide work statistics have long shown women making up about half of the 30 million economically-active Thais over the age of eleven. But since the early 1970s another trend has been forming beneath this national picture. During the past 20 years Thai women between the ages of eleven and 24 have been pouring into the cities in search of factory jobs. According to the Gender and Development Research Institute there were approximately 6.5 million male farmers and 6.5 million female farmers in 1971. Twenty years later there were more than 8 million male farmers, but less than 6 million female farmers. The reason is one of both 'push' and 'pull', in the jargon of demographic studies of migration patterns. Increasing opportunities in factories and a clear preference on the part of factory owners for cheaper, female labour, combined with development policies which assisted only male heads of farming families to create this social distortion. And Thailand is not an exception.

According to a 1991 United Nations report on women, the rapid expansion of industry right across Asia has produced a 104 per cent increase in the number of women in factories, compared to 70 per cent in men. In some sectors—such as textiles, clothing, electronics and toy manufacture—factories from South Korea, through China and south-east Asia and across to Sri Lanka are almost exclusively staffed by women.

Industrialisation has had—and is continuing to have—a very profound impact on social structures across the region. Women, removed from the expectations of rural villages and empowered with the economic independence of a regular wage, might be expected to be demanding a more vocal role in society. There is clear evidence that young women are choosing to marry later and refusing partners chosen by their parents.

There is also clear evidence in the booming shopping malls of Bangkok that young female factory workers are enjoying a freer social life, window-shopping much of the time, but with enough money in their pockets to eat out together and buy fashionable clothes at the markets.

But at the same time industrialisation is reinforcing stereotypes of powerlessness. In the lowest-paid manufacturing jobs (less than A$35 a month) women outnumber men two to one; in the top pay bracket (more than A$250 a month) the ratio is reversed. It is only in commerce that women have maintained their historic advantage and still outnumber men in the top income bracket of over A$250 a month. And there is also much evidence to suggest that working conditions in factories with predominantly female workforces are the worst.

In May 1993 the issue was briefly raised to an international level when a fire swept through a Hong Kong-owned doll and soft toys factory outside Bangkok, killing more than 200 female workers, the highest death toll ever recorded for a single fire in Thailand. Another 400 people were injured. But most chilling was the scene inside the factory when rescue workers first managed to break in. Piled up against the exit doors were the bodies of scores of women who had died trying to get out of the building. Investigations revealed that the doors of the factory were routinely locked to prevent workers from taking additional breaks or pilfering the toys, according to the management.

'Our section chief told us not to leave our work when the fire broke out,' one survivor recounted. Outside the smouldering shell riot police were brought in to control grieving relatives who had gathered at the site.

Early the following year a group of survivors travelled to Hong Kong where they heckled the Chairman of the Hong Kong Toy Council, Mr Dennis Ting, as he cut the ceremonial ribbon for the 1994 Toy Fair. Mr Ting also happened to be the Chairman of Kader Holdings, the major shareholder in the Thai toy factory.

Large numbers of Hong Kong and other foreign factories have also relocated to China to take advantage of cheap labour and less stringent industrial safety standards. Many of the factories employ women who receive lower wages, are considered 'easier to control' and are routinely housed in factory dormitories which are locked at night.

In China, Government statistics for 1994 listed 146 major fires, or fires in which at least ten people died.

THE NIGHT BUS TO BANGKOK

In November 1993, 84 workers, mainly women, died in a single factory fire in Shenzen. In December 1993 another 61 people, 60 of them women, were burnt to death in a Taiwanese-owned factory in Fuzhou in a fire started by a disgruntled employee while her colleagues slept in a locked dormitory upstairs. At the same time factory wages for women across the region have proved insufficient to cover private child care costs. Women with children are forced to send their babies back to the villages to the grandparents, often seeing their children only once a year, further accelerating the pace of family breakdown in cultures which have, for centuries, placed considerable importance on the bonds of the extended family.

Tic used to live in the countryside. (This is actually the beginning of a joke, well understood in Thailand.) She didn't move to the city, the city moved to her. Like a creeping malignancy the factories and the billowing fumes and the dirty canals followed the main roads out of Bangkok, swallowing up rural villages along the way. And then the horrendous traffic jams followed, reaching out from the capital like long continuous snakes of crawling cars and trucks.

'I used to live about two hours away from Bangkok, now it takes about four hours to get there,' she says by way of the punchline.

Tic was the youngest of six children, but her four brothers died leaving only her sister, the eldest. The hospital was far away, her family had little money. Her mother, she says, just came to believe that she could not give birth to sons who would survive.

'My father died when I was eleven and we had to

145

leave the farm because it was only rented and the owners sold it for a housing development. 'My sister was already over twenty and she had four children. She was married to start with but her husband left when the youngest was two, so she brought the children back home. Then there was my mother, the children aged two, three, four and five and me. My sister remarried and went to live somewhere else.'

Her mother started to take care of other children in the house, a small wooden structure with two rooms. For every child she took in she earned about 200 baht a month (A$10). So Tic had to look for work to help, especially to feed the four nieces and nephews.

'I was about thirteen, I got a job in a fish-canning factory putting on the lids. I earned eight baht a day. Then eggs were three for a baht and noodles were two baht a packet. There was no security and the pay was low so when I heard about a Japanese auto parts factory from my friends I went to work there.'

Tic doesn't know why she was different. She says she didn't even think about her own ambitions. All she thought about for years and years was how to support her sister's children.

There is a great deal of injustice in these stories in the way a burden is carried by individual family members if they are seen from the Western perspective of parental responsibility for children. In South-East Asia children are commonly regarded as the wider responsibility of the extended family and it is not unusual for female relatives, rather than parents, to bring up children. The issue of her sister's responsibility is not an issue for Tic. Nor is there any suggestion that their father may have been responsible.

But, when Tic started work at the auto parts factory she realised that while the men's pay increase was five baht a day, she was getting four baht. The difference, she noted, was not the one baht, but the fact that the other female workers received no pay rise at all. 'I was very efficient and very good at my job and I got a good pay rise. The owners didn't treat the other women in the same way. They were paid less for the same work as the men.

'In my own family there were only women, apart from the little boys, so I didn't really think about the difference between men and women. But when I think back I realise that in other families if there had to be a choice in sending a child to school then it would always be the boys who would be educated because they would pass on the family name and be the head of their own families.'

Tic advanced from chrome plate checking to screws. There was no union but she was always vocal. She would go to the Japanese managers and complain. She asked them directly for equal pay for everyone.

'I became the workers' representative because I was one of the brave ones, the others didn't have enough self-confidence to speak out. The Japanese bosses were surprised to see me because I was so outspoken; if they were trying to take advantage of anyone it was me who was the big mouth.'

In 1982 the Japanese owners asked her to take a rest, a euphemism for forced unpaid leave. Unionism had already arrived, however, and they found they could not force her out. Tic was the union representative in the factory, of course. The problem was that no-one had worked for 64 days. Tic had led the workers into the canteen where they stopped work and prepared to stay.

'It was really, really hard. It was very hot and we had to stay in the canteen and make our food together and sleep side by side. Some people couldn't last that long and they went home, which was understandable. But, we couldn't give in, because otherwise all the suffering would have been for nothing,' she says.

Her factory employed only 150 workers. She jumps when I remark that it was actually quite small. 'It made a profit of 600 million baht (A$30 million) a year, so it is not small,' she says, correcting me.

The strike succeeded. The workers won the right to a weekly wage, a little more job security over the day rates of the past. Tic took every kind of course the union movement had to offer: how to organise, how to be an administrator. She never, however, took a promotion at work. 'I can only be a worker, no-one in the union ever goes up.' But outside the factory she advanced—now she heads a Federation of Unions with seven member unions.

'In the old days life was more simple and women did not have to go out to work in factories. But today both husbands and wives have to work because everything is so expensive. In the past land to live on was the most important thing and TVs and other material possessions came after that. But land is so expensive that it is out of reach and people have to rent. Now they want all these consumer possessions and they spend all their money and don't think ahead.

'But in a way this new life is good for women in terms of decisions, they have more clout. In the old days if they disagreed with their husband they would just have to put up with it, now they have more power to say what they think.'

Somewhere along this angry, frustrated road Tic got married. She was 27, relatively old. She laughs with some embarrassment. She has recently given birth to her first child at the age of 39. No, she says, she did not use the Government birth control programme. She thinks her body was just too tired from all the work to fall pregnant.

This baby has brought a new issue into sharper focus. Her sister has come to stay to help her, the wheels of family obligation finally turning to her advantage. But, most women are not so lucky and have to send tiny babies back to the villages. 'There aren't many women union leaders and I have to defend both men and women. But I do think I have to make a special effort to defend women because if there aren't women union leaders then nobody thinks about issues which affect women. I want to find out which factories have a lot of women with children and try to get childcare centres in the factories, that's what I'm working on.'

I would like to know what Tic feels about her life. Is it better or worse, or is there no point in attempting to judge? In her childhood this area was a hot, flat plain of rice fields, the green expanse dotted with the golden spires of temples, glinting in the sunlight, the sky huge, blue and empty above.

This canvas is too familiar to interest her. It is easy to describe a scene taken in with new, fresh eyes. But with familiarity the details drop quickly out of view and it is often difficult to say anything at all about the things we see every day. So I ask a lot of specific questions to which she finally replies: 'It is factories now, just factories and more factories. The air is polluted, the weather is bad, there are lots of cars and the water in the canals is rotten. But, my life is better despite all that. We have more money so that reduces the number of problems for my family and that means we are a happy family compared to those who do not have enough money.'

The girl in the white Mercedes-Benz

She had come such a long way but when she finally arrived she realised she could not tell her family the truth. The end of the road for the young woman was the border post between Thailand and Burma. The red earth track wound through the green, quiet hills to the spot where a handful of soldiers stood guard over the border crossing. The young woman dared not cross back over the river to the Burmese side, to the silence, the morning mist and the faint memory of the crisp, cool air of her childhood.

But, the soldiers let her use their radio, the army radio station one of the few means of communication in such a remote and troubled region. So she called across the barbed wire barricades out into the distance: 'Does anyone know me?' she asked, giving her name and that of her family and her village. 'I was about ten years old when I was brought into Thailand. I will wait here for my family,' she said.

On the first day nobody came, but she was not surprised. She remembered her village had no cars or bikes, only a horse. She remembered her family home, a thatch hut built right onto the earth, a fire always smouldering in the middle of the floor, the constant smell of fine dust and smoke. On the second day she saw two men sitting together waiting. They saw her waiting. She sat clutching her package of gifts. They waited for a few hours. Then, as she sat listening, she recognised one of the voices. The men were about to leave when she got up and shouted that it was her.

Daeng is not her real name but it is the name she has chosen to use to tell her story. She thinks she is about twenty years old. It was her sister's husband and friend whom she finally found on the other side of the barbed wire. She had come to tell her own terrible story, to relieve herself of the burden of her grave misfortune. But, when her brother-in-law began to speak, his own tragedy spilled out.

Daeng was looking for her brother, the one who had left her at the home of a married couple on the Thai side of the border where he had been told she could work helping to take care of their children. He had been paid 2000 baht (about A$100). When he came back to get her two months later, Daeng, his youngest sister, was gone, missing, the couple said, after running off during a family pleasure trip. In truth she had been sent a very long way away to the far south of Thailand. There she had been bundled into a white Mercedes-Benz and delivered to a fancy hotel room, her path in life chosen by strangers before she had even reached puberty. Her brother had been devastated that she was lost. The family was very poor, but he had never used the money. And he had not come today because he had since died.

'I was so excited, I really wanted to see my brother but he was dead,' she says. 'Only my sister's husband came and I didn't tell him what had happened to me. It was not because I was ashamed, it was because I thought my family had gone through enough already.' Daeng gave her brother-in-law the sweaters she had brought for them and left. She has never heard from her family again.

To be alone, without a family, has been her recurring

nightmare. All the more so now as she waits out the last few weeks, slow footed and swollen, for the birth of her first child.

Daeng was born in the wild hills that divide Thailand and Burma where the troops of the Burmese army from the plains have been at war with the mountain tribes for all her life. Where the rule of government has long been replaced by the rule of the gun. Where the tribal armies and the bandit gangs run the opium trade into the lucrative Thai heroin industry to the south. In the mountains of the Golden Triangle Daeng lived a miserable life. But nostalgia can so easily distort reality and make believe that a family reunion could somehow make everything all right.

Daeng cannot remember her father. When her mother was still pregnant with Daeng he was kidnapped by bandits and the family was ordered to hand over all their personal possessions as ransom. They paid up but the bandits shot him anyway. There was no hospital, Daeng says, so he died. Daeng grew up with her mother and five siblings in the hut. There was no electricity and little food. They grew mountain rice and corn on the steep terraces, which they mixed with bamboo shoots if they could find them in the jungle.

'There was no electricity, no TV, there was no school. There was opium and some of my family were addicts. I knew about the war with the Burmese soldiers but I didn't even know about Bangkok,' she says. 'It was very beautiful, we lived right on the mountain, right on the earth. All I wanted was to have enough to eat and some material possessions like the children of the village head who had nice clothes to wear.'

Without a father her eldest brother was the head of the family. He ruled the household with fear and violence. 'My mother was thinking of getting married again and my brother was very angry so he took a log from the fire in the house and burned my mother badly. My mother got very sick with a high fever but she was too scared to tell my eldest brother, she only told me,' says Daeng. She cannot remember how old her mother was, and thought perhaps she was seven or eight years old herself. Her mother died. Then the family broke up. Her eldest brother went away, leaving her alone in the house. 'My brother wasn't running away from something he had done wrong, he was just leaving to find work,' she says.

No-one came back for her. Two days later an older woman took her in, not so much to comfort her but to put her to work. From there she began a series of jobs caring for newborn babies in the villages nearby for which she received no money, just her food and a space on the dirt floor. 'I was so, so frightened when my mother died. I just sat in the house crying and crying for days.'

Some time later she found one of her sisters and was given a job caring for her two children. Then, her middle brother, the one she came to look for at the border, got married and his wife fell pregnant. So Daeng was moved on again. Her brother and his wife were opium addicts, neither of them worked, there was not enough to eat, they were always fighting, she says. She felt so sorry for her tiny nephew.

Eventually her brother took her across the border into Thailand to the house of a married couple. She stayed in the house for one night and then was taken on a very, very long journey by train. The couple were dealers of young women. Her brother, she insists, thought she was going to work as a babysitter.

Actually, for a while Daeng did become a babysitter. In the town of Pattani, in the far south of Thailand, where the air slides in from the coast, thick, hot and humid, Daeng went to work. There were two houses. One was occupied by a man with a white

Mercedes-Benz, his wife and children. The other was a brothel. 'I took care of the children. I didn't think I was going to have to work there [next door] because these people had always told me they would look after me like their own child,' she says. 'When the girls got sick they would come to the house but I didn't really know what went on in detail. Some of the girls had tried to warn me, but I just didn't believe them.' Daeng says she thinks she was about eleven years old at the time, before her periods had begun.

'Then one night I was taken to a hotel in the white Mercedes-Benz and was brought up to the room by the man who owned the house. I was extremely frightened and I was crying so much that the man in the room didn't touch me,' she says. The customer, having paid out for a virgin, was very angry. He demanded his money back. The man with the Mercedes-Benz was very angry too. In one blow he knocked her out. Daeng remembers nothing more until she woke up, intravenous tubes sticking out of her arms.

There seem to be no appropriate adjectives left to describe what happened next, overused as they are to tell of much lesser traumas. So she just tells it straight. Quickly.

'The second time I was taken to the hotel there were two men in the room. One held me down and one raped me and then they took it in turns. I was bleeding.' Daeng is speaking in Thai, not her native Akka. Her Thai is being translated into English. The translator chooses not to bother her with my obvious question. 'Yes, it was a really traumatic experience, she has already told me that,' the translator says. A moment of silence follows.

For a short time Daeng remained at the house until she no longer fetched a high price, relegated to the ranks of the ordinary prostitute by the age of twelve or thirteen. 'They would say to me that I was not a

Thai citizen so I could not run away. Every week the brothel owner searched every corner of my room and if he found any money he would take it. I was very, very angry. I was angry at myself for being born. I was angry at my family. I was angry at everybody and everything. I just kept myself going with the thought that one day I would get out.'

Daeng says she had about ten customers a night. The going rate was 200 baht (about A$10) per service, or 500 baht for a longer stay. All the money went to the man with the Mercedes-Benz. The Burmese girls were illegals so had no rights. She did not know if the Thai prostitutes had any more choice.

'There were only two kinds of men,' she says. 'They weren't good and bad, they were only lonely and bad.' The lonely were the hundreds and thousands of seamen, many from Burma themselves, who worked for low wages in poor conditions on the freight ships that plied the busy Asian routes. The bad were the sadists, those who were not satisfied until they saw her hurt and bloody. She did not try to escape because everyone knew there was nowhere to run to. The local police, she had heard, would just take the girls on to another brothel and sell them off to a competing owner. So she waited.

Those who ran were caught and beaten. None of the girls was killed, she says, but several died during her time as the result of infections from forced abortions. 'There was one young man who came to the brothel every week. He was from the north of Thailand near my place, he had come to the south to get a job on a fishing boat. He just came to talk.'

Daeng did not think it was strange that he did not want to have sex with her. He was a traditional boy and he said he loved her so he would not sleep with her until they were married. Eventually, Daeng told him that she was a virtual prisoner. 'I had never told anyone I was trapped in the brothel. He was nice enough, but I lied to him and said I loved him so he would get me out.' The promise she made was marriage.

One evening when the girls were sitting behind the pane glass showcase, their numbers clipped onto their bikinis for the convenience of the browsing customers, the police raided the brothel and pulled Daeng out. 'They asked the girls if anyone else would like to come with them, but only two said yes. No-one else believed the rescue was for real,' she says.

Her boy had gone all the way to Bangkok and paid for six officers to come south, circumventing the local police network. But he had wasted his money. The police brought Daeng to Bangkok but told the boy to go home. Daeng, they said, was clearly under age so it was against the law for him to marry her. He fled, she says, back to the north.

'I haven't thought about all this for two years,' she says. 'At first I was always scared, I always thought that the brothel owner would find me and force me to go back.' Daeng has never moved away from the place where she was left by the police. It is one of the few women's shelters in Bangkok, a spacious spread of neat concrete buildings on a plot of land right under the flight path of the airport approach. Now she runs the refuge coffee shop. She has completed her schooling to Year 9 and has married a nice young man who works in a Pepsi factory. He knows about her past, but does not mind.

Recently, Daeng received her Thai citizenship papers so, finally, she is legal. In the future, she says, she will have the courage to cross the border and look for her family again. But she has heard nothing from them since her trip more than a year ago. 'Right now, I am just worried that there will be something wrong with my baby after everything that has happened. The doctor says the baby is okay, but I can't help worrying,' she says, self-consciously stroking her belly.

Sex is business. In Asia the commercial sex industry operates region-wide and involves the trafficking of women and children from some of the poorest rural areas to the most affluent cities. Opportunities for profit begin with the families who sell off their daughters in exchange for a brick veneer home or a colour television. Much of the money parents receive from middle men comes as part of a loan to be paid back by their daughters, thus ensuring that they are enslaved to the brothel for some time to come.

The recruitment of girls in poor rural areas is normally handled by small-town brothel owners, local king pins. The trafficking of women and children to second and third countries, though, is where the stakes become really high and organised crime steps in. A map showing the main trafficking routes in south-east Asia published by the *Far Eastern Economic Review* illustrates the movement of girls and women from Burma, Indo-china and southern China into Thailand and from Thailand to Japan and Taiwan. The other main source of migrant prostitutes in the region is the Philippines which provides many of Japan's 'dancing girls and hostesses' as well as smaller numbers to Malaysia and Hong Kong.

Superficially, the map tells the age-old story of poverty and wealth, supply and demand. As economic growth enriches Asia's men so the demand for sexual services increases. And as economic opportunities beyond prostitution reach women in Thailand's villages, new sources of prostitutes are discovered in the poorer regions of Burma, southern China and Laos, Cambodia and Vietnam. But, economic disparity is just part of the picture, according to Thai anthropologist, Dr Cholthira Satyadhna.

Her theory is extremely controversial and seeks to explain why northern Thailand and the neighbouring regions of Burma and the southern Yunnan province of China so clearly dominate as sources of prostitutes. It is not just a matter of poverty, she says, but a matter of culture and heritage. 'Why is it that in these areas the fathers don't feel any guilt about selling a daughter into prostitution? To outsiders this is very, very immoral.'

Men from these areas do not feel an obligation to support their women economically. On the other hand the women have economic responsibility for the family and daughters are brought up to expect to have to support their families in some way. Ironically, Dr Cholthira links the movement of women into prostitution with a matriarchal heritage in Thailand's north. 'From my fieldwork I came to the personal conclusion that in the past the status of women in the Thai/Yunnan area had been very high. The traditional social structure was matrilineal. There were women's spirit houses and among many stories told about northern Thai women is that of a young girl whose father taught her to pay homage to a statue of a golden deer that she called her mother. The girl married a Thai king and he had to adapt himself to worship this golden mother and because he did so he gained success and happiness.'

Dr Cholthira said her work had uncovered evidence of land ownership being passed from mother to daughter and examples of 'big women' in positions of authority with their own hills or mountains. She said she believes that the long history of families' economic management being handled by wives and not husbands represented the very deep-rooted power of women. Thai men superficially want to expose themselves and dominate but Thai women have an important role in family affairs, and in the south-east Asian context family affairs have a wider economic role.'

Prostitutes from northern Thailand and the Yunnan area, she said, did not see themselves as victims. The girls, she said, 'don't feel they are victims of men, they are merely making money for the family and at this point in history this is the best way to do so. Of course with this kind of occupation there is personal suffering involved but many girls see it as part of progress, just a step to a new life'.

The demand for a new life in the villages of south-east Asia is being fuelled by social envy. The arrival of television in so many villages reinforces the very visible gaps emerging between the cities—apparent centres of *nouveau riche* orgies of consumerism—and the villages where farming life goes on much the same as ever.

'TV comes into the village and all the kids want to eat pizza and go shopping in Central [the Thai department store chain]. Money has become equal to status. It is not a moral issue. The income from a daughter gives a family big face, they can buy a new house and get a front-row position in the social gatherings at the temple,' says Dr Cholthira. The sex industry is just a means to an end at a time when the explosion of consumer goods on sale has far outstripped the capacity of the majority to buy.

According to Dr Saisuree Chutikul, Adviser to the Thai Government on Women, Children and Youth, prostitution cannot be discussed outside the context of the society as a whole. 'In the East we still have a concept of good and bad women. They are quite separate. Good women don't have sex before marriage, bad women are prostitutes.' It is customary for young men to gain their sexual experience in brothels and for married men to use prostitutes for recreation. 'They will go out and have some drinks and just like I would go for a cup of coffee afterwards, they would go for a prostitute. The sexual habit of visiting prostitutes is very deep and will take a long time to change,' she says.

It is difficult for young girls to reject the double standard, even in the comparatively anonymous atmosphere of such a vast city as Bangkok, away from the eyes of the village gossips. There is now the girl of the *jai da*, the 'scattered heart'. She is no longer a virgin in a society which still demands moral purity from good girls. She may end up with a string of partners and drift into prostitution for entertainment or to buy material goods. 'In many ways these girls are victims of consumerism. Poverty is a relative concept. Girls of the *jai da* are not starving.'

Instead of rubbing her crotch up against the silver pole on top of the bar at the Bangkok nightclub the dancer is feigning sexual pleasure with an inflated condom as her prop. Tonight, the 'Midnite Upstairs' go-go bar has turned its stages and mirrors over to Empower, a local prostitutes' collective working against AIDS. A foreign tourist puts his hand down his pants and pulls out a banana and wraps it in a condom.

The show is amusing and the message is clear. 'Hi, dear, do you want to AIDS with me?' No? Well, slip on one of the hundreds of condoms being passed around the bar. 'Some men just can't stand watching it and walk out,' says Empower coordinator Khun Chantawipa. But Empower persists. The group passes no moral judgements. It is a collective for prostitutes and aims only to protect and assist them. It is a constant source of frustration, says Chantawipa, that prostitutes and not their male customers are always blamed for the spread of AIDS. 'We consider women the receivers of the disease so if we can teach them how to protect themselves from contracting AIDS, we are teaching them not to pass it on. We have 2000 members who are sex workers and none of them sees this as a real profession. But most of them have a very limited education and are either forced into prostitution by poverty and ignorance or lack of other opportunities. We are trying to promote condoms as part of their lives. You wear underwear every day, so you should use a condom every day.'

So far Empower has made real inroads into the more expensive brothels that are open to foreign men. But at the cheap Thai-only brothels, prostitutes who insist on condoms still face the prospect of losing their customers or of being beaten up. The enduring double standard which requires that a man take control of sex, even with a prostitute, is much of the reason why. 'The man wants the girl to appear innocent, not to talk too much. If she comes with a condom, that destroys the myth of her naivety and his control,' Chantawipa says.

In the long term, Empower's goal is to change the way women are viewed in Thai society so male children do not get preference for schooling, leaving their sisters unable to sign their names and qualified for little more than the sex trade. The goals of Empower are not outside those of recent Thai Governments spurred into action by the alarming AIDS statistics and concerns that Thailand's international image as a rapidly growing new industrial nation could be damaged by its extensive commercial sex industry.

The statistics now available for Thailand present an alarming picture. Since the first detected HIV case in 1984, approximately 200 000 people have been infected by the disease. Even the 'best case scenario' estimates that more than 250 000 people will have died here from AIDS-related conditions by the year 2000. A more realistic projection suggests that over 1.8 million people will have tested HIV-positive and about 350 000 of them will have died. But what is of even greater concern is the nature of the spread of the disease. The rate of spread of AIDS into the general population—the supposedly low risk heterosexual married couples and their children—is faster in Thailand than anywhere else in the world, except India.

According to the Ministry of Public Health just over 10 000 working Thai prostitutes are HIV-positive. But the disease has spread to as many as 184 000 of their Thai male clients. In turn, about 13 000 housewives have been innocently infected and have since given birth to more than 1000 HIV-positive babies.

A Bangkok-based official of the World Health Organisation said: 'Prostitutes generally keep working even after they have been tested HIV-positive. I've talked to girls who've said, "It's OK, I feel healthy, maybe you foreigners get sick from this." AIDS is the worst health problem in Thailand. The situation is very, very serious and will cost millions of lives. It will damage an entire generation. In many ways the AIDS education programme is already too late.'

A condom campaign, originally launched as a family planning programme, has broken down 'macho resistance' to the extent that condoms are used regularly by possibly half the country's prostitutes. There has, however, been little change in the pattern of sexual behaviour in a society which demands innocent and feminine wives and girlfriends but sanctions the regular use of prostitutes by men. 'It is an old tradition in Thailand that men visit prostitutes, starting as teenagers. The number of people using condoms is increasing but you need 100 per cent condom use with absolutely no concessions for effective protection,' said the WHO official. 'The other big problem with condom use is at home. Men who visit brothels are then not using condoms to protect their wives.'

Can a good Thai wife tell her husband to put on a condom? 'Have you asked any Thai women?' said Dr Meechai Virvaidya, a prominent Thai politician who launched the condom programme. 'At the moment that would be very difficult. It would be like serving your husband a meal and announcing, "We're having dog meat for dinner tonight, dear." But things have to change, husbands have to change. We have to go out to schools and start teaching children that going to a prostitute is not an acceptable form of behaviour. We have to tell young girls that this is their business too because they will be marrying into it.' And, Dr Meechai said of Western sex tourists visiting Asia, 'There must be some concern about men from so-called advanced societies coming over here to exploit uneducated women and children because they can't get away with it at home. These are sick people and I would like to invite their women—their wives, mother, sisters—to come here and see where these men go.'

Two years ago Da's de facto husband visited an STD clinic where he was randomly tested for AIDS. The test came back positive so social workers tracked her down and had her tested as well. The result was also positive, despite her husband's fervent denial that he had even been tested for the disease. Shortly afterwards she found out she was pregnant and against the advice of her doctors she refused to abort. Her baby was born HIV-positive. Da then agreed to sterilisation.

'At first it was addicts and prostitutes but now we are seeing a complete cycle,' said Dr Saowani Chumdermpadetsuk, Associate Dean of the Faculty of Medicine at Chulalongkorn University Hospital. 'Every pregnant patient has to be treated as at risk because we are now seeing housewives whose husbands have been with callgirls. At the moment the most dangerous link in the cycle is the husbands.'

Screening at the Chulalongkorn University Hospital is done on request or as part of the Government's random testing programme for pregnant women. Often, said Dr Saowani, it is already too late for abortion. As a result this hospital alone is monitoring nineteen HIV-positive babies. 'The AIDS problem reflects a general failure in Thailand to change community attitudes to prostitution—both by preventing poor women from becoming prostitutes out of need and preventing men from going to them. Telling the women to stop working is not very effective, they still have to make a living.

'When an AIDS baby is born we give the mother and father the facts, we don't just paint a bright picture. We give the mothers free milk so they don't have to breast feed, teach them about the best possible nutrition and assign them to a social worker. But in most cases HIV-positive babies die within one or two years.'

When an HIV-positive mother is released from hospital she may face a problem being re-accepted by society. Her baby may be accepted and loved because for the moment it looks normal, but she may be shunned. In Da's case her baby boy is as bright as a button, smiling and bouncing and grabbing at every-thing within reach. So far, his health problems are minor. Da's social worker explains that we could not meet at her home because the neighbours would become curious. Only her husband's relatives know she is HIV-positive. She has not, and will not, tell her own parents, mainly out of shame.

Da lives in the slums and works as a washerwoman. She is a thin 23-year-old with tired eyes. Nowadays, she says, she and her husband either fight or do not speak. His skin is covered with sores but still he refuses to admit he is sick. Da has lost five kilograms but remains naively hopeful that somehow she can delay the advance of the disease. The original source of the family's infection is not clear. Da is on a methadone programme and although she is no longer using needles she was a teenage addict. Her husband is a user still.

She says she is not angry about her own fate, but scared about the future of her child. 'Without my baby, I would not be able to live.' At home, she says, crying, she creeps around like a leper while her relatives talk about her out loud and avoid everything she has touched. 'I am very careful about hygiene, about not sharing even the nail clippers,' she says, but the campaign of discrimination continues all the same. 'But I am proud of myself being able to cope alone. The neighbours comment that I love my baby. I never miss an appointment at the hospital.'

Da has little education and started working in the markets at the age of twelve. She knew nothing about AIDS and seems quite confused still. She thinks her baby is healthy, she says. Will she, too, be fine one day? she asks hopefully.

The social worker said the middle-class housewives, who tested positive at antenatal screenings, were much more ashamed than the poor. 'They won't talk to anyone about it because they think this is a disease for IV drug users and prostitutes, but it is a problem that's entered the respectable family unit.'

Her father's daughter

In a brief, reflective moment Aung San Suu Kyi acknowledges her fear. It is around fear that the fortunes of her people turn. To the generals who have run Burma like a boot camp since 1962, fear is power. To Aung San Suu Kyi, Nobel Peace Prize Winner, daughter of Burma's national independence hero, former political prisoner and leader of the pro-democracy movement, fear is failure.

Daw Suu, as she is known, is not afraid of the young men from military intelligence who studiously photograph and list each visitor to her rambling family home on the edge of the lake in Rangoon. She is not afraid of the barely concealed surveillance team which trains a long lens on her gate day in and day out. Nor is she afraid of the thinly disguised tirades against a certain woman 'traitor' churned out daily by a local press long devoted to government propaganda.

Of such truly terrible fears as the possibility of assassination—like the attack which killed her father—she says she cannot afford to worry, 'Because then there would be no end to it. If you are afraid you first bow your head, then the next thing you know you are on your knees, and then you find yourself completely crushed,' she says.

She recognises the debilitating fear that drains a

nation ruled by armed men, but does not accept it as an excuse for obedience. 'What I would like people to understand is that if they give in to everything out of fear then they will have to go on being afraid for the rest of their lives.'

But Daw Suu is herself afraid of one thing. 'I am always,' she says, then pauses, 'Well, not always . . . but if I think of it, I am afraid of doing the wrong thing, of making a mistake.' The sharpness of her judgement right now is more critical than ever.

Released a few months earlier after almost six years under house arrest she has little but her own integrity and the adoration of her followers with which to oppose a military government and its formidable armoury of intimidation, surveillance, censorship and force. At the top of her list of concerns is how to prevent a popular uprising being met again with violence and death. How to outmanoeuvre a government that does not even offer her the courtesy of dialogue. 'By the wrong thing I mean something that might hurt my cause or my people. But, this is not a gnawing fear, obviously this is something any sensible person would fear,' she says, swinging the discussion back under control.

Daw Suu is an unlikely looking warrior. Smooth-faced, petite, graceful, charming, repetitively humble and a 50-year-old mother of two, she is talking in the house where her public life began in earnest: her late mother's family home, a now decrepit colonial mansion resting on the shores of Inya Lake in the once elegant residential district of Rangoon.

In 1962 a military coup ended Burma's shaky experiment with parliamentary democracy and turned the nation inward. Within the walls of the hermit kingdom a bizarre and damaging experiment combining socialist economic theory with military authority and managerial incompetence set the stage for financial ruin.

Burma, a bountiful tropical land of steaming red earth, lush forests and rich mineral and gem deposits, slid into inexcusable poverty and desolation, an isolated nation frozen in time. What was left of its British infrastructure—the symbols of colonial humiliation—slowly withered under the hot sun.

All efforts to oppose this unique 'Burmese Road to Socialism' were quickly suppressed, but in the early 1990s—following the collapse of Communist and socialist regimes around the world—the generals changed their mind. Money, they decided, was what they now needed. Lots of it. Capitalism was back. Natural resources were up for quick sale. Tourists were now free to brave the appalling roads and run-down guest houses. A flurry of building began in Rangoon: ugly, second-rate modern hotels sprang up where peeling, yellow colonial mansions once stood, markets were filled of overpriced televisions and video players. Rice prices skyrocketed for the majority of Burmese who could only afford to window-shop for the dazzling array of new consumer goods.

(For the record, the generals also changed the country's name to Myanmar and the capital to Yangon, but Burma and Rangoon remain widely used as a protest.)

In the seat of the bay window looking out at the water Daw Suu holds herself like an old English school ma'am, her stiff, straight back never slouching into her seat. But her hands move freely as she speaks and the odd wry smile softens the edges of her rigid posture. Her presence as a leader is most often attributed to 'charisma', but charisma is far too vague a term. As a woman she occupies a rare public space. She is feminine and engaging, but not so personable as to allow her credibility to be compromised by vulnerability. She is determined and serious, but not so steely as to appear grim.

Since 1988 she has been leading the perilous crusade against the Burmese generals, not so much out of choice, more out of fate. Daw Suu returned to Rangoon in that year to nurse her ailing mother. Then she was the wife of an English academic living in Oxford with her two sons, having spent much of her life in India and the United States before moving to England. At the time she was quietly preparing her doctoral thesis on Burmese literature.

In the country she had left as a school girl a new wave of discontent was simmering. Marching students and public servants were gunned down in the streets by columns of soldiers. In one incident 41 wounded students suffocated in a police van. Thousands escaped overland to the Thai border, condemned to a shadowy life of political exile.

Daw Suu was the daughter of Aung San, the nationalist hero credited with winning independence from Britain, who was himself martyred in a political assassination in 1947 shortly before independence was formally granted. Then, Daw Suu was two years old. As her father's daughter she was afforded national recognition and respect. Such was, and is, the power of the family in Burma and many other Asian nations.

Unlike many of the activists inside Burma who had been cowed, muted or killed by a brutal military government, Daw Suu had not grown up accustomed to silence. 'Fear, like so many things, is a habit. If you live with fear for a long time you become fearful. That is why I think, when people say I am so brave perhaps it is just that I am not frightened,' she said at the time.

When the military strongman Ne Win resigned to take a backseat role, chaos ensued and Daw Suu stepped out to address mass rallies on the streets, assuming a natural leadership of the fledgling democracy movement. 'Her inflexible sense of duty and her sure grasp of what was wrong and right', wrote her husband Michael Aris, 'qualities which can sit as a dead weight on some shoulders, she carried with such grace.'

Within three months a military coup brought the SLORC—the State Law and Order Restoration Council—to power. The names and faces at the top had changed but, in effect, it was the same revolving door of power, open only to those from within the ruling military clique. It was a clique Daw Suu knew well. Ne Win was one of the original 'thirty comrades' led by her father in the independence struggle.

It was with much suspicion that many greeted the announcement of free and fair elections to come. Daw Suu, though, and her close associates quickly formed the National League for Democracy and began campaigning around the country, the military always circling closely in the shadows. 'The tiger always takes one step back before it pounces on its prey,' said one elder Burmese oppositionist at that time. The pounce is now history.

Rallies, packed with hundreds of thousands of people released from almost a lifetime of silence, grew by the day. The very worst moment, said Daw Suu's former personal assistant Mathan Gi, came when a group of soldiers lined up Daw Suu and her entourage in their sights, their guns already cocked, as she addressed a massive crowd from a makeshift podium in the dusty outskirts of Rangoon. 'I thought it would be so sad, such a waste to die in the street like this, when we had so many things to do,' Mathan Gi said.

On 19 July 1989, the annual Martyrs' Day commemorating the death of her father and his colleagues, Daw Suu had called her people out onto the streets for what was to be the biggest challenge to military rule yet. But, when she saw that the streets were filled with troops she called the march off to prevent another bloody confrontation. Then the arrests began and hundreds of her followers disappeared into jails. The following day the gates of her mother's home were sealed, her two teenage boys—on a visit during their school holidays—were locked inside with her and six years under house arrest began.

'My children were with me when I was placed under detention and then they had to go back [to England] and so it was as if I started in the deep end,' she said. 'It was something I had to face immediately and get over. In effect they made me face whatever fears I might have had on that subject and I have been able to cope.'

From the window seat Daw Suu is answering the questions graciously but warily. In a society long denied trust she cannot afford to give much away. The elections did go ahead while she was under detention and the NLD won a landslide victory. The military did not step down. Right now Daw Suu is entrenched in a psywar operation. Today's offering from a certain 'sage' of the Government press: 'The more one says, the more one reveals oneself,' lectures a comment piece in the *New Light of Myanmar*, a journal that has more in common with a self-congratulatory boys' club newsletter than a metropolitan newspaper.

To mark National Day earlier that week Daw Suu had brazenly sent out invitations for celebrations at her home where she conducted a prize-giving ceremony. On a makeshift stage, she loaded up the young winners with enormous piles of books, a symbolic slap in the face for a Government that at various times closed universities and banned social science courses to stifle dissent. And Daw Suu talked, her words carefully recorded and dissected by foreign diplomats charged with assessing the current balance of power in the

171

shadow play, like the guessing games once played by Kremlin watchers in the former Soviet Union.

The symbol of the National Day, she said, is the 'dancing peacock', but the symbol of the students' movement is the 'fighting peacock'. 'We are doing the job of the fighting peacock so that one day we will be able to appreciate the life of the graceful dancing peacock,' she told the young people lined up in attentive rows on reed mats by the lake, a tatty marquee acting as an ineffectual shield against the tropical sun.

At the Government's official ceremony in one of the vast squares dedicated to national glory, medals were being pinned on hundreds of 'patriotic' chests. One woman speaker loudly criticised 'traitors who think highly of aliens'—who do not get the leading role themselves so attempt to mar the efforts of others. Daw Suu's marriage to an Englishman, an alien, is a repetitive theme in the effort to blacken her name. Like the crude and clumsy acronym, SLORC, and the ridiculous national slogans ('Only with discipline will there be progress', for example), such attacks border on farce except that the consequences of crossing the generals are anything but funny.

For many years Daw Suu warned her husband that there might come a time when she would be needed in Burma. The military regime would prefer her simply to leave and has repeatedly offered her a chance to resume her life in exile in England. She has refused other invitations outside Burma because she does not believe she would be allowed to return. She sees her duty in terms of carrying on her father's mission.

'Basically, I think people do believe I will uphold my father's values, they trust me because they trusted my father and they believe I will carry on in his tradition which was one of integrity.' Her mother, Daw Khin Kyi, was an exceptional woman in her own right, bringing up three children on her own and going on to become Burma's first woman Ambassador—the Ambassador to India.

But, said Daw Suu, 'My mother very much brought us up as our father's children, she was the one who instilled in us a consciousness that we had to live up to our father's values. She brought us up with very, very strict values.'

How would she characterise those values now? In one word, she says: 'Integrity.' And, she says, with a brief flash of humour, 'hard work counts a lot as well.'

The room in which we are talking serves as a kind of outer chamber; her office is one door further inside. Today, she has already lectured a sympathetic group of foreign journalists, the questions thrown like 'Dorothy Dixers' in Parliament. What about forced labour? 'Now, I am glad you asked that: it is a terrible disgrace.' The real issues, like what kind of tactics can be used against a military Government, are taboo.

She has so many meetings to personally attend to, despite the presence of other officers of the NLD. Publicly, Aung San Suu Kyi is the embodiment of her cause. On Saturdays and Sundays she stands on a ladder, the upper part of her body visible over the gate to her compound, in a kind of public dialogue opportunity. It is not a huge audience, several thousand every weekend, but it is significant. Every person present is photographed by military intelligence, material for future arrest lists.

Aung San Suu Kyi's personal security consists of dozens of young students, with homemade arm bands, who hold hands in line to form a human barrier merely as a basic means of crowd control. Above them Daw Suu is a vulnerable target, an essential public statement of the principle of courage. She defers regularly to her colleagues and, properly, refused to speak for the organisation. But the men at her side are clearly overshadowed by her aura.

173

'The people are very unsophisticated when it comes to politics and they wait for a superior magical being to descend from heaven to save them. I'm afraid they have put her in this role,' said Mathan Gi. 'This is very unreasonable and unworkable. The trouble is people have to see her as human.'

For her own part, Daw Suu keeps repeating the same theme. 'Personalised politics in the long run is not good for democracy but at such a time I think it does help to focus interest on an individual. I think people always like what they call human interest and it just happens that in this world I stand out in the organisation,' she says with a modesty bordering on annoyance. 'I certainly look forward to the day when we have democracy and it will no longer be necessary for the organisation to be identified with me.'

But, she says, leadership is 'something I accept as a responsibility. I do not feel it is a burden. I have always been surprised when people have said how difficult it must have been for me, because so many other people have had far more difficult situations to deal with. I have a certain degree of protection because of international recognition and because I am my father's daughter.'

But one's suffering is not negated by the experiences of others. No. But she insists her suffering was nothing unusual—the hardest thing about her time under house arrest was not being able to help people. Her first thought on being told she was free was, 'Well, just start working.'

Of course Daw Suu is not merely her father's daughter. 'When somebody says to me you must do this and I don't think it is right it is automatic for me to say well why should I?' That in itself is exceptional.

In northern Burma lies a magical ghost town, a deserted city of thousands of pagodas rising, shimmering, from the hot, red, dusty plain. Pagan was founded around 850AD, the site of the first capital of the Burmese kings, and the seat of power for more than 400 years. A stone inscription at the base of one of the pagodas, dated 1260AD, tells the story of a woman who prayed for five years to attain Buddhahood. After that time she realised her mistake—only men can achieve the highest state in the Buddhist religion—so she prayed instead to be reborn a man.

Tradition in Burma affords men 'the leading role', in much the same way that women describe themselves as the rear legs of the elephant in neighbouring Thailand. In public, Burmese men frequently walk several steps ahead of their wives; at the table women carefully pick through a meal of fish to remove the bones for their husbands. Little girls are taught at an early age not to jump over their brothers: a woman's place is below a man's. If a husband is sitting on a chair, a wife will sit on the ground.

Girl babies are welcomed, writes author Khin Myo Chit: ' "A daughter in the family is the best slave" was often considered a congratulatory expression. Daughters cook, wash and sew while sons study and play.'

But while Buddhism, the main religion practised in Burma, excludes women from the monkhood, it does not exclude women from seeking many other levels of enlightenment. Nor has religion or culture prevented the participation of women in public life.

Burmese women do not take their husbands' names. At home they are the bookkeepers and custodians of the family's finances, including their husbands' wages, and in the local markets commerce is largely controlled by networks of women. There is no wage discrimination in either the public service or the private sector, and more girls enter university than boys. Where women stand is a question, then, of perception.

'Burmese women never seem to have had any need for liberation movements throughout history. They have never known impediments like *purdah* or bound feet,' writes Khin Myo Chit. 'Their right to own property has never been challenged. Men just hand over their earnings to their wives.' This last fact, says Khin Myo Chit, never fails to bring 'ohs' and 'ahs' of admiration from women of other nationalities.

However, one of Burma's most popular novelists, Juu, has written a string of bestsellers around the less tangible notion of machismo. Her latest novel, *Confessions of a Woman*, is partly autobiographical. It is about a woman who is wealthier and more successful than her husband and the conflict this causes. In her own life she has forsaken a long-term love for similar reasons: she is unprepared to minimise her own achievements to spare the man's pride. 'I agree that Burmese women are more equal than many other Asian women but whatever you say men still have their pride and so many women don't try to be equal or superior.'

In Burmese society there is an expression: 'One step down from the family home, the husband is a bachelor'. Says Juu: 'In this society men are allowed to ignore the law of monogamy. Women, on the other hand, even widows, would be disgraced for taking another partner.'

In downtown Rangoon, the handpainted movie posters of the local film industry advertise this month's offering—the story of a man with two wives, his official wife and what is known as a 'parallel wife'. The tale cannot be graphically told: censorship bans sweaty backs and bare breasts. Women appear on screen covered from neck to ankle with not even a plunging neckline to titillate the audience. But, nevertheless, the story is readily understood.

The parallel wife finally gives the man an ultima-
tum, leave his first wife or lose her. He returns to his
first wife. But in the meantime she, too, has made her
choice: to leave him. And so the man is abandoned to
live alone. An unlikely fantasy ending, but one that
met with great approval by many Burmese women.

Aung San Suu Kyi says she does not see herself as a
woman leader. In fact she would prefer not to see
herself as a role model at all, 'because I do not think
I am so exceptional that I should be a model for
anyone else. I think compared to a lot of Asian countries the position of women in Burma is stronger but
I think men are still the privileged gender.'
    She acknowledges her own gender only in so far as
it has been used to attack her movement. 'Sleeping
with the enemy', being married to a foreigner, an alien,
continues to be held up as evidence disqualifying her
from patriotism. 'I think they [the military] have
attacked women a great deal because of me,' she says.
    'At first many people thought, "She is just a
woman",' said Mathan Gi. 'The traditional idea of
Burmese men is that they are the brave and the women
are the timid and need to be protected, but when they
found her doing things that men would not dare go
through they got the idea that she was smart and
brave.'
    Says Daw Suu: 'I don't take it all that seriously—all
this women and power stuff—because the pursuit of
[personal] power has very little to do with my real
situation.' (It is obvious that she has been asked these
questions too many times.) 'I mean men don't have
rights in Burma so when people ask me how about

women's rights I say we've got to get everybody's basic rights.' The subject appears closed.

But, later on, as I get up to walk back out into the thick, afternoon heat, Daw Suu composed and neat, me dripping with sweat, she asks if I would like to come back to meet with some of her female colleagues. When I return I see three jolly ladies, laughing. One elderly, two mothers in their forties. On the table on the verandah sits a pot of tea and little plates of coconut sweets.

'We seldom walk in front of our menfolk, we are usually a few steps behind, but in the house we are the boss,' says Ma Ni. More than four decades ago Ma Ni entered into an arranged marriage with a man eleven years her senior. 'No such luck,' she says, when asked about notions of romance, 'but we got along fine anyway. In those days you would never have been able to go out with a boyfriend. Even with our male cousins once we reached thirteen or fourteen we were not allowed in the same room with them. And later, working outside the house would never have crossed our minds.'

Ma Ni is a politician's wife. In her case, her husband is a leading dissident in Aung San Suu Kyi's camp, which means she has spent many years raising four children alone, with only fifteen-minute visits to jail twice a month, during her husband's three stints as a political prisoner. 'I spent two weeks preparing what to say. Fifteen minutes, you can imagine just fifteen minutes,' she says.

In the end she talked to her husband of practical matters, checking what he needed her to bring, confirming that the food and goods she had brought last time got through the guards.

'I just saw him through an iron grille and the guards had tape recorders on both sides. I wasn't going to show them my weak points so I always talked about anything else but my feelings,' she says. 'Of course, I felt sad but I had to keep a different face for my husband's sake; I wasn't going to show how weak I could get.'

Of course, she said, her family was scared. They lived off the money from family jewellery she pawned each time her husband was away. In 1988 when he joined Daw Suu, she said, she was emotionally prepared. She knew he *would* be arrested, it was just a matter of *when*.

The two younger women listen with interest. One generation later they hold university degrees and positions of their own in the political opposition. But, they are still in charge of their families, from running the family budget right down to the details of their children's daily activities. In 1988 they, too, knew it was just a matter of 'when'.

'On that day we were travelling by car and we met many road blocks and somehow we got through and when we were finally stopped and questioned they let us go. I was frightened then. I just went cold. But when we were actually arrested half a mile down the road I wasn't frightened anymore,' says Ma Hla. 'There were four of us and we had one thing in common. We must never show them that we were afraid. It wasn't something we agreed on, it just happened that way. I knew we were in for big trouble, a very bad time.'

There are two doors leading into the women's wing of the notorious Insein Jail. The large outer doors open into a kind of alcove where the prisoners are met and examined by the doctors before being taken to their cells. The inner door is very small, just large enough for one person to pass through at a time.

'The instant that I crossed through the inner door—going from the darkish enclosed area to the open air in the inner courtyard—I felt very strange, like I was oblivious to everyone and everything. Then I was through and it was suddenly light. I didn't know what it was then, but after a few months I recognised the feeling as utter loneliness, nobody could help me,' Ma Hla says.

Her opinion, though, is not shared by Ma Yee. 'I was crying,' she says, before correcting herself. 'Bawling, actually, for my daughters and my husband.' Neither Ma Yee, then mother of seven-year-old twin daughters, nor Ma Hla, mother of two daughters, aged seven and ten, had warned their children that they might be caught.

'At home the children would be asking, "Where is mother?" I said they should be told that I was coming back soon, that I was with grandmother,' said Ma Yee. 'We were just disappearing in our children's eyes, that was all.' But at Ma Hla's home the children were watching television when they heard their mother's name read out on the arrest list.

Both women agreed that they had to deal with the separation from their children in the same way: alone and immediately. 'I just cut them off,' said Ma Hla, of the two-and-a-half years she was in jail, an imaginable separation, perhaps, for an adult but an eternity for a child. She banned her daughters from visiting her, as did Ma Yee, to protect them from a memory of their mother in jail.

Ma Hla has worked hard at her toughness, Ma Yee is willing to follow her lead. The conversation turns quickly to the practical: descriptions of the cell, awash in the wet season. The two huge toilet pots with difficult, humiliating rules: one must urinate in one, defecate in the other: never both at the same time.

For nineteen days they slept on the concrete floor in the same clothes they had on when they were arrested. 'When the senior officers came to inspect us the first thing we said was, we are women, we need sanitary pads. A Burmese woman would never, ever talk to a man like this. They were so shocked that we dared to ask for such an intimate thing straight out that then we were moved in with the prostitutes.'

The intelligence chaps, says Ma Hla, had been working night after night so when they came to interrogate us they didn't bother much because we had been caught with physical evidence, the leaflets. So when they took us in they told us to get the questions over with quickly.

But, still, they did bother with the ritual. In the middle of the night the women were woken up, their heads were bagged, they were forced into trucks and taken off to an old building somewhere, they didn't know where. Female guards came along for the ride, but, says Ma Hla smiling, 'they brought their woven mats and had a good sleep.'

How did they feel then?

'Not scared, no. Angry,' they both say, together. 'If you humiliate a person, they will not fear you, they will hate you.'

Their trial took fifteen minutes. They were not legally represented. They were given no notice of the court appearance. They were surrounded by armed soldiers. Ma Yee says that as the time passed she became braver, but, day by day, her legs became weaker until one day she could no longer walk. When Ma Hla, a dentist, realised that movement was not returning and Ma Yee's muscles were beginning to atrophy she started a campaign to have her friend moved into a hospital. Her illness was not physiological, it was purely psychosomatic. In the meantime the women took turns in carrying Ma Yee around. At home, they were later told, their children, too were always sick: flu, measles, dengue fever—every mother in prison had the same experience with sick, pining children.

It seems foolish to ask whether there was anything positive about their time in jail but the response is enthusiastic, a bright, three-way jumble of Burmese voices until they switch back into English.

'I met people I would never have met in my life. I had a chance to talk to prostitutes, murderers, drug addicts, thieves. I got to talk to these women and get their points of view,' says Ma Hla. 'Prison is a place where you can't hide your true nature. I discovered I had been quite intolerant in the past.'

'I changed my opinion of people, too,' said Ma Yee.

But boredom and close proximity also wore them down. Six hundred women in one jail, with no books, writing material, jobs or exercise and few visits, began squabbling like battery hens about anything and everything: from politics to the personal.

Ma Yee eventually was taken to hospital for twenty days under heavy guard. And she did regain the use of her legs. All the women served their full sentences but on the day they were due to be released Ma Yee was kept in another twenty days to make up for her hospital time. Her children came to meet her, but she was not there. All the other mothers were out, but not theirs. 'They were angry with me,' she says. 'The children are quite distant from me. I think I have made up for the missed time but they never seem satisfied.'

Says Ma Hla, 'My elder daughter had a very bad time and my younger was unnecessarily spoilt. So, when I got out I had to sort out a lot of things with my children and my husband.'

On this Sunday morning Aung San Suu Kyi's compound is quiet. Outside the barbed wire, barricades are going up for the afternoon's public meeting. The whispers are of five young male students arrested, plucked apparently at random, from yesterday's crowd.

Yes, they say, they have been cowed. They are here in this compound, but they would not like their real names to be published. They have come because they are proud of Daw Suu Kyi—as they called her—and she has asked them to talk. Their children have suffered a lot, they are more reluctant than ever to resume an active role in political life. 'Daw Suu is very brave. A lot of people [who were jailed] have moved away and the field is smaller. Those involved are in more danger now,' says Ma Hla.

Mathan Gi, who was sentenced to ten years in jail but released recently, has not come back.

Aung San Suu Kyi says that not so much has changed in Burma since the beginning of her detention in 1989. But superficially much has changed. No change is more important than the illusion of prosperity. For the first time in three decades new opportunities are opening up in private business.

It seems almost treacherous to say that the military have the upper hand. It is true that the basic price of rice has jumped and that the very poor are probably, relatively speaking, even poorer. But it is also true that the markets are now crammed with cheap, reasonable quality consumer goods where the grey, third-rate products of such organisations as the 'People's Soap Factory' once stood.

The twin human weaknesses of greed and fear are intangible qualifiers in any political analysis of the current stalemate. Everyone wants a television set. From absolute poverty and destitution comes revolution. From the quest for material comfort comes political indifference.

Daw Suu would like the junta to know that there will be no pay back, that there is life after dictatorship. 'It is very, very difficult to convince a regime that is very, very oppressive that we are not interested in vengeance. I think those who handle people very, very harshly find it difficult to understand that we are not interested in meting out the same treatment.' But, right now, the junta is simply ignoring her.

The regime, explains a senior journalist on the *New Light of Myanmar*, is not as intolerant as many outsiders think. He cites as evidence an occasion on which his newspaper accidentally printed a photo of a senior general back to front, his wings on the wrong side. There were no repercussions, he says, smugly, clearly illustrating for me the vast intellectual divide germinated in isolation and nurtured by authoritarian rule.

'I am a cautious optimist,' says Daw Suu. 'I do think we will get democracy. But I cannot promise we will get democracy tomorrow.'

Rich bitch

Daw Khin Ma is waiting to show off. Outside sits her black Mercedes and the matching black jeep 'for the kids'. Inside the café of her city hotel the waiters are hovering nervously, refilling cups of thick black coffee before they can even be drained.

Her necklace is real, a huge ruby on a thick gold chain—to match today's outfit—set in a gold mount crackling with tiny diamonds. Her earrings are real, too: large single diamonds. And from her fingers rise mounds of gold, flashing with gemstones. She changes her gems like cheap costume jewellery, she says, as frequently as she changes her clothes.

Daw Khin Ma does not speak fluent English so she has agreed to this meeting on the invitation of another local businesswoman who does (she is very well known and has not agreed to use her real name, so I have picked this name at random from an old Burmese textbook). Still, her comprehension is good. And she nods, laughing, liberated, at the words 'showing off'. Yes, that's right. After three decades under socialism, crass new money is just fine.

Daw Khin's mother had advised her to marry an army officer. It seemed like a reasonable idea some twenty years ago. She was a beautiful young maiden, likely to land a good catch. The military was, and still is, the power in Burma. But Daw Khin was shrewder than that. Her family sold cooking oil, one of the few private businesses manufacturing essential products which was permitted to remain open under strict socialist economic policies imposed by the military in 1962. Early on, despite her limited high-school education, she realised she was a talented entrepreneur. She was, she says, pretty, charming and manipulative, a veritable *femme fatale* of the plain, outdated oil factory on the outskirts of Rangoon.

At that time life in Burma was very austere, the people denied all but the most rudimentary of consumer goods produced by the lumbering Government factories. The black market, of course, thrived. Gems, timber, antiques, bank notes flowed out of the country on the backs of human porters across the jungle border to Thailand. For the élite, French perfumes and Johnnie Walker Black Label, for example, came the other way. But it was not possible to flaunt one's wealth, so it was more practical to accumulate diamonds and gold. Yes, Daw Khin says, they kept them at home hidden under the bed.

Daw Khin bided her time, far beyond the age when a young girl turns into a worrisome spinster. All the time she honed her negotiating skills at her parents' factory, learning where power really lay and how to use it. Then, at the advanced age of 30, she made her choice and married the son of the family which ran Rangoon's other cooking oil factory, thus laying the foundations for a business empire. 'A woman cannot do business alone, she needs her husband,' she says.

At her hotel, breakfast is being served. Years in isolation have not helped Burma's service industry. The buffet offers glutinous, pre-cooked eggs swimming in oil and sweet, powdery white toast in honour of the hotel's Western guests. The building itself is one of Rangoon's first new high-rise developments: low ceilings, rows of oblong boxes stacked one on top of the other, confined spaces crowded onto a single piece of land in a vast, green city of gracious colonial parks and crumbling colonial mansions.

In the early 1990s, the fortunes of Burma's black marketeers suddenly changed. The generals abandoned the disastrous 'Burmese Road to Socialism' and reopened private businesses. The problem then, says Daw Khin, was how to 'bring out' one's illegal wealth.

It is with some pride that she explains the only way around the problem was to demolish her mother's home, a large, run-down mansion surrounded by ample gardens, and to build lots of small apartments. Her mother was very upset. Then she sold the apartments cheaply but greatly overstated the sale price, providing an official explanation should the Government care to question the source of her tremendous wealth. But, now she has added a national bank to her empire so such accounting problems are not so acute.

Economic and political power have never stood apart, side by side in a society ruled by censors who prevent the local media from engaging in investigative reporting and debate, but precise information is very difficult to come by. There are many stories, however, from knowledgeable sources told at small private meetings like this.

'Women in Burma,' Daw Khin says, 'are the money managers, the negotiators, the networkers of the upper echelons in Burma's new business world.' To do business in Burma requires access to influence, that is, the military. Influence is not, both my breakfast companions agree, a relationship with the wives of the generals. It is, however, a relationship with their daughters. The current Minister for Trade, they say, has four daughters, four such brokers of contracts and permits. And, to round the arrangement off nicely, a foreign business person is required to spend US$400 at one of the daughters' shops before an appointment with her father is confirmed.

Much is also said of Sandar Win, the daughter of Ne Win, Burma's ageing dictator. Like the other members of the new breed of Burmese matriarch, she boasts her own multi-storey hotel, a converted Government office gifted to her by her father. But she is perhaps best-known for her nightclub, one of the few permitted to operate in Burma. The glass doors at the entrance feature geometric patterns of nine, the astrological number of luck so heavily favoured by her father. (Ne Win had the currency converted to denominations adding up to nine to head off challenges to his power: thus the local *chat* comes in notes of 45, 90 and 135.)

The club is not much more than a smoky, windowless room with a very third-rate Filipino band doing covers up the front, the two female singers squeezed into tight blue and yellow satin catsuits, swaying around on top of high heels. But all transactions are in dollars or a curious currency called 'foreign exchange certificates'—Monopoly money invented by the generals to be compulsorily exchanged for greenbacks by tourists arriving at the airport, thus dictating the minimum amount of hard currency spent in the country. Just to be able to afford to buy a drink there, at Sandar's place, in a city where construction workers earn 50 cents a day, is status enough.

Daw Khin's husband arrives from breakfast at another restaurant. His patterned, short sleeved polyester shirt clashes with his *longgi*, the traditional cotton wrap-around skirt worn by Burmese men. His hair is oiled off his forehead, his teeth are stained with betel nut. 'Men do not show off,' says Daw Khin, laughing.

The conversation narrows, spinning around money and prices. There is so much to talk about. No question is too intrusive. How much do I earn, how much do I pay for my house, my car, my air ticket, my clothes? It has been a very long time since money was on show in Burma, and then it was in the hands of the British colonial regime and their lackeys.

It is difficult for Western tourists to understand why no particular efforts are being made to preserve the stunning, gracious architecture the British left behind. The colonial buildings, explained one Burmese academic, are symbols of the colonial subjugation of the past. Daw Khin, and the small coterie of entrepreneurs rushing into Burma's development boom, prefer things modern and new. Now money is the symbol of power. Daw Khin only finished the eighth grade at high school. Her two children, in their new black jeep, attend the most expensive school in Burma. The most expensive in Asia, she says. (This is not actually correct but Daw Khin and her husband make sure I do not miss the point.)

For more than two and a half thousand years bare feet have padded up the stone steps to the golden Shwedagon Pagoda—its deep, religious history and its commanding position atop the last hill before the Pegu range drops into the flat river delta has ensured its position as the most significant landmark of the city of Rangoon. Legend has it that the treasure vault of the Shwedagon contains the sacred relics of the Buddha and a fantastic fortune in gold and gems, donated by a string of kings and noblemen seeking merit to carry them favourably into their next life. But, more than anything else, the Shwedagon has been a place of quiet and tranquillity, its hundreds of tiny bells tinkling constantly in the breeze. From below it is seen standing reassuringly, visible from almost any street of the city.

But it was a queen, not a king, who established the Shwedagon's domination of Rangoon. Queen Shin Saw Bu, who ruled the Mon people from 1453 to 1472, retired to Rangoon where she built the dominating terrace, 50 feet high and 300 feet wide, and the immense balustrade. During her life Burma was a collection of competing kingdoms, usually ruled by men, but, on occasion, taken over by consorts or queens. In her book *The World of Burmese Women*, Mi Mi Khaing reports that Shin Saw Bu ascended to the throne following the death of her father, the king, and then her brother. But, she was not universally accepted and on one trip in the Royal Palanquin an old man on the side of the road shouted, 'Old fool am I? Not so old that I can't beget a son which is more than your old Queen could do.' After that she referred to herself as the 'Old Queen' and later retired, granting the hand of her daughter to a monk who had defended her from the taunt. The monk left his order and became king on the instruction of Shin Saw Bu who chose not to pass her authority through the female line.

Now, for the first time in history, the uninterrupted sweep of green leading up to the pagoda is under threat. New high-rise towers are being built on almost every corner with armies of women construction workers carrying bricks and concrete across their backs. The sweet tropical air is marred by the fumes of too many cars. For female workers the new jobs are mainly on building sites and in the private markets. It is not considered unusual for women to be out doing heavy physical work. Culture in Burma has never denied women a public economic role and, while political power remains in the hands of the male military élite, women are gaining more and more power in business, from the entrepreneurs at the top to the ordinary wives and mothers who have always controlled the local bazaars.

Defining the position of women, says Professor Yi Yi Myint of the Institute of Economics, is difficult anywhere in the world. Women in industrialised countries face the problems of being bound to their homes and children because of the lack of domestic help, whereas women in developing countries, on the other hand, have the freedom of an extended family and affordable household help. 'Burmese women have always been active in many fields, though there are special tasks that mostly women perform. The involvement of women in economic activities beyond the home is part of local culture and tradition originating in agriculture.'

In the social élite more girls than boys graduate from university in Burma and women dominate technical and health-related jobs such as medicine and pharmacy. In the rest of society, however, a history of education controlled by the Buddhist monks has favoured boys.

In many cases women have less education than their husbands and seek out work in less formal sectors such as casual construction, labouring or selling. A study of Rangoon's four main markets, quoted by Professor Yi Yi Myint, found women stall holders worked to supplement the family income and more than two-thirds of them ended up earning more than their husbands. In fact, even women of upper-class families sometimes choose to join a market rather than a profession, the study found.

Every morning in every town women congregate at the bazaar, some selling, some buying. Men are rarely found among the hagglers. The business dealings are diverse, from secondhand clothes to wholesale food purchases. Some women specialise in the trade of jewellery and gold and become money lenders and real estate agents.

The boom of downtown Rangoon has not reached the town of North Aklarpa. The brilliant red dirt road cuts through a row of simple shops to the flat, thatched roof of the open market. Around the perimeter the crude open drains are filled with rubbish and stagnant water. Under the thatch canopy, kids are playing and lounging on the wooden platforms that serve as their mothers' stalls. Ma Than Win is 33—her oldest child is sixteen and her youngest is four. She is selling secondhand clothes, bought for about 20 cents US a piece, repaired on her pedal sewing machine and resold at a profit of 100 per cent. Her income is about US$30 a month, just enough to supplement her husband's income and live a very basic life. Her clothes hang above her wooden platform, their fabric too old, thin and crumpled to be genuinely restored even with the most delicate repairs.

It is impossible to talk to one person in a market-place. Soon Ma Than Win's stall is packed. A young boy of about three tugs at his mother's bright pink blouse, helping himself to her breast while she talks. Babies are passed from shoulder to shoulder, curious, poking fingers running, grasping, along sweaty skin.

'If my husband decides what to do then we have to follow, the man is the leader,' she says. But, the money her husband earns he gives to her so she feels their position is equal, that there is no restriction on her life. Women, she says, are better at selling. 'Men are not patient enough to negotiate a price. Women are better persuaders.'

No, she says, men do not regard women as second-class citizens. But not all agree on the notion of equality. From out of the crowd comes a loud guffaw, a beaming smile of ragged, missing teeth. 'The woman has to add on the work of caring for the children and cleaning, of course,' says the old lady, to rousing gestures of agreement. 'And sometimes a man can go out of the house to enjoy.'

Could a woman go out 'to enjoy'? I ask the group, a sea of faces painted with the yellow paste that keeps a Burmese woman's complexion fair. 'No, no, no,' they laugh even more, as much at the novelty of my interest in their lives as anything else. A woman can choose her own husband when the time comes, usually by the age of eighteen. But she mustn't get a boyfriend first.

They have heard of men with more than one wife. But not here. This is a poor township where life is hard for both men and women. Polygamy is not an option their men could afford. Anyway, they say, most of them would disagree so he would not be allowed to take a second wife. The final word on such matters rests with the first wife and here, they say, their morals are quite strict.

The women once went into Rangoon with their families and watched a movie and visited the zoo and walked through the 'rich markets'. Maybe the rich are getting richer, they say. 'But the poor just stay poor, life just stays the same.'

An arranged marriage

Picking through the turmoil and tragedy of her life it is possible to discover where the happy ending should have been. It was truly a humbling, magnificent moment in the history of the world, a rare triumph of good over evil, a brief flash of order, momentarily arresting the chaos.

On 1 December 1988 Benazir Bhutto, the 35-year-old mother of a six-week-old baby boy, was named Prime Minister of Pakistan. She was the first female leader of a modern Muslim nation and one of the youngest Heads of State in recent history. The military dictator who had hanged her popular father, Ali Zulfikar Bhutto, the founding Prime Minister of Pakistan, was gone, killed in a mysterious plane crash in the remote, dusty reaches of the east. Behind her lay her own years in detention, her exile in Europe, her brother's suspicious death from poisoning and her exhausting personal campaign to wrest back the political power of the famous Bhutto clan.

More than nine years earlier her mother had fed her with Valium capsules as they lay unable to sleep, imprisoned in a deserted police training camp on the outskirts of the capital, Islamabad. The drugs, she says, had little effect and at 2 a.m. she suddenly sat bolt upright in bed screaming, clutching at her throat, gasping for breath. In her autobiography *Daughters of the East* she wrote:

> I felt the moment of my father's death. 'No', the scream burst through the knots in my throat. 'No'. I couldn't breathe, I didn't want to breathe. Papa. Papa. I felt so cold, so cold, in spite of the heat, and could not stop shaking.
>
> There was nothing my mother and I could say to console each other. Somehow the hours passed as we huddled together in the bare police quarters.

It was the moment that would define the rest of her life, and those of her surviving family members. In the morning she stood, stunned, hugging the pathetic bundle of clothes delivered from the jail, the fabric still smelling of her father's cologne. Long after his death, Benazir would sleep with her father's last shirt under her pillow. And from that moment on she would be a Bhutto, above anything else. A Bhutto before she was a woman, in an Islamic country which asked its women to cover their bodies and heads and walk obediently behind its men. Her name would defeat the prophets of doom, the old mullahs of the mosques who ranted and raved about the perils of defying the Holy Qu'rān and allowing a woman to lead.

Her opponents would attack her Western education, her sophisticated elegance and her cosiness with the foreign press. Scandalously, they would doctor her photographs—young, attractive, long-hair flying—and accuse her of breaching the Islamic law that states that a woman must cover her head.

But, for this brief happy ending it would never be enough.

'Would you vote for a woman?' I once asked a crowd of men, scuffing the red dirt along the road after her entourage had passed. 'A woman?' offered one young man, 'Well, yes. I would vote for Bhutto's dog, so I would vote for his daughter.'

Benazir would become one of the most famous women in the world. So much would be expected of her, so much would be made of the novelty of her gender. In fact, the world would want much more than her past ordeals had prepared her to deliver. To oppose a dictator is painful but simple, a clear question of right versus wrong. To lead a raucous, poverty-stricken, divided nation is another matter altogether. And as the thousands of news magazines rolled off the presses around the world, her handsome face splashed across their covers, no-one thought to stop to ask how it came to pass that Zulfikar's eldest child, a girl, had emerged as the heir to his considerable political fortune. Was it not true that one Bhutto son, Mir, still survived, himself as keen an opponent of the former dictator as his sister had ever been?

The excited mob swept onto the highway and swamped the jeep in a sea of sweaty, jostling bodies, thousands of wide-eyed faces pushed flat against the glass. Inside, Benazir Bhutto smiled calmly as the temperature gauge edged up towards 45 degrees Celsius and the jeep began to rock. Her helpless minders watched the frenetic crowd carefully, dismissing the undercurrent of panic with the casual observation that if the jeep could move no further then the people would carry it. The minders were sure, the people outside were sure, Benazir was sure, that they all loved Benazir.

The happy ending, of course, was not the ending of this story at all. The crashing, foaming waves of Pakistani politics rolled on, tumbling even Benazir as they swept across the dry, desperate nation.

In August 1990 Benazir was thrown unceremoniously out of office by Pakistan's military-backed caretaker administration, ending a mere 20 months in power. She and her businessman husband, Asif Ali Zardari, and scores of her political allies, had been accused of corruption during their brief rule. New elections were called so she would have to start again.

Two months later, tens of thousands of people surrounded the High Court in the northern city of Lahore where the hearing of some of the charges against the ousted Prime Minister were due to begin. Thousands of stiff, neat riot police, armed with long cane sticks, several old tanks on hand, had surrounded the people. We had waited and waited, a small group of foreign correspondents, pressed against one door, hemmed in by the surging crowd. Here, in this same old British courtroom with its slow-moving ceiling fans and its highly polished wooden benches, Zulfikar Ali Bhutto had been sentenced to death by hanging, more than a decade earlier, by the ruling military junta.

The pressure from the pushing crowd grew stronger and stronger until we were packed so tightly together that our sweat began to mix. Wave after wave of movement surged through the crowd towards the barricaded door. Then, a single panel of glass shattered and the crowd exploded. The doors fell to the ground, everything and everyone within the path of the mob was trampled beneath their feet.

Benazir had blacked out momentarily and was dragged away to an alcove behind the judge's bench where she collapsed, shaking and crying. With the courtroom wrecked and hundreds of people battered and bruised the hearing was adjourned. When the men with the cane sticks finally moved in to clear the crowd, the people left just as they had come, in a wild, screaming surge, pulling the frame of the fallen door with them on their shoulders as they spilled out.

Two days later Benazir was back on the campaign trail for the new election, more bitter than ever, more determined than ever to weep a martyr's tears for her own misfortune. On that day, like the day before that and the day before that, the pulsating mob thronged the tatty streets waiting for their queen.

At first the jeep flashed by the roadside crowds, Benazir waving regally as we went. Then the reckless young boys, in white flapping tunics, threw their bodies in front of the wheels imploring Benazir to stop. The jeep braked and accelerated, two steps forward, one step back, until it reached a dusty strip of higgledy-piggledy, red mud-brick houses, festooned with bunting. We could go no further. The crowd had blocked the road so completely that we could not see beyond the thousands of dark-haired heads. So Benazir emerged from the sun roof and waved. Her minders, perched on top of the jeep, beat back the young men with canes.

Benazir was now 38 years old, and the mother of two young children. In person, she was as charismatic and imposing as her curriculum vitae would suggest. But she looked tired and hounded, her voice hoarse from the grinding daily schedule of mass public rallies. She had come into politics deeply scarred by her years in detention and her father's death. Today she was on different turf, but she was still fighting back at Pakistan's powerful armed forces. The battle, as she saw it, was simple, her democracy against their authoritarian rule.

But, on the crowded, impoverished streets such lofty ideals were meaningless. To the masses she was merely fighting to uphold the dynasty, the famous Bhutto family name. Pakistan is a punishing nation. A vast sea of terribly poor, illiterate peasants supports a small club of the worldly rich. An election is a carnival, a welcome break from the monotony of a hard rural life on the red, dusty land. A single day when the powerless are important enough to be asked—or paid—for their vote. Ballot papers are marked with symbols, votes are cast with thumbs dipped in ink. Benazir's pride is in her history, her membership of one of the most powerful feudal families of all. Meaningful political change has eluded the little people of Pakistan.

'I'm young, I'm strong, I'm determined. I grew up believing that one didn't give in. It is physically and mentally exhausting but, ironically, it is the exhaustion which gives you the satisfaction that you are doing your best,' she told me. It was a well-rehearsed, often repeated line.

She signalled the driver and her men to regroup. The sun was already setting and her final destination was another 40 kilometres away. Hundreds of thousands of people had been waiting since midday along this route, growing edgy and irresponsible in the heat.

The jeep crept forward, very slowly at first, the canes lashing wildly at all those pawing at the sealed windows, searching for a grip.

Then, suddenly, a space opened up ahead and the jeep broke free, chased by packed cars, streams of motorbikes and running, shouting youths. In a brief flash the headlights caught the wild faces of the young men. Beaten back, they rolled laughing in the dirt, the tails of their *shalwars* riding up over their billowing white pants. The warm evening air stung with the black fumes of hundreds of clapped-out cars.

Benazir wanted to direct the conversation. She is Western-educated, intelligent and well read, so this is something she is accustomed to doing. Inside the jeep she was ready with all the answers to the questions she would like to be asked. She would like to focus, in detail, on the injustice of her dismissal, the 'trumped-up' corruption charges against her and her family and her own role as the leader capable of saving Pakistan from the certain clutches of dictatorship.

The evidence against her associates, she said, was gathered under torture. But so widely circulated were the rumours about the kickbacks and preferential deals obtained by her jet-setting, polo-playing husband that surely the damage had already been done. And Zardari's image could not be helped by the enduring fascination with his supposedly footloose bachelor days when he had allegedly had a disco built in his drawing room to entertain his guests.

'A glamorous, young couple holding positions of power—people love to hear things about them. It is the celebrity status that makes people thirsty for any spicy little morsel of gossip they can pick up and gobble.' Peck, peck, peck. She spoke with open resentment. She remained, in public, loyal to the man many blamed for her political demise.

Pakistan is a nation of patriarchs, arranged marriages, dutiful daughters and obedient wives. Benazir had accepted an arranged marriage in 1987, bowing to the reality that an Islamic nation would not accept a single woman as their leader. Pakistan was formed following the splitting of British colonial India, the two poor pockets to the north-east and the north-west reserved for the former colony's Muslim minority. East Pakistan later became the independent nation of Bangladesh and Pakistan continued to spat, bitterly, across the border with the new majority Hindu Indian nation. Islam defined Pakistan as a country and the rules of the Holy Qu'rān played an important political role.

Benazir had learned to cover her head modestly in public, she had learned not to flaunt her ease with the English language and the ways of the decadent West in the face of the country's religious leaders. She had accepted the impossibility of divorce. But her public achievements went unrecognised by many. 'They aren't interested in the 8000 primary schools and the 4000 villages electrified . . . only in the spicy bits of gossip about myself and my babies and my husband,' she says. And, 'of course, I miss my babies,' speaking of the campaign trail, separated from her children. But this is what she has to do.

Actually, I wanted to ask her many more questions about her personal life, but she had already turned the conversation back to her script. I tried, meekly, to call upon the universal sisterhood of women in this male-dominated world, and so asked her about her life as a prominent woman in a nation retreating into conservative Islam.

But, today, Benazir does not see herself as a woman, rather as a struggling politician. I wanted to ask if she was pregnant again, a rumour circulating widely and supported by her rounded lines. (A British journalist, hungry for a spicy little morsel of news, later plucked up the courage to ask. The answer was 'no', she had merely been snacking on sweets on the exhausting campaign trail.)

We turned off the narrow highway and into a compound with a high gate. But the best efforts of the minders failed to keep the crowd out. In the confusion, an old man had fallen under our jeep, his beard caught in the wheel. The crowd lifted the car off and pulled him out. Then there was a scuffle and a moment of genuine alarm as members of the official convoy tried to squeeze through the narrow opening of the front door before it was slammed shut. Several men were left yelling outside, pushed up hard against the windows. Inside, English tea was being sedately served.

The reality of politics, one of Benazir's minders explained, is that you need family money as well as friends and relatives in the military, the police and the bureaucracy. Benazir's mistake, according to this analysis, was to hold too great a grudge against the armed forces and to fail to acknowledge the reality of their power. The frenetic mob outside became a mere back-drop, of little relevance to the real power game labelled 'democracy' currently being played out in the drawing-rooms of the rich. Others said that Benazir gathered around her incompetent ministers and advisers, rewarding them for their suffering under the dictator. She appointed the largest Cabinet in Pakistan's history and gave 20 000 party workers Government jobs.

Benazir does not like to be pushed. Impatiently, she said: 'The inheritance of a tottering and troubled economy made mistake-free management an impossibility. Yes, we made some mistakes.'

She would not care to elaborate. Instead she would like to explain her idea for an organisation of nations such as Pakistan and the Philippines, newly liberated from dictatorship. But, surely, both nations were still reeling? Was not, perhaps, the problem that both countries were still controlled by a handful of squabbling moneyed families, rendering the voice of the people mute, no matter what political label had prevailed? But Benazir is talking only about the past and her plans for the future are vague and academic. She is obsessed with her own personal battle, she is counting on martyrdom to win for a second time. She does not like my questions, the conversation is over.

It is a very long, hard road, I cannot deny her that. Millions more sweaty, aggressive young men along the way. Rally after rally to raise with the same battle cry.

Benazir lost that election of 1990. But she narrowly won again in 1993. By then, her brother Mir Murtaza Bhutto had begun the process of challenging the will. Their father's political inheritance was his, not hers, and Benazir's mother had stood up publicly to agree. In truth it was the matriarch, Begum Nusrat Bhutto, who had been made leader of her husband's Pakistan People's Party (PPP) when he was first arrested, a temporary measure at the time to hold the party together until his release.

With her son seeking to challenge Benazir at the

polls *in absentia*, she turned around and told her daughter that now it was time for her to take her husband's name and pass the mantle to her brother. Benazir sacked her mother from the PPP, but both Nusrat and Mir still won seats in her Government.

In her autobiography, Benazir had referred only in passing to her conflict with Mir. But before her return from exile in Europe they had clashed many times over how best to challenge the military dictatorship. Both Mir and their dead younger brother, Shahnawaz, had been convinced that violence must be met with violence. Both had been targeted men during martial law and even while in exile in France.

Mir finally returned to Pakistan in 1993. Benazir promptly had him arrested and jailed for seven years on terrorism charges. The family was sucked into a vortex of bitterness that left Benazir isolated from her closest relatives, with only her husband at her side. Meanwhile, spot fires of violence erupted around the country, the economy limped forward and accusations of corruption and incompetence followed the Bhutto queen.

I returned to Pakistan in 1995 for an interview with Benazir. I waited in Islamabad for ten days as she dealt with crisis after internal crisis. Before making the long trip from Australia, via India, I had read a particularly nasty profile of Benazir in an English magazine. She had had nothing to contribute, that was the trouble. The journalist, a woman, had spent two weeks chasing the Prime Minister around the country, brushed off by the arrogant minders who surrounded the feudal queen. Finally, she returned to London with nothing.

I actually wondered whether earlier I had met Benazir by accident, not design. Naturally, I had filed my written interview request and had turned up at the appointed time at one of her family homes, this one in Lahore. Sitting under a canopy on the street outside were the ordinary people, denied entry even into the garden. On the grass inside sat the next group up the hierarchical scale, then on the verandah those with a little more access and, inside, in the outer living room, those who had managed to get closer still. But, there was yet another inner waiting room for those who just might meet the queen and from where they would be plucked. Whatever appointments her staff had made seemed irrelevant. Benazir's power was personal. I stood up as she was leaving town in her jeep and pushed forward. She signalled me to get into her jeep. I'm sure she had no idea we actually had an appointment.

So I am not overly surprised that my second interview does not materialise, nor overly annoyed. I am dubious of the expectation of some female journalists that preferential access should be granted in the name of the sisterhood, but I am very interested to discover more about what Benazir thinks of the position of women in Pakistan. She has not been able to escape the expectation that a female Prime Minister should pay particular attention to the country's women, nor the grinding disappointment that so little has been achieved.

I didn't really believe her when she told me that she did not see herself as a *female* politician, but just as a politician. So I searched back through her autobiography, and reread the many references to the plight of women in Pakistan. Benazir's grandfather, she writes, was the first to break away from the feudal ethos.

> Until this time Bhuttos had only married other Bhuttos, first or second cousins. Islam entitled women to inherit property and so the only way to keep the land within the family was through marriage.
>
> When there was no suitable cousin in the family, the Bhutto women did not marry at all. For this reason my

grandfather's daughters from his first marriage had remained single all their lives. But, despite great opposition from the family, my grandfather had allowed his daughters from his second marriage to marry outside the Bhutto circle, though they were not love matches, but strictly arranged affairs.

A generation later, my sister Sanam would become the first Bhutto woman to make her own decision. Contrary to my expectations, I would follow the traditional path and have an arranged marriage myself.

When Benazir's mother married her father in 1951 she entered *purdah* with the other Bhutto women, hidden behind the high walls of the compound and allowed to leave only once a week to visit her family, despite having had a degree of freedom before her marriage that included learning how to drive.

'The old ways, however', writes Benazir, 'were getting tiring'. When it came time for her mother to bring out for Benazir the black *burqa* that covers a woman from head to foot—only allowing her to peer out through an embroidered panel across the eyes—her father turned around and asked her to take it off.

Despite the male-dominated Pakistani culture Benazir was not discriminated against within the family and, in fact, was encouraged by her father to pursue an overseas education and thoroughly congratulated when she won the Presidency of the Oxford Union at her father's former university in England.

Her style forthright and open, her education and experience international, Benazir grew into an international stateswoman even in her twenties, a life far from that of the women behind the veils in Pakistan. To a certain extent her ease with Western culture made her a darling of the Western press and many were surprised when she entered into an arranged marriage.

An arranged marriage was the price in personal choice I had to pay for the political path my life had taken. My high profile in Pakistan precluded the possibility of my meeting a man in the normal course of events. Even the most discreet relationship would have fuelled the gossip and rumour that already surrounded my every move.

To many Easterners an arranged marriage is the norm rather than the exception. But my own parents had married for love and I had grown up believing that the day would come when I would fall in love and marry the man of my choosing.

As an undergraduate in the USA during the flowering of the Women's Movement, I was convinced that marriage and a career were compatible, that one didn't preclude the other. I believed then, as I still do, that a woman can aim for and attain all: a satisfying professional life, a satisfying marriage and the satisfaction of children.

At the age of 34, Benazir finally consented to consider her family's choice—Zardari, heir to the chiefdom of the 100 000-strong Zardari tribe and a man of similar feudal power.

I felt torn apart. I knew my friends in the West would find it difficult to understand the peculiar cultural and political circumstances that were leading me towards an arranged marriage. Feminism in the West was very different from that in the East, where religious and family obligations remained central. And there was also the personal side of the question. In my position as the leader of the largest opposition party (at the time) in Pakistan, I could not afford the scandal of breaking any engagement or ever getting divorced, except in the most extreme circumstances.

I was being asked to make up my mind about living the rest of my life with a man whom I had only met three days before and in the company of our respective families.

Behind Benazir's decision lay loneliness and the reality that it would only be a matter of time until her brother, Mir, returned to Pakistan with a new wife to take over the family home. 'What would my position be in the home of my brother and his new wife?' Of Zardari, she wrote:

We did not love each other yet, though my mother assured me that love would come later. Instead there was a mental commitment between us, a realisation that we were accepting each other as husband and wife, totally and for always. Though I certainly did not—and do not—want to be seen as an advocate of arranged marriages I realised there must be something to a relationship based on acceptance. Our love could only grow.

In her announcement of the engagement Benazir told the Pakistani people: 'Conscious of my religious obligation and duty to my family I am pleased to proceed with the marriage proposal accepted by my mother.'

I had plenty of free time in Islamabad to visit Benazir's showcase, the nation's first women's police station.

'Women in Pakistan,' said Inspector Shamshad Ashraf, 'are not greatly respected,' laughing to herself at the humiliation of a man subjected to questioning by one of her female police officers. 'Here,' she said, gesturing at the three small rooms in the tiny new building, 'we feel much confidence and independence.'

Most women who seek help have been raped or abandoned without financial support, she said. 'The face of the man goes very pale. Husbands feel much shame in being brought before a female police officer.' But, she conceded, they did not encourage women to file charges against their abusive husbands because a man can simply divorce his wife and leave her without any financial support.

I am confused rather than impressed.

For Pakistan's fledgling women's movement, Benazir is an ineffective role model who has made too many concessions to conservative Islamic values and whose women's policies are bandaids that do nothing to address blatantly discriminatory laws.

In the local papers I read of a Prime Ministerial mercy mission and the resources of the Government being put at the disposal of a poor rural woman horribly mutilated by her husband in a sexual assault using a red-hot metal poker. The national Human Rights Commission reports that a woman is raped every three hours in Pakistan, every second victim a child, every fourth the victim of gang rape.

Under the Islamic *hudood* ordinances a woman must provide four adult male witnesses to prove a rape or must face being jailed for adultery, which is a criminal offence for females beyond puberty. Between 80 per cent and 90 per cent of women in the country's jails are on adultery charges, according to legal activists, resulting from rapes.

When Benazir first came to power in 1988 she announced a one-time amnesty to clear the jails of thousands of women, but the laws have not been amended. Nor have the laws of evidence, in which a woman's written testimony counts as half of a man's. And a Pakistani man has the automatic right of divorce but a woman must prove misbehaviour and forfeit her financial claim if she initiates the action.

'One of the greatest impediments to development in this country is the automatic barring of almost half the population from decision-making and public life,' said one diplomat. Twenty per cent of girls under eleven attend primary school, compared to 37 per cent of boys. Only two per cent of public servants and one third of teachers are women. On average every Pakistani woman bears 6.7 children.

'The biggest barriers to women in work are cultural and social such as, "You are not going to an office to work, that is an insult to the family honour",' said one middle-class professional woman.

In the fields the women must toil alongside the men but the dowry practice continues, marking female children from the day they are born as burdens for most families of limited income. In extreme cases young brides who have brought an inadequate dowry to their husbands' homes die in mysterious 'kitchen fires', in which the stove supposedly explodes while they are cooking.

'Benazir is fighting for her political survival. In order to be acceptable to a wider public she had to get married,' said another professional woman.

But Benazir maintains her marriage has turned out well, anyway. It is a supportive partnership, she has said, and she would like in the future to arrange the marriage of her children.

In September 1996 gunmen cut down Mir Murtaza Bhutto in the violent port city of Karachi. Investigations showed that Benazir's brother did not die in the first volley of shots but that he was 'finished off' as he lay bleeding and helpless on the ground, most likely by members of the Government's security forces. Even Benazir's closest supporters asked how it was that she could not protect her own brother, regardless of the political rift.

Two months later Benazir was again sacked from the Prime Ministership, the decree dissolving Parliament citing corruption, abuse and mismanagement by her Government. Benazir had made her husband Investment Minister. Now he stood accused of official corruption and was jailed. He was also under suspicion of involvement in his brother-in-law's death. The national economy had stagnated, sectarian violence was escalating and her Government was widely criticised for failing to improve the lot of the country's women and the poor. There was talk of a new political exile in Britain under a deal that would see charges against her husband dropped.

'Benazir Bhutto is rehearsing one more time for the role she knows best,' wrote one foreign journalist as Benazir again prepared to go into a new round of elections. 'It is a character she has played so often in her tumultuous political career: the martyred patriot and champion of democracy, defending her noble family name against the dark forces of dictatorship. But, who is going to buy the histrionics this time?'

Benazir suffered a humiliating defeat. She did not, however, retire from politics or leave the country freezing her accounts. It is fair to assume she will be back.

In September 1997, Swiss authorities froze the bank accounts of Benazir, her husband and her mother saying they had seen 'solid evidence regarding their corrupt practices and accumulation of ill-gotten wealth'. Deposits totalled about US$18.5 million and Benazir's political opponents claimed the money had been traced to commissions from offshore companies.

Benazir strenuously denied the accusations but Swiss police maintained the accounts should be frozen 'as a preventative measure'.

Mothers of the
uprising

'I am sorry, but it is very embarrassing for me to talk about myself,' says the stout grandmother, self-consciously adjusting the jacket of her neat, knitted twin set. 'I have always been introduced as the mother of my son,' Mrs Lim Ki-Nan explains, apparently genuinely surprised that I have come all this way to talk about her instead. But, for almost a decade I have wanted to make this trip to find Mrs Lim.

Now that we are finally sitting down together in an ordinary coffee shop in the centre of Seoul I feel my confident sense of purpose beginning to slide in the face of misunderstanding. 'But your life is very important,' I say, through an interpreter, in a weak attempt to salvage the moment. There is no nod of agreement, but I plough on, none the less.

I would like to start at the very beginning when Mrs Lim was a child, a girl burdened by the shame of her mother's failure to produce a son, a girl who had learnt that she must cast her eyes downwards lest she meet the gaze of the boys in her class at school. I would like to ask her about her marriage to a man she barely knew, a union she accepted without ever thinking to ask herself about love. And, then, I would like to ask her about all her children. Not just her well-known son who had campaigned against South Korea's

211

military dictatorship in those treacherous street battles of the 1980s, before disappearing first into jail, and then later into the shadowy, illegal life of the underground political opposition.

Mrs Lim is polite and answers my questions, still confused about the purpose of our meeting.

It is a hot day in Seoul. The coffee shop is now filled with her colleagues, ageing mothers and grandmothers, mopping their faces and bustling around our booth with concern, just to make sure Mrs Lim already has her drink. Mrs Lim is now 66 years old. She is sturdy, not frail, her forearms still thick and firm. Today, she has come to Pagoda Park, just as she has come every Thursday for many years now. With a megaphone and home-made banners Mrs Lim and her mothers' group have today publicly berated the latest in the line of South Korean Governments they have opposed. Theirs is a small group of unlikely radicals: floral frocks and pearls, folded handkerchiefs pressed against warm foreheads.

The towering office blocks and boxy department stores of downtown Seoul dwarf the small patch of green, the sun refracting harshly off the endless walls of glass. The high heels of the office girls on their lunch breaks click rhythmically as they breeze past in chattering bunches. The traffic drones on.

It is a matter of principle, really, Mrs Lim explains. Almost ten years ago I caught my first glance of Mrs Lim's group of mothers on these same streets. The wide avenues were empty, the air stinging with tear gas. On one side stood the formidable rows of riot police, the eyes of the young conscripts concealed behind their visors. On the other side stood the mothers, marching towards them, handbags swinging, their faces and lungs exposed to the burning toxic fumes. They were the mothers of South Korea's jailed pro-democracy activists: the so-called 'Mothers Against Tear Gas'. Their sons were in jail, so they had come to face the riot police themselves. At the age of 56 Mrs Lim did not avert her gaze.

'When I was a student in middle school [primary] I could not so much as look a boy straight in the face. Later, I had to bind my breasts to hide them when I went out in public I was so ashamed. But, when I looked at the riot police and I saw that they were afraid of us I knew we were doing the right thing,' she says.

In retrospect many political analysts identify the appearance of the mothers on the streets as the beginning of the end of three decades of military rule. It was through Mrs Lim and her friends that political opposition made the critical shift from the radical students to the mainstream middle-class families, and from that point the power of the dictators began to unravel very fast. In 1992 South Koreans elected former political prisoner Kim Young Sam as their President, in a democratic ballot. President Kim released many of the remaining political prisoners who had opposed the military, but not all of them. Which is why the mothers are still here, Mrs Lim explains, despite their victory in their quest for democracy.

Numbers are dwindling now, she concedes, and few of the ageing mothers have the stamina to go on once their own children have been released from prison. She understands that. 'They are human beings, they are tempted to live a comfortable life,' she says. At which point I switch off the tape recorder and avert my own eyes from her tears.

For the first ten years of her life Lim Ki-Nan lived with her parents in a small provincial town where her father was a trader. She was well looked after by her grandfather and father, she says. But, then, her father took a second wife. Her own mother had failed, and produced only her, a single daughter. 'It was taken for granted that those men who were rich were allowed to have two or three wives and for men who had no sons there was a great deal of shame. Sometimes it was even the first wife who encouraged her husband to take another wife, because she felt so inferior,' she says. 'My father complained a lot because my mother couldn't produce a son. Finally, my mother had to allow him to take a second wife, but even then they never stopped quarrelling.' In retrospect, Mrs Lim says, all her mother wanted was just to have the one family and a husband for herself.

The second wife quickly gave birth to four children, two sons and two daughters. Her father's duty was to support them all, so both the families were very poor and very unhappy.

'At the age of 24 I thought I was obliged to get married, I had already reached that age. I was a teacher and I was the only girl from my area to have passed the exams and that was something really special. But, once I got married I gave up my job. I wasn't forced to, that is just what you did.'

In 1953 there were few young men available, she says, because of the Korean War. A local match-maker set up a series of meetings with a soldier who had been conscripted from university where he was studying engineering. She thought he was a sincere man so they were married the next month. 'I didn't really think about whether I was lucky or happy, I just got married.'

Her answer had been very long and the translation offered very short and to the point. It was really an irrelevant question anyway. 'Romance' and 'love' were low priorities in the chaos and starvation that followed the war. The chaos swamped Mrs Lim on a personal level as well. Soon after her marriage both her parents died leaving her and her new husband with financial responsibility for the step-mother and young children she blamed for her own miserable upbringing.

'The second family was suffering a great deal. Then,

their mother had a stroke. We had to help them but the youngest couldn't go to school because we ran out of money,' she says.

This is clearly a very painful topic. 'I don't want to think about it,' she says, and then confers with the translator. 'Why are you asking these questions?' she asks.

We have been talking for about half an hour. I want to know about her motivations for her obvious courage. She wants to talk about her son. Later I am told that Korean people do not like to show their grief or weakness. All I am hearing is a literal translation of her words. I realise that I cannot hope to fully understand. So we pause, wait a few minutes and regroup.

'My first child was a daughter, then a son,' she says. 'That was very nice.' But at the age of four her first son died from diphtheria. Her next two children were girls. 'So I then had three daughters in a row. I don't deny that at that time I would have preferred to have sons.' So she had more children, two boys.

'In my case I had to produce two sons after three girls,' she explains. 'And if I hadn't had my youngest son then I wouldn't have become involved in this kind of activity.'

The city of Seoul is dotted with ancient palaces, their thick stone walls enclosing leafy gardens, sanctuaries from the crowded streets. The most famous landmark, perhaps, is 'The Secret Garden', a vast, shady sweep of tree-lined paths, ponds, springs and elegant resting pavilions. In one corner of the grounds stands the Palace of Illustrious Virtue (Changdok), the seat of power of thirteen successive kings of the resilient

Yi Dynasty that was founded in 1392 and survived until the Japanese military annexation of Korea in 1910.

The guided tours shuffle past the panels of sliding wood that form box-like cubicles along one side of Changdok Palace—the quarters of the royal concubines. Other plain rooms with cool wooden floors were the domain of the king's wives, their status determined by the order in which they were chosen and their skill in retaining his favour.

The Korean myth of creation of the first royal dynasty says the Son of Heaven came down to earth where he met a female bear who wanted to become a human being. When the bear and the Son of Heaven united he became the first king and she the first queen, creating a bridge between Heaven and Earth. The Korean view of the universe is based on the principle of yin and yang: that life is governed by the interaction of two opposite poles. Yin is the female, or negative pole and yang is the male, or positive pole. From that basic position any kind of balance can be derived. A male, simply because he is male, is yang, but as a son to a parent he is yin. As a brother to a sister he is yang, but he can become yin again when he grows up and becomes a subordinate to his boss in the workplace.

Much of the form of social organisation and government in Korea was based on the teaching of the Chinese philosopher Confucius who is assumed to have lived in the sixth century BC.

'Designed to uphold a static agrarian order, Confucianism was a paternalistic system of benevolent rule by civil bureaucrats acting in the name of a monarch who was technically absolute and the nominal owner of all the land in the kingdom,' Lone and McCormack wrote in their book *Korea Since 1850*. As such, the roles and status of all members of society were fixed, and little opportunity existed for changing one's position in life.

In traditional Korean society a woman carried with her an ornamental dagger, the purpose of which was not to strike out at a man bent on stealing her chastity, but to kill herself rather than surrender to a man's desire.

The Korea Handbook, published by the Government, notes:

> Women were required to learn the Confucian virtues of subordination and endurance while being denied opportunities to participate in social and political functions: their major role was to give birth. No matter what social stratum they belonged to they were inferior to men and the social institutions and customs of avoiding the opposite sex did not permit women to become involved in life outside the family.

'In no relationship did a woman enjoy prestige except as a mother to a male child,' write Lone and McCormack in their analysis of the Yi Dynasty.

Kings took many wives and mistresses. Their women lived confined by the heavy stone walls and when they ventured outside they were carried in a windowless wooden box, an Oriental variation on the *purdah*, or veil, of Islam. In the rice fields, however, the restrictions of the Royal families were not as practical. Men and women both had to work. But the rules of male lineage remained, and wives became the property of their husband's family. Many a daughter-in-law became her mother-in-law's new maid, poor compensation for the misery she herself had endured as a young bride.

Shijipsari, the term women used for life after marriage, literally means 'life with one's in-laws' but it is more commonly understood to refer to the suffering of a young wife.

'Suddenly at the age of sixteen I found a marriage arrangement being made for me. When I was informed that my wedding date had been chosen I was very upset. I was too young to be married,' Kang Bok-Nye told Marion Kim, author of a collection of oral histories of Korean women.

'When my prospective mother-in-law came to see me for the first time and to eat rice made by me, I served her, but then hid in the corner and wept continuously. She was impressed none the less and bestowed her approval on me as a daughter-in-law,' she said. 'Marriage was a linking of families, not an individual thing. My husband and I didn't even see each other's faces until the day of the wedding when—according to custom—he and his relatives came to my house to escort me to my *shijip* [in-laws]. He rode a horse and I sat in a closed palanquin on poles carried by his male relatives.

'I could not see out of the box so I did not know where I was being taken. As a new bride I was not allowed to visit my family until three years had passed and then only with a male escort from my husband's family. Likewise I could not go to the market, only men and old women were permitted to travel so far from home.

'For some reason I never discovered my young husband [also 16] hated the very sight of me. Without a husband who loved me I was totally consumed by *shijipsari*. My father-in-law was partly paralysed and so my mother-in-law had to work the fields. This left me to take care of everything in the house and I was always exhausted. I had to prepare all the food, cooking the rice, the soup and several kinds of side dishes. During meals I had to wait in the kitchen, then when everyone else was finished I ate the leftovers and the scrapings off the bottom of the rice pot. That was normal *shijipsari*.'

A well-known Korean proverb went: 'If you want to know a household, try its condiments', and referred in particular to *kim chi*, the fermented cabbage a Korean housewife was obliged to prepare. Regardless of the skill invested in the preparation of the condiments they can be ruined through insufficient attention during the fermentation process, in a large earthenware pot set in the corner of a room.

'On a sunny day the lid must be open to let in the sun, on a rainy day it must be closed,' writes Dr Lee O. Young in *Korea in its Creation*. 'The housewife has to keep one eye constantly on the condiments. We say that we can taste the quality of her devotion and her love for her family in the condiments she makes. In the traditional family when the new wife's life under the thumb of the mother-in-law gets too hard she will let go of a few tears in the bay where the condiments crock sits.'

Dr Lee also writes of the wooden stick called the laundry bat: 'Together our women, as if they were playing a percussion ensemble, drum away on the washing rock in harmonious rhythm'.

But Kang Bok Nye, who was born in 1917, at the beginning of the process of change, says: 'At that time Koreans were still dressing almost entirely in white, so any dirt was visible. If I did not get the laundry sparkling clean I was severely scolded by my mother-in-law. Squatting by the steam or the well I beat the dirt out with a thick laundry bat. Some people these days refer to the romantic sound of the sticks, rhythmically pounding the laundry, but for me that sound recalls an aching back, eyes drooping with tiredness and a heart aching for the sight of my own mother.'

When the Constitution of the Republic of Korea was promulgated in 1948 women achieved equal status before the law, but, in reality, considerable social restrictions remained. It was not until 1991 that a new

Family Law came into force that sought to interrupt the automatic cycle of inheritance of authority and power from father to son. A husband remains the legal head of a South Korean family, but custody of children is no longer automatically granted to the father on divorce and sons no longer automatically inherit a father's property ahead of his widow and daughters.

'I think that the legal and structural changes have been made but the consciousness has not changed much. The Confucian male-centred attitude is still there so this delays implementation,' says Chung Sei Wha, President of the Korean Women's Development Institute.

'If we have to pick out one thing about Confucianism's attitude towards women that would be the ideology of purity. Women are supposed to have only one husband in their lives and to respect their parents-in-law, but this ideology requests not just purity but the subordination of women.

'When a son is born everyone still claps, when a daughter is born there are soothing words. Most women still want to have at least one son so the family lineage is not broken.'

At a decision-making level, she says, less than one per cent of bureaucrats and company executives are women. In politics only two per cent of representatives in the National Assembly are women, half of them appointed, and in local councils the percentage is only 0.9.

'Even these days women think that women are not supposed to be in the political arena and they feel negatively when they see women in politics,' Sei Wha said.

When Congresswoman Ms Oh Sun Kim first took her seat in the National Assembly there was not even a ladies' toilet for her convenience. So she decided to wear a man's suit. Now in her third term in office she still does so.

In June of 1987 South Korea was preparing to host the 1988 Summer Olympic Games. It was an occasion of immense national importance and an important source of international legitimacy for the government of military strongman President Chun Doo Hwan.

When my flight touched down in Seoul I had a busy press schedule ahead of me: visits to Olympic stadiums and villages and tours of local attractions on offer alongside the Games. But, on the first taxi ride into the city, my nostrils burned and my throat hurt from the wisps of tear gas seeping out into the atmosphere.

Every day there were demonstrations, mostly centred around the universities. The student groups opposing the regime were well organised, almost along their enemy's military lines. Every student had his prescribed role: one to taunt and provoke, then fall back quickly, another to race in from behind armed with a Molotov cocktail. The riot police moved, like daleks from *Doctor Who*, hidden behind shields and gas masks, routinely blasting the rioters with tear gas, then lashing out at them with rattan sticks.

The Korean riot police normally did not carry guns, but sometimes a tear gas canister struck and killed a student. Sometimes news leaked out of a student who had died in jail, tortured to death under interrogation. And sometimes a student or two set themselves alight, the grimmest and most dramatic of protests against almost three decades of military rule.

It was often said the tear gas used on the streets of South Korea had originally been purchased from the Marcos regime in the Philippines, that dictatorship having lost the nerve to use it on its own political opponents because of the gas's debilitating potency. It was a matter of pride that the students of South Korea

221

faced the riot squads without gas masks. Toothpaste, they said, worked to neutralise the stinging and clear plastic sandwich wrap could be used to provide some kind of protection for the eyes.

For several days in late June the Olympic village public relations tours continued as the crowds of protesters swelled. Then, across town in the middle of the busiest business district I watched the group of middle-aged women, arms linked, march past the rows of shops, swinging the focus of the protests right into every middle-class family home. By the end of the week the protests had taken over the city and the streets were deserted.

'At that time the role we were expected to play was to chant slogans and rescue the students from the police,' said Mrs Lim. 'At first when we rescued the students the riot police couldn't attack us because we were mothers, but gradually they didn't care about that anymore. By that time I had police guarding both the front and back of my home and so I had to sneak out. I was forcibly taken to the police station many, many times. It was very risky.'

By mid-1987 Mrs Lim's youngest son had already disappeared into the underground world of political opposition, leaving just a letter to say goodbye. Two years earlier he had been arrested for the first time during his third year at university, after being involved in the storming of a Government office.

'I was involved in the YWCA movement then, it was a typical middle-class women's organisation which was pro-Government. I just thought my son was a beginner in the student movement and all I needed to do was to separate him from this dangerous peer group and then he would be okay. Then, he disappeared. I went everywhere, even to all the hospitals to find him. I finally got news five days later from one of the other mothers that he had been taken by the National Security Agency. Then I realised this was not just a problem for my son, this was part of the pattern of human rights' violations.

'In May 1986 I joined my first demonstration. The mothers who came together were very convinced of their cause, they were not afraid. I had to give up my high position with the YWCA because of my activities. Many other women said, "Why are you doing these things? Just leave your son alone and he will come home soon; is there something wrong with you?".'

'There were all kinds of bad things said,' she remembers, before modifying her statement and selecting instead the word 'misunderstandings'.

There were so many demonstrations, she says, shaking her head. 'I can't remember them all. Sometimes we were dispersed, sometimes some of the mothers were injured and taken to hospital.' She gestures to her own forehead, split during a street beating with a rattan stick. A young armoured soldier beating a middle-aged mother into the ground: it was a powerful symbol of disorder in a society so concerned with the allocation of proper roles.

'Because of the tear gas I was suffering from skin diseases. Sometimes we used wet handkerchiefs, sometimes we put plastic film on our faces or toothpaste, but we never used gas masks,' she says. 'In the beginning we started this type of demonstration out of our motherhood, because we loved our children, but gradually we became convinced that the cause of our children was right.'

When her son was released from detention, his return was brief. It was then that he decided to disappear underground, out of contact, indefinitely, with his family.

At this point, this interview cannot be continued, there are too many tears.

On a Friday afternoon in June 1987 about half a million people took to the streets of Seoul. Some said it was a million, but from on the ground, within the pack, it was impossible to tell.

The shops and office towers were hurriedly closed, and for a moment, the city just stopped. Between the opposing sides lay a ghost city of faceless towers and empty subway tunnels and the unnatural quiet. Cities are usually so noisy that it is difficult to think. We complain about the racket, but often go home and turn on the television automatically, it is easier that way. So, when a city is empty the silence is frightening. Every single movement crystallises sharply in the absence of the background hum.

Then the street battle began. The charges and the retreats, the billowing clouds of tear gas, seeping under every closed door, burning every patch of exposed skin. By nightfall the pattern of the battle was lost in the dark, and the random lunging of the packs became more dangerous still. A small band of protesters burst into the lobby of the upmarket business hotel, the Westin Chosun, seeking refuge. The tear gas followed them in. In the dark it was no longer possible even to guess who had the upper hand. The crisis continued into the next day.

Then came the Government announcement. President Chun Doo Hwan would step down as party leader and commence a series of democratic reforms.

When South Korea elected President Kim Young Sam five years later Mrs Lim's son finally came home— she had not seen her youngest child since he disappeared underground. President Chun Doo Hwan was sentenced to death for treason and corruption in 1996, later to have the sentence commuted to life imprisonment.

'The students used to ask me where I got my strength. This is not for the sake of power, this is not for ambition, because I am nothing. What I am doing is right, so I am not afraid. Sometimes I cry when I look back on my life because there is so much pain and suffering. But, partly, I am very happy because for ten years I have thought about nothing except my family and human rights. I feel, sometimes, though, that journalists look at our story out of curiosity.'

At this point I doubt the translation is correct. I can't measure the weight of her words, but I can understand the message. 'Voyeurism' would be more accurate. The intrusion of an outsider into another person's suffering.

The CEO

'I have always liked to win,' she says, laughing, her frankness immediately disarming. 'In the school playground I used to play marbles and card games to beat the boys, because they had power. They were useless games and I didn't need that kind of power. But as a child I read a lot of biographies of heroes and heroines like Joan D'Arc and I understood that one person could have a lot of power. I wanted to get that power, I wanted to be a changer,' says Lee Yung Hae, the 39-year-old president of one of South Korea's most successful publishing houses.

In South Korea few women run their own businesses. Of those who do, many have come to their positions through what is widely perceived as a family misfortune: the failure of a father to produce an heir, allowing a daughter to inherit his economic power by default. Even fewer have made their own way through the system like Lee Yung Hae, probably sacrificing their chance of marriage and children along the way.

Lee apologises, unnecessarily, for her less than perfect English. She is translating her words herself in her head as she speaks. Many spill out in strings of unfamiliar pictures, images outside the boundaries of imagination of the English language.

'I was born in the mountains. So every morning

until I was in third grade at elementary school I saw the sun rise and set on a mountain. Then we moved to the coast and for the first time I saw the sun rising out of the sea. I was so shocked, it was so huge. It was only then I realised how big and interesting the world must be,' she says, by way of introducing herself.

'I always believed I was special, but I never talked about it at school. I liked to read about people who were brave or wise in the face of challenges, people who had the strength to overcome. The other girls read fairytale books so I never had a friend to discuss my books with.

'In Korea we have 5000 years of history, mostly of woman as a kind of servant to man. I thought this kind of preoccupation was very discouraging. So I wanted to find enough wisdom to avoid that kind of thinking. It is often said that Korean women are sheltering under the branches of a big tree. Many women believe this shady place is very nice and very honourable. But, I do not, because if you look at the small plants lying in the shade of a tree you will see them rising very weakly, almost unable to grow.'

Ms Lee cannot remember a time when she did not break the rules. Her parents, she says, were tolerant at first, encouraging her to study and excel. Her family was 'average middle class'. Both her parents were teachers but her mother gave up working to look after her young family.

At college she studied design, but not as a genteel art, more because she was interested in South Korea's place in the world. Then, in the 1970s, South Korea was emerging as a new industrial power, one of Asia's first 'tiger economies'.

'In our factories we were making brand name shirts for export for about US$9, which sold in Europe for around US$150. That meant design was adding about $141 dollars worth of value to that product, give or take the shipping costs. I realised that the design field would be very important to South Korea's future because we didn't have oil or other natural resources to fall back on so we had to find some way of adding value to our manufactured products.'

Her professor, she says, was very kind. 'But when I visited him with my concerns about design he said to me, "Yung Hae, please get married".

'Of course, I had a boyfriend. He was three years senior to me. He really loved me, and I liked him as well. But, I told him, You are a good person, but if you marry me you will be unhappy, because I will not be satisfied with just being your wife. So, of course, he married someone else,' she says, as though this was the only possible outcome. His understanding of her ambitions was something she could not realistically expect.

On graduating, Ms Lee took her first job as a designer for a local leather goods company. She was, she says, dismayed. Her creative work was limited to copying bags and belts from Europe and the United States.

'I was very unsatisfied and I wanted to know from the buyer what people wanted, but the designers never met the buyers. So one day I deliberately changed all the model numbers and my employers had to bring me into all the meetings to sort things out. They were very angry but at least I could ask the buyers what products they wanted and why. That was the first time I began to understand about fashion colours and styles.'

Next, she had discovered a small magazine on the topic of design, a kind of private hobby horse for a rich young architecture student funded by his father. 'I knocked on the door and said I wanted to be a reporter. I had no idea how to be a reporter but I just kept on asking until he took me on.' Three years later the son decided to continue his studies in France and wanted to shut the magazine down.

'I went to everyone I knew, all the professors of design, and begged them to buy the magazine but no-one would agree. I knew my mother had some money, so for four days and three nights I pushed my parents as hard as I could to borrow that money until they finally gave in.'

At the age of 25, Yung Hae became president of the tiny publishing company and boss to a staff of nineteen. Six months later South Korea's military government, headed by President Chun Doo Hwan, shut down all private media organisations, as part of a sweeping move to place all media outlets under direct Government control.

'What a stupid history for our country,' Yung Hae sighs. 'My parents were very happy to hear that. My mother didn't want to lose her money but she said, "don't worry", it is a relief.' Maybe now Yung Hae would get married and settle down while she still had a chance.

'Korea's military stars had power so I wanted to meet them, but of course they ignored my requests,' Yung Hae explains. 'So I decided to write to President Chun Doo Hwan personally and explain to him that Korea needs design, it needs to create something Korean in character, like the Italians have created their own designs. Just having industrialisation is very poor for this country, I told him. I never met the President but I was called in to see the Minister for Culture and in three months' time I had permission to publish again.'

Actually, Yung Hae says, she had no idea how to run a business. 'I had to pay the salaries and pay for paper and printing costs. I didn't realise at first that I had to make all this money. I lied to my parents and said it was going well, but it was not going well. I borrowed money from friends, I worked for other people on the side, I slept maybe only two or three nights a week.' That great big world shrank very fast.

'I felt so lonesome, like the Little Prince, running all the way around the world to discover he was the only one there. My parents just kept talking about when I would be getting married. Finding a husband wouldn't be a problem, they could arrange that. I thought good things would be easy to share with a husband, but not problems. I knew I had to be patient and I could see my goal, but other people couldn't. They thought I was a crazy lady, most of my friends thought they would never get their money back.'

Korea's economy works on two levels. In the homes the purse strings are controlled by the wives. In the outside world private businesses are controlled by men. 'In Korea men do business after working hours, they network by drinking and playing golf and going to the sauna. Women have to go home and cook and tidy up the house so they can't keep up,' says one business analyst.

'In the beginning, it was very difficult. When a paper company representative would come to the office one of the staff would introduce me as the president, but they didn't take any notice of me and just kept looking around for the real president. Korea is a heavy drinking society and drinking is the base of business contact. When I went out with the men and the topic was women and sex then they didn't like me to listen,' Yung Hae says. 'Sometimes they wouldn't invite me when they needed to visit a geisha girl.'

So she decided to turn her tactics around. At night when her competitors were out drinking she would be at her desk working extra hours. First thing in the morning, with her clear head, she would knock on their doors seeking advertising deals. What Yung Hae also understood was that the women were the main consumers in Korea's rapidly growing economy. So she bought the rights to publish a Korean version of the US *Homes and Gardens* and opened her own women's magazine alongside the original *Design* title.

'The men of Korea earn the money, but the women spend it. I was determined to publish a magazine on creative interiors because even rich women didn't know about taste—they would buy a Persian rug to put with a Swedish chandelier which is very expensive but lacks harmony. I wanted to show them that you could buy even cheap goods which fitted together harmoniously. Because many women were housewives they wanted something to do and they wanted this kind of information.'

Her next magazine was targeted at a younger generation after conducting a market survey of 10 000 young men and women in their early twenties. 'What I found out was very interesting. The majority of young women said they wanted a career more than they wanted marriage. Of course, when it comes to the crunch most women still get married, but they want to do more and know about more in between, so the technique for preparing articles for this X generation is different.'

In the bustling streets around Yonsei University, the centre of Seoul's student life, the traditional tea shops and market stalls have been replaced by 'rock cafes', booming discos and multi-storey department stores. Since 1961 rapid industrialisation has transformed a nation of impoverished farmers into a major economic power with an increase in average per capita income of around US$10 000 from around US$300. Increasingly women have been drawn into the workforce and, increasingly, the first generation of young people born into industrial affluence are rejecting their Confucianist past.

At the City Pop café, 23-year-old Oh Su Jin and her boyfriend, Kim Tae Ju, are nursing cocktails laced with coloured ice cubes in a booth equipped with its own colour TV. They say they like to go out every night to drink, listen to Western music and wear Japanese fashions.

'Basically, I am not interested in my parents' lifestyle, they are quite different and I don't think it is necessary to learn about their life. I understand what my parents want me to be but I am looking for my own life,' says Su Jin.

Further across town, in the swanky river belt, three young office girls are tossing back Miller beers and waving around the Malboros, giggling. Away from the eyes of their parents they are confidently flaunting the Confucian taboos. They come out like this almost every night, spending half their weekly wages on their social life. 'Our parents are very conservative and their way of thinking is quite different. Smoking is considered very bad for girls, for example.'

Some parents give their daughters pagers and mobile phones to track them around the city. Others see their daughters return home, rebellious, to family conflict over their behaviour. Many members of the older generation bemoan the apparent moral decay of Korean society.

On the streets and in the cafés the young Korean girls say they want to have it all: careers and financial freedom as well as marriage and children. But the Korean Women's Development Institute's more formal surveys show that most young men still want wives who stay home although most young women want to go out to work.

'Girls say they can take or leave marriage but they must have a career,' says President Sei Wha Chung. 'Men have stayed conservative because they don't want to lose what they had, so there is conflict [in many marriages].'

Yung Hae believes the biggest problem now is the attitude gap—most men have not changed. And there's the matter of power.

'I am a feminist, of course, but I don't like shouting because Korean women are very different from women in other countries. They are patient, they are always behind the scenes but in the home they control their husbands. The men's whole salary goes to the wives, they spend the money. Behind the scenes women already have power but when we appear powerful in public, in the outside world, men don't like that kind of women, and that is the problem. Korean men have to change their attitude.' Which is not to say Yung Hae is the least bit like a victim.

'I think Korean women have power, so I don't have sympathy for them. But most Korean women have to find out what kind of power is good value. Women like diamonds and fur coats. They have a passion for those things, they have a passion for their children's education and push them to study, study, study. But in life isn't there something more important than this? I believe Korean career women have a lot of potential yet to come out. We have a lot of energy and because of 5000 years of subordination, we have waited a long time to use it.'

Yung Hae says she would still like to get married, but remains realistic about her options at the age of

39. Her publishing company has expanded considerably, and several recent books she has printed have sold over 600 000 copies.

'Nowadays, I am thinking about marriage. I am so busy that sometimes I get scared that I wouldn't be able to share my life any more. I work at least ten hours a day, I always have dinner appointments and I like travelling and sports and computers. So, if I never get married it is also okay. Whatever is my destiny.'

The love boat

A young woman in a neat, short skirt arrives at the pier, alone. The sleek, white, luxury cruiser is tied up, waiting, the gangplank down, a hostess gracing the entrance. The young girl produces her ticket and the hostess nods: 'You are sitting over there with the gentleman.' He is also alone. It is a blind date, of sorts. The difference is that the entire boat is full of young people, certified single by the Singaporean Government, doing exactly the same thing.

Fifty single young women and fifty single young men are brought together inside an air-conditioned cruising restaurant complete with DJ, dance floor, and views of Singapore's busy harbour. Once you get on you can't get off until the party is over. This evening's 'love boat' cruise has been organised by the Singaporean Government's Social Development Unit (SDU) and is open only to university graduates so that when boy meets girl the common higher educational qualifications assure that the match is suitable.

The SDU came into being in 1985 when the latest census gave the Government planners an alarming picture of what was ahead. The country's most accomplished women were so busy that close to 40 per cent were never expected to marry and those who were marrying were having fewer children. Meanwhile the least educated sectors of society were procreating as enthusiastically as ever. The Government's chief concern was the potential net loss in intelligence society would suffer, based on the belief that high-achieving parents produce high-achieving offspring, a concept that remains open to debate.

'It is not the Singaporean Government's style to just let social trends evolve. We try to manage things to achieve particular goals which are good for the nation. Is it an individual's right to stay single or have fewer children, or a society's right to say "Have more children"?' one Government Minister explained.

Enter the SDU, the state-run 'cupid' charged with identifying and monitoring the personal habits of the single high achievers and developing programmes to realign the marriage and reproduction statistics so that the curve takes an upwards trend.

'In a society like ours, young people have no more time to date,' says SDU Director, Dr Eilleen Aw. For the thousands who earned their university degree, got a good job, worked long hours and woke up one day to discover they were approaching 30 and still living with their parents, there is the SDU to turn to. Through it, the Government runs courses for certified singles in everything from 'getting to know you' to social dating and conversational French. It also has regular 'blind dates' *en masse*, and a computer dating service.

'We have given our women education and independence, they only want to get married to men they think they will be happy with,' says Dr Aw. 'In the past, status and family were the criteria and marriages were arranged through matchmakers. This is a different kind of matchmaking service. At the same time we found that 63 per cent of men wanted to "marry down", to marry girls who are younger and have less education, for example. This is a problem many societies face when there is a mismatch between the rising expectations of women and the chauvinism of the men. The men still want their wife to stay home and raise the kids and look after their interests and now women say, "Well, why should I?".'

When the Government first looked at the problem in 1985 it found that 39 to 40 per cent of women aged over 40 were unmarried and never expected to marry, and that the least educated young men were also unable to find partners. But in Singapore there are also other specific causes related to rapid economic development and the emergence of a workaholic, materialistic society obsessed with national development.

'In Singapore paper [academic] qualifications are very important, you can't get on in this society without a university degree. And young people think, the faster I get my degree, the better, so they don't go to parties, they don't go on dates. When they start working they are at the office from 7 a.m. until 7 p.m. I think young people nowadays value material possessions and career success more than a family,' explains Dr Aw.

On board the *Equator Queen* the 'twenty-something' engineers, doctors and managers are as nervous as teenagers. Dr Aw sits up front, somewhat school-ma'am-like behind a microphone, and announces a competition that will force the guests into groups where they will have to reveal their name, qualifications, profession and hobbies.

Susan is 'about 25' and is on her first SDU trip. 'It doesn't take much courage to sign up but it takes a lot of guts to come down to the pier, show your SDU ID card and put the SDU sticker on your lapel. It sort of says "Government-certified single", doesn't it,' she says, with considerable embarrassment. (Even in achievement-conscious Singapore the local cynics have dubbed the SDU, 'Single, Desperate and Ugly'.)

Susan is a chemical engineer who is neither ugly nor desperate. 'We are supposed to work nine to five but we stay back until 7 p.m. and come in on the weekends,' she says. What about the time spent in Australia at university? 'I was too busy studying,' she says.

The two men sitting at her table are less forthcoming. In fact, they say nothing at all.

The 'love boat' stops at a manicured island park with a white sand beach. The beach stroll is scheduled to last exactly thirty minutes, then everyone is herded back on board. The Government's 'cupid' is, some say, as subtle as a scout master. Programmes regularly include time slots for jolly, organised fun such as 'joke time along the beach' and 'song time'. Back on board, the DJ is warming up his smoke machine and lights while the participants queue for the buffet. His first number is far from subtle—'Too Many Broken Hearts in the World'. Many more thumping, disco numbers follow before the first couple venture on to the dance floor. Soon, everyone is dancing and getting to know each other—by exchanging business cards.

'Yes, I believe in inherited intelligence,' says Dr Aw. But, she adds, she does not believe that the SDU can solve the problem of single, educated women. 'I don't think I can correct this, but if I wasn't here it would go down the drain faster. Personally, I would like to see the problem return to society.'

To understand how Singapore produced such an imbalance of the sexes it is necessary to look back for a moment. There is a local slang expression, *kiasu*, that is not in the dictionary but is widely understood.

Translated from the Chinese Hakka dialect it means 'afraid of losing'. It is used for the university 'swot' who writes down exactly what the lecturer says in class, word for word, or the student who rushes to the library the minute the reading list comes out and takes the books and hides them on the wrong shelf so only he or she can use them.

On holiday one can also be called *kiasu* by pushing to the front of a buffet queue at a package tour resort, but only if you leave with as much food as you can physically cram onto your plate. 'At best,' says one local sociologist, 'it means going to a business meeting and discovering four extra people "sitting in" for no better reason than that they might miss out on what is going on. At worst it means protecting your own chances of success by destroying the chance of others. Everyone talks about this *kiasu* mentality. What young Singaporeans want on the whole is to earn lots and lots of money. They are very self-centred and not very concerned about others. This is the symptom of a young generation that is pretty insecure, because it is pushed so hard to perform.'

Kiasu is the ugly side of the much-lauded Singaporean economic miracle. In a single generation former Prime Minister Lee Kwan Yew fashioned an affluent, efficient and internationally competitive island state out of a backwater of migrant labourers the British colonisers left behind. Officially, Singaporeans work only 44 hours a week. But the lights in the office blocks burn well into the night. Employees come into work when they are on leave. Exams start in kindergarten, children graduate from primary school speaking two languages and the after-school private tuition business is booming because everyone is scared of falling behind.

Success in Singapore is based solely on merit. Study hard, work hard and the Government will look after you, and Singapore will stay one step ahead on the international scene. Almost every one of Singapore's 2.6 million people has a decent place to live, a job and enough to eat. In a single generation the Chinese Confucian discrimination against the education of girls has been swept away.

The problem now is that Singaporeans are too busy to remember the values of family life. After an initial 'two is enough' population control programme the Government has attempted to shift into reverse. In 1965 population growth was 4.7 per cent, financial and educational incentives were offered to small families and Government hospitals started to offer abortion for a nominal fee. By the mid-1980s population growth had fallen to 1.44 per cent, way below the replacement rate of 2.1 per cent.

Demographers estimate that the number of fifteen to 29-year-olds will have dropped 30 per cent by the year 2000.

'I must say the level of stress in this society is higher than elsewhere. This is a very high performance society, as a country we keep drumming into people that they must work hard. I work twelve hours a day and that is pretty normal. I get a kick out of my job and there are lots of Singaporeans like that, they just work, work, work. It doesn't leave much time for marriage,' says one professional.

Apart from the SDU the Government has come up with a number of measures to try to turn the trend around, aimed particularly at encouraging high-achieving women to have children. While financial incentives have been offered to poorly educated women to use contraception or seek sterilisation, high achievers have become eligible for big tax rebates based on second or third children.

'Is your self-sufficiency giving men a hard time?' asks one poster advertisement, showing a young woman working into the night. 'After all, you don't want to give men the wrong idea,' it continues, to the considerable annoyance of many young, professional women.

In the SDU's regular magazine, *Link*, psychologists, counsellors and singles exchange views on common problems. 'It is not just men,' says Dr Aw. 'The trouble is women also still want to "marry up" despite the change in their educational and career status, and their higher exceptions of marriage.' Women still generally want someone more educated, older and even taller than themselves, so the SDU advises women not to be too choosy. 'You cannot look for Mr Perfect, so we ask our women to play softer, to play a little dumb if possible,' says SDU deputy, Helen Wang. And of the men's performance on the dating scene, she says, 'They do not know how to behave, what to do with girls. We have a lot of nerds around here.'

In *Link* the nerds and the over-ambitious can glean some useful advice. This month there are condolences for an anonymous young man who reports that his first 'follow up' phone call to a 'pretty lady' he met at an SDU function consisted of a barrage of questions including whether he owned his own home, what position he held in his company and whether he supported his family. The lesson to be learnt, *Link* advises, is 'not to be too transparent' early on and reminds all members that when using the telephone you are engaged in a 'conversation, not an interrogation'.

A Dr Cheung offers readers some 'plain talk about hard facts'. A confusing series of graphics claims to assess the relative performances of children of graduates and non-graduates, an issue he claims is a national one, not a personal one. 'The problem is that the better educated are not replacing themselves. We will end up with a net loss in human capital. And since human resources are Singapore's strong asset, then we can't afford that.'

The SDU currently has about 19 000 members and has married around 10 000 couples in the past decade. 'Romance is still there in the realm of the teenager,' says Dr Aw, 'but, we deal with graduates and as each year passes the notion of romance dims. We have men who cannot fall in love. They've been waiting for years for their pulse rate to go up.'

The re-education
camp

Laos: the only country in the world with no prostitutes.

Our host casually scratched at his crotch, his initial
politeness obviously exhausted, and continued with the
same pointless, circular discussion. He was, he
informed us authoritatively, the 'Director of Research
and Control' of this strange place and would not
answer any questions he did not like. In fact, he just
might not speak to us at all. Here, he was king of the
castle. He had been the king since 1975 when the
Communists had rolled into town, armed with their
wisdom of secrecy, security and social control. And
what a kingdom it was: two tiny mounds of red earth,
tufted with shrubs, in the middle of a vast dam, in the
middle of nowhere. We were, we presumed, in his
office: a long, thatched hut with a dusty dirt floor,
watched over by a row of grim portraits of senior
members of the Politburo.

He was apparently not troubled by the demands of
modern communications. There was no phone, no
electricity, no radio and no typewriter, just a couple of
pit toilets outside and a few scrawny chickens scraping
at the dirt. Beyond the dirt a wide expanse of hot,
white glare hovered above the water. But the Director
had already confirmed that this was the place we were

looking for. These patches of red dirt were the re-education camps known as 'Girl Island' and 'Boy Island', where those judged to be social deviants by the Communist rulers of Laos were reoriented, with the help of Marx and Lenin. It was to these islands, in the middle of a huge dam at the end of a very bad road to the north of Vientiane, that the prostitutes, pimps, drug addicts and hippies were banished following the Communist victory of 1975.

The Director was apparently not troubled by the contradictions of our ridiculous debate. Here we were, already talking to him, but we would have to—he absolutely insisted—go back to Vientiane to get permission for this conversation from the Ministry of the Interior. Unfortunately, we had already made the appropriate inquiries at the appropriate official level, a fact we left out. The Ministry of the Interior had already told us that the camps were now closed and the inhabitants of the islands were farmers, free to come and go. Officially, this important man did not exist.

I had been visiting Laos for four or five years and the rumours had persisted. I had heard whispers of new batches of women being taken off to 'Girl Island', enough to make me wonder, never enough to confirm that the stories were true.

In Asia, a certain amount of shame and embarrassment falls upon the one who loses his or her temper first, the so-called loss of face. So the Director rose to our challenge by ordering one of his two silent assistants to take notes in response to our own furious scribblings. Then, they all sat back in their rough, bamboo chairs, arrogant and suspicious. They were typical of the petty bureaucrats who rise to positions of mediocrity in any system that requires the unquestioning imposition of rules.

We Western believers in the right to intrude sat back, also arrogant and suspicious. We all drank tea.

But as the guardians of the secrets of the regime, they were not quite in control. Already the director's assistant had divulged the fact that a typical day on 'Girl Island' started with re-education seminars from 7 a.m. to 11 a.m. with another two hours in the afternoon. For the rest of the day, the women tended the vegetable plots. How quickly a woman was released 'depended on herself. If they advance quickly in their studies, then they can go. First, they have to work hard, they have to deeply understand the policies of the Party and to know well what is right and what is wrong'.

If a fallen woman did not study hard she was forced to read more and more Party documents (provided she could read), was denied the right to work in the garden and made to attend extra seminars instead. 'There should be no prostitutes, but there are some young people who do not know how to control themselves, how to be good women. We had hoped these types of people would not appear after the revolution.'

In the distance, small female figures moved slowly around the thatch huts on the island across the water. We had interviewed a Government health officer responsible for 'Girl Island' in the town near the dam who said that 50 women were there. Most, she said, were former prostitutes in the process of rehabilitation but some were long-stayers and were now insane, unable to learn the lessons correctly and so unable to return to the fold.

On 'Boy Island', home to drug addicts and other male social deviants, there were still about 40 men, she said. They could seek the permission of the Director to marry one of the female inmates after successfully completing their re-education. The islands are divided by deep water and there are no boats for the prisoners, so whether the inmates actually met or made their choice from a long-distance glance was not clear. But, this was about as close as we would get to the women, too.

Our host sat staring, continuing to rearrange his pants. It was 1991. Marx and Lenin were having a hard time helping any Government these days, we said. How could they help a prostitute reassess her life? This is a question the Director would not care to address, apparently untroubled by reality, so far from the crumbling Berlin Wall and the new restaurants and dance halls in Vientiane. And if the Party line changed, as it had significantly over the last five years, the inmates merely learned new lessons and the revolution went on. It had to, otherwise the Director and his assistants would no longer be important men.

The Director then politely informed us that he would file a report on our unauthorised visit (to whom?), the tactical *coup de grâce* in our psychological skirmish. The visit was over. Permission to see 'Girl Island' was cancelled. We all smiled, shook hands and said our thank yous as we backed down the stairs, carved out of red mud, to our rented boat.

For many years I had been fascinated by the proud claim on the part of the Communist Government of Laos that this was the first country in the history of the world to succeed in stamping out prostitution. Poor, powerless, landlocked and sparsely developed, Laos has the dubious distinction of being ranked by the United Nations as one of the least populated countries in the world, alongside nations such as Ethiopia and Bangladesh. So economically and politically weak is Laos that there is a frequently repeated joke that goes: 'Laos, Land of a million elephants (referring to the fourteenth-century Buddhist kingdom), Land of four million irrelevants'.

Under French colonial rule, little more was achieved for the scattered, self-sufficient communities of farmers than the building of 5000 kilometres of poor roads and a short stretch of railway, the construction of the occasional French language school and some lovely French villas and restaurants for the hapless colonial administrators.

During the Vietnam War, American B-52 bombers dropped two million tonnes of bombs on Laos, in secret and in violation of official Laotian neutrality, in an attempt to cut the supply line to the Vietnamese Communists along the jungle paths of the Ho Chi Minh trail. In Vietnam, the strings of the Government were pulled happily by the CIA, an operation largely funded by illegal heroin sales. So overwhelming were the USA's military and political blunders inside neighbouring Vietnam that the dislocation of one-quarter of the entire population of Laos was referred to as a 'side show'—a complication—rather than the international scandal it really was.

When Saigon fell to the Communist forces in 1975, Vientiane soon followed. The Pathet Lao leaders came down from the limestone caves in the northern hills that had so effectively deceived the B-52s and began laying the foundation for their 'Workers' Paradise'.

Three decades of guerrilla war—first against the French and then against the Americans—had produced a regime obsessed with secrecy. Thousands of educated Laotians swam across the Mekong River to Thailand as the round-ups began for the re-education camps. The men who had waited out the Indochina War in the caves shut down private markets and shops and placed the entire economy under state control, forcing the nation to the brink of starvation.

Laos went about closing its borders and removing

itself from the map. Every now and then a bleat was heard from the refugee camps along Thailand's northern border, but the country's self-imposed isolation from the West was almost complete. Laos became Asia's Albania, one of the harshest and most hermit-like Communist states in the world.

In 1986 the doors opened just a crack, following economic reforms in the then Soviet Union. Laos was virtually bankrupt, its average annual income estimated at US$150 a year. Only 1300 kilometres of roadway in the entire country were passable and only 2.5 per cent of the population had progressed to high school. There were no laws, no Constitution and no individual rights. There was just the absolute rule of the Party with its two television transmitters and 181 loud-speakers (a gift from the Vietnamese) that awakened the residents of Vientiane at dawn with ludicrous public information broadcasts featuring the latest rice production figures.

When I first visited Laos in 1987 Vientiane was a silent and gracious town. I was assigned a female Government guide who accompanied me everywhere, even to the bathroom. I saw the lovely crumbling French colonial villas and the stark, concrete-block apartments of the Russian advisers. I learnt almost nothing about Laos. It was in this environment, of almost total control, that the redefining of the Laotian woman came about.

One year later Laos held its first elections: there was only one Party standing, of course, but the people had a bit of choice out of the single Party field. At the same time the Prime Minister announced that the state ideology was now about making people richer. The return of capitalism, under Communist rule, had begun. And, as was necessary, so had the process of reopening to the outside world.

The daily life of Vientiane still followed the flow

of the thousands of bicycles that glided through the dry season heat. The old, twisted frangipani trees were still in full bloom, a particularly intoxicating summer pleasure, already sacrificed to progress and cars in other Asian capitals. The markets had reopened and the US dollar and the Thai baht made a mockery of the local currency, the kip, printed by the Government like Monopoly money and still decorated with the motifs of proud Soviet-style cement factories that Laos never even had.

At night the streets were not quite empty. A handful of clubs and discos had opened their doors now that dancing was again permitted. And it was here that the proud claim of the prostitute-free nation was most under threat.

At the headquarters of the Women's Union, the politeness of our hosts was inexhaustible. The four officials sat back primly, glowing with the kind of self-righteousness that only comes with truly believing that you are right. The women were neatly dressed in modest blouses and traditional wrap-around Laotian silk skirts, fastened with silver belts. The Women's Union is the Party's official guardian of women's rights and its agent of discipline.

Under the old American-backed 'puppet' regime, one official said, 'women had no rights'. The Vietnam War was the golden era of establishments such as 'The White Rose' (now a faceless student dormitory) and 'Madame Lu's' (then specialising in French). 'Nowadays what is required is to be a good wife, a good mother and a good citizen, participating in the construction and the safeguarding of the nation'. The process of fostering goodness began at the age of fifteen when teenage girls were recruited by the Union. Every member was required to participate in a monthly self-criticism, a kind of Communist confession, that did not come with the comfort of confidentiality. 'The monthly reports are sent to the central authority, which studies the weak points and goes out to talk to the women about them. Those who do not respect the requirement for self-discipline are punished.'

The central authority was apparently looking for confessions of such social crimes as prostitution, infidelity, premarital sex and gambling. Those not brave enough to confess themselves could be reported by more reliable workmates and neighbours. Offenders were given three opportunities for counselling to mend their ways before being dismissed by the Union. With dismissal came a declaration of the offender's failings as an ideal socialist woman. The declaration was sent to the Party authorities as well as distributed at her place of work and around her neighbourhood to maximise the sense of humiliation and shame. If even that failed, there were still special places for re-education and there were moralistic round-ups that were never publicly announced and so can never be confirmed.

It is difficult to comprehend how this centralised reporting process ever worked, given the fact that many rural villages are 50 kilometres from the nearest road. For the failed woman, the officials explained helpfully, there was also physical evidence of her sins against the Party. 'The woman will have a baby,' one said, coyly, running her hands over an imaginary large belly. And, of course, she would have a baby because contraception was not legally available to unmarried women. The Women's Union has ruled that Laos remain a traditional and conservative society in which virginity before marriage is the expected norm. There is no mention made at all about the role of men.

I met the Women's Union in 1991. Then, Laos officially had only one case of AIDS. In the foyer of the Union's office traditional handicrafts were on sale, the muted hues of their vegetable dyes already unable to compete with the bright, cheap, polyester imports pouring across the borders from Thailand and southern China. The officials talked on and on about their system. I kept on asking the same question, in many different ways, and eventually elicited an acknowledgement that sex outside the rules just might be creeping back.

There were no obvious brothels, that was true, but deals were now being discreetly and individually brokered for about US$10 'a turn', for a Laotian man, and twice that for a foreigner. Across the river lay Thailand, land of 600 000 prostitutes, land of 200 000 HIV cases.

The problem was, they concluded, that some women 'just like to do it'. The answer, they had decided, was 'still more surveillance'. Patrols of trustworthy officials were dispatched, armed with pocket money from the Union, to the handful of nightclubs. Women observed with men who were not their husbands became the subjects of investigations. 'Yes, there are a small number of women doing this kind of thing. We have ways of finding out who they are and where they live.' Again, they would be given a chance to repent. If they did not they would be sent to some unspecified place of retraining. We all nodded and drank tea.

I have been back to Laos several times and each time I find Vientiane greatly changed. The graceful, crumbling colonial villas were being pulled down to make way for glitzy shopping malls, the bicycles were— bit by bit—being edged over to the pavements by new cars. The billboards of new consumerism towered over the streets. I never went back to the Women's Union because I already knew how the story would end. I preferred to hang on to this tiny part of the history of the women of the world, the only nation ever to claim to have stopped prostitution.

There will never be any final answer to the question.

Is sexual freedom part of the liberation of women, or merely part of a process of redefining a woman's value in line with her sexual appeal? Is the imposition of modest dress a denial of a woman's choice or a protection against the exploitation of a woman's body in advertising and films, for example? For many, many centuries Laos has been a small, insular country and the prudes of the Women's Union genuinely believed that what they were doing was protecting the status of women in the eyes of their society.

In Laos, as in China and Vietnam, the Party still rules. But its leaders are old. Much of the tradition of respect for age still remains, so the next generation is waiting patiently for its turn, like the Communists waited in the caves. It is called the biological solution. The old men will soon die and Communism will go away of its own accord. The new God of capitalism is already in town. The process of re-education has begun again.

The only man
in the Cabinet

'He was shot here, on the verandah, you know,' she says, flatly, immediately demolishing the introductory niceties that would have led us, inevitably, to the same point. 'He didn't believe in security, "Why would they kill me?", he would say. So the gates were wide open, and the man dressed as a Buddhist monk walked right in. He was the first politician to be assassinated in this country,' she reminds me, by way of perspective.

I accept her invitation to break eye contact and glance outside. The south-west monsoon had just begun, sweeping in low and dark over the ocean, its waves of torrential rain breaking one after another across the city. The garden was dripping rhythmically outside, the giant fig trees, towering high and wide over the sodden lawn, heavy with moisture.

The house, I imagine, is still much the same as it was then, in 1959, when Sri Lanka's reformist Prime Minister, Solomon Bandaranaike, was murdered on the porch. The country was then Ceylon, not long released from the yoke of British colonialism. The family's gracious Colombo residence retains its distinctive style, fashioned partly after an English country manor, its walls neatly white-washed, a crunching gravel carriage-way leading up to the front door, mock turrets gracing the roof line. But downstairs at 'Rosemead Place' the

French windows are flung wide open on to cool verandahs, a refuge from the tropical heat.

The country, I know, is not the same. Where the gates once stood open there are now barbed wire barriers and guard posts. On the streets of the capital daily life rotates through check points of armed soldiers and police, with the nonchalance of a long-term habit. And, at night, much of the tatty, old city of colonial stores, houses and shops is deserted, the roads leading to the homes of the powerful closed off by truckloads of troops.

In 1956, Solomon Bandaranaike, son of the landed élite and just 'down from Oxford', had been swept into power on a radical ticket, promising to turn away from the moneyed class into which he had been born and redraw the lines of privilege and influence in the young independent nation.

In a moving public statement, issued from his hospital bed before he died of his injuries the day after he was shot, Solomon Bandaranaike called on his widow, Sirimavo, and his three children to face the future with 'courage and fortitude'.

'His time was bad,' says Mrs Bandaranaike, now 81, sitting back in an armchair in their living room, his portrait hanging on the wall behind her. 'By that I mean, inauspicious. An astrologer had told him his time was bad and the advice was for him to leave the country. People believe that if you leave the country in which you were born and go elsewhere then those bad influences will not affect you. But, he didn't believe in astrology,' she adds, waving her hand in mock dismissal. Which, in itself, became her own destiny.

Unlike her husband, who was raised a Christian under the influence of the British and later converted to Buddhism, Mrs Bandaranaike was brought up as a Buddhist, her own mother a healer and astrologer who put a great deal of stock in *karma*—the concept that this life is determined by your actions in previous lives, just as your next life will be determined by your deeds in this life.

'My life has not been ruled by astrology, but I do take it into account,' she says. Her faith is not strange in this rich, green country of temples and legends. The pulse of fate beats strongly beneath the deceiving veneer of Western 'modernity' the British left behind and the clipped, precise, English accents of the Sri Lankan élite. 'Your life is pre-destined; it must be,' she says.

When her husband died, she says, she was 'struck by sorrow'. She had no expectations beyond coping with raising her three children alone and repaying the mortgage on the family home her husband had taken out to fund his 1956 election campaign. She had no inkling of what the future would hold.

In 1960, Mrs Bandaranaike was leading her husband's Sri Lanka Freedom Party in a new election campaign. On podiums across the country she stood in her 'widow's weeds', the plain white sari of mourning, her delivery blunt where his had been chatty, her forcefulness taking those who may have sought to use her by surprise.

'I think it was partly sympathy, or mainly sympathy,' she has said of her campaign. 'I was a widow and, when I spoke to them, the women were crying and—I was surprised—the men also. Otherwise I couldn't have won. I think they all realised that because my husband was so popular someone was coming to take his place.'

Thus Mrs Bandaranaike became the first female Prime Minister in the modern world and began her rise to the status of national matriarch, the leader of the country's most influential political dynasty. In South Asia many widows and daughters would follow her into leadership: Indira Gandhi in India, Benazir Bhutto in Pakistan, Khaleda Zia in Bangladesh.

Thus, too, began Sri Lanka's tragic and terrifying slide into political violence and ethnic war.

Solomon Bandaranaike ruled as a ghost, his widow entrusted to interpret and apply his socialist policies. Her sweeping nationalisation programmes dragged the economy to its knees, forcing the very people she championed into Soviet-style food queues in the streets. Her chauvinistic favouritism for the country's majority Buddhist Sinhalese fed into dangerous ethnic tensions that would eventually erupt into one of the world's most brutal wars.

Two armed uprisings would fail to unseat her. She would gather around her many enemies, but still she would be widely praised as a strong leader, an expert in the political game of playing competing powers off against each other, thereby staying on top. '"We've got this poor widow who has to be helped", said all sorts of political courtiers who wanted to use her for their own agendas. And, of course, she proved them all wrong,' said one political commentator.

'The whole world was shocked,' she says. 'I was given so much attention—in fact too much attention, to the point of embarrassment, because there was only one female Prime Minister in the world for such a long time.' In the 'progressive' West, she says, the astonishment seemed the greatest, apparently based on the widely-held notion of the 'submissive nature' of Asian womanhood. The West, however, did not elect a woman until 1979, when Britain chose Margaret Thatcher.

'I pointed out that the women of Sri Lanka have never been chattels, have never been in enforced ser- vitude to the male sex. Whatever 'servitude' we render is voluntarily undertaken because there is a deep rooted respect for the dual and different roles of father and mother in our society,' she says.

She pleaded with her three children not to follow her into politics, but only her eldest daughter obeyed her. When her second daughter, Chandrika, married the popular politician, Vijaya Kumaratunga, her own destiny was sealed. Like her mother before her Chandrika took over his political legacy when he, too, was assassinated in 1988. Six years later it was Chandrika, and not her younger brother Anura, who led the revamped People's Alliance to victory over the widow of the assassinated leader of the conservative bloc.

Mrs Bandaranaike was still influential behind the scenes. She anointed her daughter as her successor over her son, allowing pragmatism to override her maternal ambitions for her only boy. Her daughter, she says, 'was better organised'. Sri Lanka's political system had been changed to bring in an elected President and Chandrika won an easy victory. The Prime Minister-ship, then, she handed back to the matriarch, creating the first mother–daughter leadership team in the history of the modern world.

At 81 Mrs Bandaranaike's health is failing, but her intellect is not. Nowadays she is, says her private secretary, a kind of senior advisor, the head of numerous committees in her daughter's Government. But it is probably more accurate to say that she is the glue, the person who sorts out the power struggles within the party. And nowadays, from her drawing-room chair, she fears for her daughter's life, and the lives of her grandchildren, as Sri Lanka's modern political history is littered with the bloody corpses of those who have sought to lead.

'Does political violence discriminate?' I ask.

'Oh no, not any more.'

Perched on the dark, polished wood sideboard sits

a silver framed photograph of her with her old friend Indira Gandhi. In 1966 Mrs Gandhi was elected Prime Minister of India, carrying on her father's political dynasty. In 1984 she was assassinated by her own bodyguards.

Mrs Bandaranaike, or Mrs B. as she is more commonly known, would like to mark the beginning of her political career with her husband's death. That way the tale would unravel in neat, easy clichés. She, a mother and political wife, endlessly circling the downstairs drawing rooms, discreetly sweeping up overflowing ashtrays and rearranging cushions, while her husband attended to the steady stream of visitors that flowed through the family home. 'I didn't have very much in the way of expectations. The marriage was arranged, at that time you were not going to find your own husband,' she says, dryly, concealing a slight smile.

'He was okay, just okay,' she says of her first impression. 'He was also a politician, so my role was to support him. I believed the primary role for a woman was as a wife and mother, yes, so one just carried on. But, I didn't agree with everything he said,' she adds, quickly.

Mrs B. had grown up in the hill district of Kandy, the spiritual heart of Buddhism in Sri Lanka and the gateway to the tea plantations of the British colonial élite. Her own mother had been one of three sisters so had entered into a *binna* marriage in which local tradition is reversed and a son-in-law is brought into a wife's family, as a kind of honorary son. His role, though, is manager of his wife's property and not replacement heir, so the property of the wife will be handed down to their children.

Mrs B. was born into one of Sri Lanka's most prominent landed families, as was her future husband. As a young girl, however, she spent much of her time with her mother—a healer—grinding herbs, using natural remedies and trekking through the hills between the miserable villages where the poor farmers and plantation workers lived. Her mother, she says, 'was the strong person in the family, the one who dominated us all.'

'There was an old astrologer my mother used to consult,' says Mrs B.'s brother, Clifford Ratwatte. 'When Sirimavo was six, he was reading her horoscope and looked up and told my father, "Sir, one day this young lady will be king of the country". My father laughed the biggest laugh of his life. "We are under the British, how can a girl become anything in this country?" he said.'

This story is widely known in Sri Lanka. It is offered up as evidence that from an early age Sirimavo was treated differently because those around her believed she was destined to rule.

Accounts of the late 1800s and early 1900s paint a suffocating picture of life within the élite of Ceylon. 'The source of what we called "culture" was believed to lie in the kind of education England gave its aristocratic young. English tutors were entrusted with the early education of many young men,' writes Yasmine Goonerante in *Relative Merits*. Governesses, she writes, 'taught the mysteries of the piano, the violin and the harp to high-born young ladies. Higher education for women was firmly discouraged, but once the young men of these families had outgrown their tutors, Oxford or Cambridge became their almost certain destinations.'

And so it went on. Beneath the slow-turning fans, the young members of Ceylon's élite circulated politely, the young ladies swapping recipes for 'love cake' in drawing rooms, catching a glance or two of the young men as they passed from beneath properly down-cast eyes. There were horsemanship and country holiday homes and teams of faceless servants in the background.

It was into this protected, languid world that Mrs B. was born in 1916. Even for tennis, there was a chaperone, she says. 'I was never allowed to go out alone.' Her marriage to Solomon Bandaranaike was, naturally enough, dubbed 'the wedding of the century' and characterised as the 'consolidation' of power of two of the country's more prominent land-owning families. But it was not the social whirl that dominated her daily life. Those around her, stopping just short of being rude, described her variously as 'uninterested in fashion' and 'straightforward'. As such, she tramped many miles with her father through the Kandy hills, where entire families were wiped out in a malaria epidemic, and began to ask why the poor succumbed so quickly to disease.

It was a question that would fit perfectly with the ideas of her husband, Solomon, who had come home from Oxford with a radical new perspective. He rejected the Catholicism of much of his clan and turned back to Buddhism, shed the fancy Western clothes of the élite and donned the simple, homespun suit of the rural villagers and announced that the tiny plots the rural families held could not possibly support them.

Solomon became more and more disillusioned within the mainstream of Sri Lankan politics, although he already held a Ministerial post, because he was unable to push through any meaningful reforms. One morning Mrs B., having quietly observed her husband's frustration, advised him directly to quit his post and form his own political party.

'It was a great risk, I took a lot of risks,' she says. It was a risk for her husband and her children. It was also the turning point in their lives. And it was not, offers her private secretary from the sidelines, the kind of advice usually offered by demure wives. 'So, the short answer is yes,' he says, 'she did have a political role. Sometimes when people had a big problem and felt they could not approach the Prime Minister they used to go to the kitchen and canvass her support. There were many other women at that time who weren't involved in the same way.'

So when Solomon Bandaranaike died, his Sri Lanka Freedom Party rallied around her, seeking her help. Even her children were approached to lean on her, bringing with them the message that their father had died for the Party and was she now going to allow his sacrifice to be wasted? 'I felt I had no choice, there was no other leader.'

'Of course, they could have found another leader,' says the political commentator who is close to the family. 'But then the whole drama would have been lost. They could not have found an alternative leader who could claim the mantle like she did and weep on political platforms like that.'

Pushed? Yes, she says, but not manipulated. She was not merely a figurehead whose personal tragedy could be used to pull in the votes. 'I believed I was there to lead,' she says, bluntly.

The joke at the time was that Mrs B. was the only man in the Cabinet. 'When she walked into a Cabinet meeting she walked in looking very stern, holding her files in her hand. The Ministers would all rise up in silence. She'd pull her chair out and sit down, very sternly,' says her eldest daughter, Sunethra. 'That set the tone for the meetings.'

'I had a hard time, I had a lot of enemies, but I had the Ministers with me,' says Mrs B., without elaborating. She is not fond of the sound of her own voice and does not fuss over the details of the past.

Of her husband's socialist policies his political rivals used to say: 'If we redistribute the wealth now, then we will all be paupers'. But the post-colonial mood of the Indian sub-continent, too, had embraced the island to the south then known as Ceylon. There was much popular support for the concept of moving away from élitism towards self-reliance and nationalism. Mrs B. showed no reluctance in pursuing radical change. She immediately pursued her husband's policy of imposing upon the multi-ethnic nation the single national language of the majority Sinhalese and ensuring a privileged place for Buddhism. Thus she dangerously alienated the country's predominantly Tamil minority. She sought to bring all private schools under state control and, in doing so, antagonised the powerful Roman Catholic church.

She nationalised a wide range of both local and foreign enterprises including the tea plantations, in an attempt to wrest control from dominant capitalists, hitting foreign businesses and those controlled by ethnic minorities the hardest. 'It was about reducing the gap between the rich and the poor,' she says. But her first term in office was marred by ethnic and religious confrontation and long periods under emergency rule.

After losing power for the first time in 1965, Mrs B. did not return to home life. 'I had no choice,' she says again, determined not to portray herself as a forceful and skilled political player, but one swept along by the tide of fate.

Behind the scenes, she says, she regrouped for another electoral assault on the conservatives. Five years later she won again, but inherited an even more explosive set of problems with the dangerous alliance between the educated youths and the unemployed.

One year later, armed with homemade bombs, a group of youths attempted to kidnap the Prime Minister and attacked police stations around the country.

'The Ministers used to come (to her), the Army Generals, the Police Chiefs, with their knees knocking together and saying, Madam, Madam, we are all going to die,' says Sunethra. "Tch, Tch", she would say, and walk out to the kitchen to check if there was enough food to feed the quivering masses.' 'I wasn't scared, no,' says Mrs B., 'I don't know why'.

About 10 000 youths were arrested or killed in the security crackdown that defeated them. 'But, later I talked to some of them and it wasn't really political, it was about unemployment,' she says. In response she speeded up the process of socialist reforms, giving away most of her own family land to demonstrate her faith in land reform. In the international arena she played a prominent role in the Non-Aligned Movement, the bloc of developing nations that pledged to follow a middle path between the Soviet Union and the US during the Cold War. While she swanned around the world, her reputation as a stateswoman growing steadily, her own country was in shambles.

'If you had a baby brother or sister you had to queue for milk. The rich complained that even if you had money there was nothing to buy. For many she became a target of hate,' the commentator says.

'What she did in extending nationalism, with the gift of hindsight, was pretty disastrous, but at the time it was seen to be empowering in some way. And despite all the socialist policies it was still pretty feudal. The feudals gave their land away, they showed their sacrifice, it was very much *noblesse oblige* from those born to rule. But one thing that should be said is that she did face two coup attempts and an insurgency and she did not waver a bit, so she gave us that stability. Here was a woman for whom once she put her foot forward, there was no turning back.'

If she could be compared to another leader, perhaps it should be to Margaret Thatcher, he says. 'It is the flip side of machismo and sexism. She gathered around her all sorts of (male) courtiers who were bending over backwards to help this woman. She thrived in male company and in many ways she used her sex to her advantage. She knew how to delegate, she was a fast learner, but she knew it was she who would make the tough decisions.'

For the women of Sri Lanka in general she did nothing, he says, rounding his fingers in a 'zero' in the air. And nor has her daughter, Chandrika. Between them they have not brought in a single policy to uplift the country's women nor have they, widows of the élite and backed by servants and nannies, been forced to challenge the dominant image of the woman as a wife and mother. Those in the élite can juggle both roles.

But, surprisingly, several Sri Lankan feminists were much less harsh. 'No, hers was not a deliberate vision which involved empowering women,' said one. 'On the one hand you could say it was expediency, you could count on popular support to put the widow in power, so that was a very cynical and opportunistic move. But in reality she did play a very key role, she was not a subservient tool and she did change the balance in terms of how women were perceived because, now, if a woman wants to run for political office, she can.

'At the same time her overall policies assisted women which is why literacy is higher here and infant mortality lower than in the rest of South Asia. Her policies were to provide free health care and education and to spread these services across the country: it was very much a welfare state.'

Mrs B.'s official home was known as 'Temple Trees', a gracious colonial mansion, backing on to the seafront along the southern coastal road to Galle. At home, and in her office, her son Anura would trail behind her, clinging tightly to his mother from the time of his father's death when he was ten.

'My children were scared, they did not want the same thing happening to me as happened to their father.' In many official photos Anura is seen at his mother's side, and it was her only son many expected would inherit the family's political mantle.

Anura, it seems from most accounts, was indulged by his mother and developed a genuine interest in politics. On one occasion, he says, he decided to call a Cabinet meeting on her behalf, summoning the entire Cabinet, who walked in one by one. Only then, he says, did his mother lose her temper with him. On another occasion his pet leopard was sleeping under a chair during an important Cabinet meeting when one of the Ministers disturbed it, unaware that it was there.

'At the third lick on the foot he realised something was wrong and looked down to see a growling leopard. My mother was screaming, he jumped up and was screaming. Then, she turned around to me and said, "Do you realise we have lost every by-election to date and if this man dies we will lose Minuwangoda as well?".'

Mrs B. says she actively discouraged her children from entering politics. 'With the level of violence in this country, I was worried about their future. I wanted my son to study, to get through his exams and go to London.'

With her expulsion from politics in 1977 by the conservative bloc Mrs B.'s socialist policies were slowly unravelled, but even today the evidence remains—the offices of the People's Bank, and the charming, if grubby, face of a nation that has escaped the roar of capitalism, East Asian style. It is a mixed blessing, of course, the sweet air and the clean beaches just as

much evidence of rural poverty and the isolation of
civil war as of environmental care.

A new threat emerged, far more chilling than the
social unrest poverty provokes. In 1983, communal
violence broke out, mainly directed at the nation's
Tamil minority, and so began the ongoing war between
the Tamil Tigers of the separatist movement and Government troops. So, too, were born the suicide bombers
of the Tigers, many of them women who slipped
through security cordons unnoticed—seemingly incon-
sequential wives or sisters just tagging along. In 1991,
it was a young woman who touched the feet of former
Indian Prime Minister, Rajiv Gandhi, in mock respect
before blowing both of them to pieces, to revenge
India's support of Sri Lankan Government troops in
the war against the Tigers.

It was a suicide bomber, in a truck piled high with
explosives, who drove through the gates of the Central
Bank in Colombo, the massive hole still visible behind
barbed wire barricades. And so, too, died Chandrika's
popular husband, then the conservative Prime Minister
Ranasinghe Premadasa, and, later, the replacement
Presidential candidate, Gamini Dassanayake.

The war, of course, was not new. For millennia the
Sinhalese and the Tamils had struggled to build their
empires on the island once known as 'Serendipity', so
ideal were the vistas of rich, green hills and balmy
white sand beaches on the coast below. But this time
around, the weapons of modern warfare and terror
have extracted a much higher toll. At the international
airport that bears the Bandaranaike name the con-
course is fenced off behind machine-gun nests and
sandbags. When darkness falls the city empties hurriedly, the trucks of soldiers moving in to close off the
key roads, the little groups of curry and sweetmeat
stalls patrolled by men brandishing their guns.

In 1994, with the conservative candidate dead and

the war grinding on, Chandrika ran on a platform of peace. She would seek to turn back the violence and meet the Tamil Tigers face to face. Within her own family she had been fighting another battle. She had challenged her brother for the right to carry on the dynasty and won. Sulking, he joined the opposition, where he remains. 'Oh, he is still in politics, it is just that he is in the wrong party,' says his mother, with her characteristic dry wit.

'There is a very strong bond between the mother and son,' says a family friend. The son, many believe, may yet come back and challenge his sister again. It is also widely believed that there will be an attempt on Chandrika's life. This deeply worries Mrs B. 'Personally, I would like to see more women in politics, they are just more conscientious,' she says, excusing herself politely to the only man in the room. Which is not to say that she agrees with all her daughter's policies. Of course. 'Is there anything else you would like to know?' she asks.

'Yes. If you believe in destiny, does that mean that there is nothing you would have done differently?' I ask.

'No, I would have done some things differently. For example, I would have said "No" to the party leadership.'

It is quite apparent she is only half joking.

On stoning for adultery

Ibu Mahdiah is a female pioneer in her field. She believes in the Islamic laws of polygamy, and she believes in stoning as a punishment for adultery, but not to death. She covers her body and her head outside her home, but not her face. She believes a woman must obey her husband if he orders her to cook for him, or bans her from leaving the family home to go out chatting with the neighbours. These are a man's rights within Islam, she says.

But she does not believe a man has a right to deny his daughters or wives an education, or the freedom to pray five times a day. And she is herself a highly accomplished and religious woman. Nor does she believe that a mosque should turn a young couple away if the girl is pregnant, as punishment for engaging in sex before marriage. There are no pregnant women without husbands, she says. The act of primary sex constitutes a religious obligation to marry.

Islam teaches that a woman is neither fit to sit in judgment nor to lead a nation, her character being swayed by emotions and both her memory and resolve weak. Yet Ibu Mahdiah is a judge.

When the Indonesian Government took the decision to establish a separate Islamic Court in 1974 it made the extraordinary move of opening the judiciary to both men and women. Indonesia is the only country in the Islamic world to permit a woman to sit in judgment. Before the court came into being Ibu Mahdiah taught civil and criminal law at a university in Indonesia, fulfilled the domestic responsibilities prescribed by her religion and raised the first six of her children, born one after another within the first seven years of her marriage.

In all honesty, my introduction is perhaps a little alarmist. But so negative is the perception of the role of women within Islam in the West that it is a struggle to find a comfort zone of shared beliefs to anchor our discussion. It is easier just to reject a string of clichés: the predominant images of women of the Middle East, swathed in black, walking behind their husbands, peering out at the world through the webbed panels of their veils. Easier, but not really fair.

I have come to her home on the first day of Ramadan, the beginning of the fasting month. Her small, neat house lies within a labyrinth of footpaths which lead to a modest, central mosque. Here, in this suburban enclave of Jakarta the air is fresh and clean, protected from the radiating heat of the crowded roads by the quiet ring of footpaths and a rare expanse of parkland a short stroll away. It is already 9 a.m., almost six hours after Ibu Mahdiah first woke up to watch the national broadcast of prayers and to eat her simple early breakfast of chicken, vegetables and rice in the dark.

She apologises for not even offering a glass of water. During the fasting month a Muslim cannot eat, drink, smoke or have sex during daylight hours. I am in her home, so these are the rules. 'The purpose is to demonstrate discipline by obeying God's orders,' she says, adding, with humour, that it is also a good time to lose some weight.

Maybe it would be better to start again.

Polygamy, Ibu Mahdiah explains, is permissible within Islam. A man may take four wives under certain conditions. He must have the consent of the existing wives, he must have the ability to provide adequate economic support, he must treat them all fairly and he must be able to provide education for both the wives and the children.

'Before 1974, when the Islamic Court was established, the general laws in Indonesia were very vague on this issue. Now the law has become clear so women are safe from abuse,' she explains. 'It is a matter of responsibility, the responsibility of a man to a woman and a woman to a man. Islam teaches men and women to look after each other. If there is no polygamy then there will only be extramarital affairs and the woman has no protection or status. It is better to have a formal second marriage with responsibility than to allow a man to have affairs.'

Her court does not deal with common crimes but with the rules of Islam that control family life. In Indonesia, polygamy is not actually widespread. Centuries of Dutch colonial administration preached monogamy and, more recently, opposition to polygamy from within élite circles, led by President Soeharto's late wife Ibu Tien, has greatly reduced the number of multiple marriages. But, on the other hand, says Ibu Mahdiah, adultery is widespread. Indonesia has not adopted a law within the Islamic Courts to punish adulterers.

Adultery is a common reason for seeking a divorce, but only light penalties are available under criminal law. 'Indonesia has not applied the Islamic law which says that adulterers should be stoned to death. Actually people believe that stoning is not a punishment educated people should use,' she says. 'The challenge for Indonesia is that not many legal experts understand Islamic law and because there is no specific law on adultery that is separate from divorce proceedings then adultery is commonplace. We should be able to look at this issue from many sides, and personally I agree with the Islamic law.' To which she quickly adds, 'But not to the point of death.' Instead, the public punishment should be 100 stones for a virgin and 80 stones for a widow, and an equal punishment for the man, of course.

Ibu Mahdiah spent her early years in Malaysia, her mother was Malaysian and her father was Indonesian. When her father became involved in the anti-colonial movement the family was forced to leave the country and moved to Mecca.

'In Malaysia I had friends who were both boys and girls, but in Mecca they did not allow that, so I went to an all-girls' school and couldn't talk to boys and had to cover myself fully with only my eyes showing, even as a little girl. The culture in Mecca was different to the culture in this country. It was not difficult to wear those robes because everyone else was,' she says. 'But in the house we could open them, with my mother and my friends.' She was the only child, so had no brothers, but if she visited a friend whose brother was home she would have to keep herself covered just as on the streets.

For high school the family returned to Indonesia where they sent Mahdiah to an Islamic high school and then to an Islamic university.

'Law was not my dream, it was my father's dream,' she says, laughing. 'I wanted to be a teacher. You see, in Islam the role of women is not only as housewife— women also have a right to education and to apply their knowledge, you can read this in many *sura* [sections] in the Holy Qu'ran. In Indonesia men and women can mix together in public, which is a matter of our culture rather than religion, and so women here have much more opportunity to gain an education than women in the Middle East who are not permitted to study alongside men.'

The conversation jumps in and out of Indonesian and English. Even now her English is almost fluent, remembered from her very short time at an English school in Malaysia as a young girl. On top of that she has learned Arabic.

Did she have only one child, too? I ask. She laughs. 'No, no, I had seven. I got married in 1968 and I gave birth in 1969, 1970, 1972, 1973, 1974, 1975 and then I had another baby in 1981, after I had become a judge. It was very difficult to keep on working, but I was very glad that God gave me seven children. In Islam a child is a blessing from God. We can use contraception to arrange spacing, but not to prevent having a family.'

According to Islam, Ibu Mahdiah explains, the role of the wife is to carry the responsibilities inside the house and to look after the husband and children. 'The role of the husband is as leader in the house and in society. In Islam a woman has no obligation to work for money, that is her husband's role.'

Ibu Mahdiah's husband supported her request to teach and then her desire to sit for the exams to enter the new Islamic Court in 1979, but the balance of responsibilities did not shift.

'We are not superwomen,' she says, 'so if I want to work then I must compensate for my absence by providing a maid to do my work. Islam doesn't say that a wife has to do all the work herself. In the Middle East some husbands provide their wives with maids so they can feel more relaxed. No,' she laughs, 'the husband isn't actually doing any of the domestic work himself.'

In Ibu Mahdiah's court most cases are divorces, including custody cases and property settlements. And she must judge them according to the laws of Islam, not according to any new ideas the couple may have about their roles in the family in Indonesia's rapidly modernising society.

'The most common reason for wives coming to the court is that their husbands have left them without support, or their husbands are drinking, gambling or physically abusive. Nowadays there are many information seminars for women about their rights so more and more are initiating divorces. About 70 per cent of the cases are brought by women. In other countries the *ulama* [religious leaders] do not give women the opportunity to become judges, they say women are emotional. I believe it is an issue of interpretation—most religious teachers in other countries only listen to one opinion. Having a woman judge helps women a lot because they have more understanding of the feelings of women and it is much easier for them to come to a woman than a man.'

A man, she says, mainly comes to the court because his wife is disobeying him or because there is a misunderstanding between his wife and his parents. Or he might make up a reason because he wants to get rid of her and get another wife by accusing her of adultery, for example, or he might want permission to enter into a polygamous marriage. As a judge, she says, she is obliged to seek reconciliation before granting a divorce. And, yes, she will tell a woman to cook for her husband and to stay away from the neighbours, if necessary.

I am floundering with my limited knowledge of Islam when the discussion turns to the process of determining a ruling. In divorce cases when adultery is alleged either a man or a woman must bring four male witnesses to prove the case. But in Indonesia the interpretation of this rule is somewhat softer than in Pakistan, for example, where it is literally enforced, making it virtually impossible for a woman either to defend herself against an accusation or prove her case.

'If you don't have four male witnesses then you can swear to God three times, and swear to condemn yourself if you are lying one time instead,' she explains. 'The rule is based on the assumption that the memory of a woman is weaker than that of a man.'

'Do you believe that?'

'Maybe, sometimes that is true.'

In Indonesia there are five state religions. About 87 per cent of the nation's 200 million people nominate their religion as Islam. But as it is not possible to claim any religion outside the official five or to profess either agnostic or atheistic beliefs there is great diversity in both the practice and rituals of Islam. At the same time Indonesia is undergoing a virtual economic revolution. Significant economic reforms that have opened the economy up to foreign businesses combined with the impact of communications technology are rapidly swapping images of the Muslim woman in her modest batik outfits and head scarf for the long, bare legs, the peeping midriff and the sculptured breasts of the raciest imported fashions.

The Indonesian Government reinforces the basic position that the primary responsibility of a woman is in the home through its Office of Women's Affairs. The biggest women's organisations in the country are associations of public servants and military wives, which assume a woman is not working for money and is principally concerned with supporting her husband's career. But at the same time the reality of rapidly increasing land and housing costs in urban areas mean more and more women have to seek paid employment in the formal workforce.

Tradition has never been static, but we tend to look back at history as though certain social practices were frozen in time. In truth they were always bending and evolving but never so dramatically as they are bending now. The balance between the expectations of a woman's role in Islam and the reality of life in modern Indonesia is increasingly difficult to achieve.

In May 1996 a nationwide controversy exploded over Indonesia's representative at the Miss Universe contest who was recalled by the Government in disgrace, accused of degrading Indonesian women by exposing her body in her swimsuit appearance in Las Vegas.

'Let's not pretend to be moralists,' the 20-year-old Miss Indonesia, Alya Rohali, said in her defence on her return, citing the wider criteria of the contest as 'brains, beauty and behaviour'.

'The winner is measured by the size of her breasts, I am sure of that,' countered the Minister for Women's Role, Mrs Mien Sugandhi, in a fierce public argument that dominated the pages of local magazines. Miss Rohali's swimsuit appearance in Las Vegas, she said, was an insult to Indonesia, and an inappropriate representation of the role of Indonesian women. Mrs Sugandhi took the issue to President Soeharto and emerged from her meeting to announce a Government ban on any overseas appearance in a beauty pageant and a review of the judgment criteria for local contests. The new ban clarified an earlier restriction imposed in the early 1980s that prohibited Indonesian women from participating in contests that judged contestants by their physical attributes.

'The ban on sending Indonesian women abroad is final. It is strictly forbidden. It's got to stop. End of discussion,' said a clearly annoyed Mrs Sugandhi. Small groups of Indonesian women, fully covered in Islamic dress, had taken to the streets the previous week in noisy protest over the Miss Universe incident and numerous officials, Members of Parliament and commentators jumped eagerly into the debate. But while Government officials and religious leaders expressed their moral outrage, Indonesia's small number of outspoken feminists found themselves lining up in defence of a woman's right to participate in a beauty contest—an institution not generally favoured for its role in the promotion of the status of women.

In neighbouring Malaysia, also a majority Muslim nation, participation in the Miss Universe contest is permitted and when Miss India, Sushmita Sen, won the contest in 1995 she was hailed as an ambassador of her country, despite the widely-followed practice in both India's majority Hindu and minority Muslim communities of covering a woman's body. And, anyway, the same Las Vegas swimsuit shot appeared on the cover of one of Indonesia's popular magazines—Miss Rohali grinning broadly, hands on hips. The sale of magazines at traffic lights and in traffic jams assured the photo maximum exposure as it was paraded by hopeful vendors past drivers and bus passengers.

Said one Member of the Legislative Assembly, Mrs Aisyan Amini: 'I disagree with women competing in this kind of contest. I worry that if we let it happen now, then later on the younger generation will want to be Miss Universe as their goal in life.' But prominent feminist Maria Pakpahan said: 'Participation in a contest is a positive way for a woman to prove herself. Personally, I don't feel that she is degrading Indonesian women or that she represents me or any other Indonesian women, this is just an individual matter.'

The debate over the beauty contest reflects the wider debate over the role of women and their responsibility towards men.

Ibu Mahdiah agrees that now is a stressful time for married couples.

'It really depends on the woman, how she manages her time and how her husband supports her,' she says. 'It is a requirement to wear the *jilbab* [headscarf] but not all women do. Maybe they think that it makes them look old, or maybe they like European or American clothes.'

Nowadays, with so many ideas and role models coming into Indonesia on satellite TV, is it becoming less popular for wives to obey their husbands when they tell them not to go out? She merely laughs, pauses, and adds a simple 'Yes.'

'Islamic jurists thought that a woman had half the brain of a man and the Prophet Muhammad is even quoted as saying that, but I don't believe this really came from the Prophet,' says Abdurrahman Wahid, leader of Indonesia's 40 million-strong Nahdlatul Ulama.

It was Wahid's father, a former Minister of Religion, who signed into law the right of both girls and boys to enter religious schools and universities in Indonesia. 'Then, when religious law was acknowledged as a separate jurisdiction we had many girls and women ready and qualified to take the positions of judges,' he says. 'This is the only place in the world that accepts female religious judges. Basically, Islam says that one of the four requirements to be a judge is to be a man, and one of the seven requirements to be the leader of a nation is to be a man. But in Indonesia it was just the signature of my father.'

He would like to tell a story about an *ulama* from Pakistan who came to Indonesia protesting to his Indonesian counterparts and dramatically expressing grave fears for his country under the leadership of that woman Benazir Bhutto. A nation led by a woman would be led to destruction, the *ulama* warned.

'I said to him "Please understand that if the Prophet said a woman could not lead, then that was said in the context of Arabian Peninsula society in the seventh Christian century. The only organisational structure then was tribal. These were warring societies where the leadership was personalised, the tribal chiefs were the head warriors, the officials and the law makers, so it was not surprising that in those conditions the function of leadership belonged to a tribal chief who was a he, not a she." And then I told him not to worry, because Benazir Bhutto doesn't rule by herself, politics is now institutionalised, not personalised. I told him that she couldn't make decisions by herself, that she would have to consult the male-dominated Cabinet at least, and even then there was the Supreme Court, which is 100 per cent male, that could overrule her. He was annoyed and told me I was just playing with words.' (Nonetheless, Benazir Bhutto was dismissed from office for a second time in 1996.)

Since the early 1970s, according to Wahid, Indonesia has witnessed a 400 per cent increase in the number of mosques and an increasing ritualisation of religion. At one level the interpretation of a woman's image seems to have polarised: on the one hand skimpily clad girls are gracing all kinds of consumer goods in advertisements splashed across billboards, but on the other hand more and more women are choosing to wear the *jilbab*.

'You have to look at the issue with a wider sense of the meaning of Islam in Indonesia,' says Wahid. 'We are conscious of the threat of being uprooted by modernisation and rapid social change and one way to go back to our roots is by wearing clothes that are as close as possible to what is prescribed by the Prophet. But, that doesn't mean women want to accept domination by men. Even some men have adopted this Muslim garb like a tunic because they want to be identified as Muslim.

'I was surprised once when I gave a lecture in economics at a university in Jakarta. Of the 1000 students attending, about 400 were women and about half of them wore *jilbab*. They are going to be professionals in a male-dominated field. It is not such a simple question. My wife doesn't wear *jilbab*, and nor do my daughters.

'Personally, I believe that the Prophet demands interpretation from us, not just blind following, and I think this illustrates the differences in the perceptions of women in the religion. But, also, I do have to say this frankly, many Muslim leaders still look at women with degrading attitudes, they still believe that the rights of women are not equal to the rights of men. So, we have a long way to go.'

The princess

The princess, I deduce, was originally the young mistress in the love triangle that would define her life. She does not make this clear at the beginning but, bit by bit, the pieces fall into place until, an hour or so later, the final link is offered up, as casually as an irrelevant, passing thought.

Sitoresmi was born into the Royal Family of the Sultanate of Yogyakarta, in central Java. Her grandfather was the Sultan Hamengkubuwono IX, a man with five wives and 22 children. Her own father was son number five, too remote a spot ever to have a chance of ascending the throne. But his position was such that his one wife and eight children lived within the Palace walls, in one of the plain, modest cottages scattered around the compound. Sitoresmi went to the special Palace elementary school and was assigned a maid of her own to attend to her every whim or wish. Nevertheless, she liked to help with the sweeping and washing and cooking. Such lowly work was her first childish rebellion, a step away from the unspoken rules of life for a high-born Javanese princess.

The Palace in Yogyakarta is not an elaborate affair, its grandeur only relative to the rural poverty that once surrounded it. The courtyard is shimmering with heat and slow gaggles of tourists drag their feet through the

fine, hot sand that lies spread between the low buildings. Inside, the ceilings are ornately carved and
painted in garish red and gold, the carpets are thick
and rich, but the rooms are modest in dimension. Only
one small part of the Palace remains sealed off nowadays to afford Sitoresmi's uncle and his family some
privacy.

The ruling Sultan of Yogyakarta, Hamengkubuwono
X, is a modern, educated man. He has married only
once and has five daughters, none of whom qualifies
to succeed him. Many have encouraged him to marry
again, if only to beget the required son, but he has
refused. So it will be a younger brother, or a nephew,
who will rule after his death. The Sultan's father's
generation was the last of Yogyakarta's Royal polyga-
mists. Like Sitoresmi's own father the Sultan has made
clear that monogamy is now the rule for the Royal
Family.

'In the past the Sultan had many wives so he would
have as many children as possible. The women were
restricted within the Palace,' says Sitoresmi. 'But, I
grew up in the transition period from the traditional
practices to the modern. The role of the Royal wife in
Yogyakarta is now the same as a modern wife, she has
a lot of freedom.'

Sitoresmi's father was the first of his generation to
campaign against polygamy. His argument was that
polygamy was being practised without attention to the
religious rules that permit the taking of more than one
wife. So numerous were the Royal wives that it was
impossible for a Sultan to treat them equally and so
powerful was the Sultan that it was impossible for one
of the wives to refuse to accept another into the
compound. Polygamy therefore became an excuse for
promiscuity.

When Sitoresmi was married at the age of twenty
her father refused to attend. It seems that she had

already become the mistress of a well-known local artist who was already married. She was not a mistress in the furtive sense. There was no attempt by the artist to hide his princess from his wife. In fact, it was his wife who suggested he marry Sitoresmi. He was, says Sitoresmi, 'a free sex kind of a man'. His wife said she would do a deal with him and allow him his relationship with Sitoresmi. But he must marry her as well, and then that was that. Enough.

'I was not a virgin and that was a taboo in Indonesian society. My condition at that time, the virginity that I didn't have any more, meant I didn't have any choice,' Sitoresmi says of her decision to accept the role of wife number two. 'My condition fitted with their need, so I came into their life and they welcomed me.'

Naturally, the marriage was a scandal. Her father told her he could not give her his permission because of his responsibility to God and to his society. Psychologically, Sitoresmi says, members of the Royal Family played an important role in society even though their authority has long been taken over by the national Government.

The wedding was cause for much gossip, particularly the rumour that both wives slept together. 'For the first year we all slept in the same bed, that is what shocked society. I didn't think about whether this was a rebellion on my part or not, I just thought that as I was no longer a virgin, I didn't want to take a risk.' It is assumed I understand that most Indonesian men demand virginity of their brides and so Sitoresmi believed her chances of making another marriage were slim indeed.

The next year the wives split up into separate bedrooms. There was not, says Sitoresmi, much competition or animosity between the women.

'I am an easygoing person, I can make adjustments.

It seems the door was already open to me. The first wife had a special reason for welcoming me. Her husband was a "free sex man", so she tried to control her husband by letting him marry me,' she eventually explains. She was very aware, though, of the whispers behind her back in her home town. The artist broke the deal.

Sitoresmi stayed at home with the four young children she bore him in quick succession, three girls and a boy. The first wife, ten years her senior, also stayed at home with her older brood. Then, one day, a third wife was brought into the home. Sitoresmi allied herself with the first wife in the new situation: two women united by a common sense of betrayal.

'The situation was becoming irrational. There were now three women in the house, all the children received three different opinions for their questions. The children from the first wife were starting to grow up and to understand the situation. My own children were still young but I knew it was only a matter of time until they understood too.'

So Sitoresmi talked to the first wife and told her she was planning to ask for a divorce. The first wife said she would divorce the artist as well. Sitoresmi went home to her father, who welcomed her and her children back.

Initially, I am quite confused by the use of the term 'widow'. Sitoresmi is talking about the next phase of her life and continues to refer to herself in that way. But that is how a divorced woman is labelled in Indonesian society: 'a divorced widow', or simply 'a widow'.

For a young 'widow' life is not easy. Even for a 'widowed' princess there is the matter of financial support. The artist offered no financial settlement and so Sitoresmi was left to bring up the children on her own. Royal retainers are modest and only go to those close to the throne, so Sitoresmi was required to go into business herself to generate her own income. There were many family members to help her so she shuttled backwards and forwards between Jakarta and Yogyakarta building a trade in local handmade crafts for export. She also joined her brother in advertising and publishing, and later in film. Within two years she was able to move out of her father's home and support herself.

'I found out how many people underestimated me,' she says, of her status as a widow. There is no doubt in her voice that the next ten years caused her a great deal of pain and that much of her struggle involved presenting herself to the business world as a 'widow'. 'When I was single I had a boyfriend. That is unusual for Indonesia and, of course, people will look at you negatively.'

The burden of surviving as a 'widow' in the business world eventually led her to her own personal liberation. In 1986, she made a crucial decision for her own sense of self worth. After a lifetime of breaking a conservative society's rules Sitoresmi put on the *jilbab* and the long, concealing clothes to match. It was then, she says, that her society began to treat her with respect. Just like that.

At the same time she had begun to study Islam more deeply and she was asked to give a public speech in her home town on the subject of religion. 'I knew they would come to fulfil their curiosity,' she says of the crowd that attended. 'They wanted to know who Sitoresmi was. A widow with four children who can get a handsome, single man [her boyfriend]. They felt sorry for him. My activities in film and business had given people a negative image about me, they doubted me.'

Her pursuit of religion became more and more zealous and so she gave up her boyfriend. In 1989, she married again, this time to a very religious man, a virgin himself and a decade or so younger. It was, she says in retrospect, a mistake. She wanted a father for her children, he wanted only a wife. They tried and failed to have children of their own and again she divorced. Her daughters took off their *jilbabs*, an expression of disappointment in the solution religion had offered their family.

Sitoresmi is now 47 years old. Her face is smooth—the skin of a woman years younger. There is no secret, she says, laughing. It is, however, widely believed in Indonesia that the Royal Families of Java hold the recipes to many special herbal potions to keep their women beautiful and young.

Today she is happy. Her clothes remain modest and her head is covered. She likes, however, to be fashionable. She likes to be rich. Her own line of Muslim women's clothing is on sale in Yogyakarta, the labels bearing her name. At her side is a quiet, younger man, who is listening to her story without interruption. He is her third husband. Recently, she became his third wife. She is seven years older than him and lives with his first wife and six children in a home in Jakarta, when she is not attending to her businesses in Yogyakarta. His second wife and four children live in another home, but those doors are not closed to Sitoresmi either.

Her third husband is a well-known Muslim singer and a deeply religious man. Polygamy requires a great deal of effort on his part to fulfil the religious requirement to treat the three women fairly. She has known him since the mid-1980s, but only as a friend, their paths first having crossed in the recording of religious music.

'In 1989 I told him I wanted to change my life completely. Our friendship was very strong, he always listened to me. He proposed to me but I didn't take him seriously because he was my best friend and he already had two wives,' she says. But he waited out her failed second marriage and then, last year, asked again. 'From the first time we met until the time we married he never touched me,' she says, an experience which seems to have earned her trust, as well as evoked her surprise.

It is more difficult to ask about this marriage with her husband looking on. 'The religion requires fair treatment for all, but we understand to be 100 per cent fair with the feelings of the heart is impossible,' she says. 'Also, my husband's job takes a lot of his time. He has to drive from place to place to deliver religious lectures, for example, and he has to be a husband to three wives. So, the nearest home from the place he is going is where he will stay or stop over. We have to behave as a team.'

Jealousy, she says frankly, cannot be avoided. Wife number one has already told the newlyweds that she does not like to see them behaving 'romantically' in front of her. 'But I like to see my husband being romantic with the other wives,' Sitoresmi says. Underlying her generosity, perhaps, is her own confidence in her husband's interest in his newest companion.

'Sometimes, though, I get jealous when he tells me he is going to visit another wife. My heart will suddenly jump with jealousy. But, you have to control your jealousy. I can't avoid being jealous but it is not a problem for me to see him being romantic with another wife because I have had experience in dealing with this kind of situation.'

I think I am more uncomfortable with this conversation than she is. I splutter out one or two more questions but feel reluctant to push the issue any further into the realm of mere voyeurism.

No, she says, there is no rule for where the husband should sleep. It is not a case of counting the days and nights and sharing them out. 'The important thing is we have to be transparent and practical, and we have to be open with each other. Last night, for example, I stayed overnight at his second wife's home because this was nearer to where he was going.'

Polygamy and monogamy both have their problems, she says. Monogamy is not a recipe for happiness. 'In any part of your life there will be many problems, in a monogamous situation you could have bigger problems than with polygamy.'

Her religion permits polygamy for men and that she accepts as fair. 'I agree that a man can have more than one wife and a woman can have only one husband at the same time. It is very clearly stated in our religion that a woman is not allowed more than one husband. Our religion teaches that you should never hide the identity of your child's father, that is very important. If a woman has more than one husband she will never know who the child's father is.'

In strict religious circles Sitoresmi is readily accepted alongside the other two wives. In wider society, however, polygamy is no longer widely practised and frequently disapproved of. So, the whispers have not yet stopped. It is really a matter of juggling the available compromises, just as she did on the day of her first marriage, 27 years ago.

Java's empty villages

Subiata was fifteen years old when her embarrassment finally overcame her and she realised she would have to leave her village, crouched between the iridescent green rice paddies of the central plains of Java. It was not that she wanted to buy a one-way ticket for the bus to Jakarta, like so many before her, nor that she particularly hankered for the bright city lights. It was just, she says, that she was the only one left.

All the other teenage girls and single young women had already gone. She felt so uncomfortable dawdling along the red, dirt tracks that wound through the fields and thatch huts that she went to her father to ask for his permission to go too. She didn't know where she was going but, she says, she wasn't afraid. At the end of the trip she was sure she would find all her friends who, one by one, had disappeared. 'My village is an empty village, so are the villages around it,' she says. 'There were only little children and mothers left and I just thought it was time for me to go.'

Subiata got off the bus on the outskirts of Jakarta in the industrial district of Tangerang, where the sprawling factories swallow up the village girls by the thousands to sew seams into kids' pyjamas, attach pockets to men's jackets and seal bags of cheap confectionery for the international market. Factory owners like to employ young, single, village girls. They are cheap and easy to control, they say. Labour agents come to the villages seeking twenty or 30 girls at a time. In some cases all the young girls from one village are bussed off to Jakarta together on the same day.

For the first time in Indonesia's history young single women and, to some extent, married women, are significantly more employable than men. In a Muslim society that places considerable emphasis on the authority of fathers and husbands the social impact is profound. The exodus that has created the empty villages is turning the rules upside down. Husbands left behind are tending to domestic chores and nurturing children, tasks that they say would have publicly humiliated them less than a decade before. And daughters, with their own money in their pockets, and free from the prying eyes of the village elders, are telling their parents 'No'. They will not come home, they say, to accept the stranger chosen for their marriage by their parents. Some even say they will not get married at all.

Since the 1970s, when Indonesia began to industrialise, rural people have been moving off the land and into the cities. In the beginning it was the men who went to the cities in line with their culturally defined role as head of the family and chief bread winner. But now, says Dr Suharso, Secretary of the National Research Council's social and economic divisions, young, single female migrants now outnumber the men. 'Men realise that women have more opportunities in the industrial sector so they have to let their wives and daughters go to Jakarta.'

In 1960 only about 12 per cent of Indonesia's population lived in cities; by the end of this decade urbanisation will have reached around 40 per cent, or more than 80 million people. Those statistics, however, only tell half the story. The largest category of migrants will be single young women, followed by married men, creating a profoundly disruptive demographic imbalance.

According to a current study on the Indonesian labour market, the textile, footwear, garment, shrimp processing, toy manufacturing and cigarette manufacturing sectors are so heavily dominated by young women that the only men in the factories are a handful of supervisors. These are the industries that rely on large numbers of cheap workers and, just as in China and South-East Asia, the least educated and lowest paid are the village girls.

'The restructuring of the village system is so great that in some areas there are just the old people and the children left behind,' Dr Suharso said. 'In the village the culture still requires women to accept social controls. They should stay inside the house, not go out with men and not allow men to visit the house unchaperoned or at night. In the past the women just had to follow the men, providing the supporting role on the farms. Now, the gap between the rural culture and the city culture is huge.'

In Jakarta, he says, young girls and women enjoy much greater freedom and economic independence. They are delaying marriage, becoming selective in choosing their husbands or challenging the long standing social stigma of the 'old maid' at the age of twenty or 25 by refusing to get married at all. 'Family ties are loosening and this is causing social conflict. Young men have always had freedom so the biggest impact is on young women. There are many family problems but people in the villages believe in saving face so they won't talk about it and will try to appear as though everything is still the same.'

Subiata and her friend Mariam have just finished their shift. They have been sewing pockets on men's jackets this week, the latest contract job at their garment factory, for about four or five Australian dollars a day. As the hundreds of girls spill through the factory doors the hawkers are setting up their stalls on the dirt verge outside. They are selling hair clips and hair bands with big, girlie bows, cheap pillow cases with ruffles, bags of sweets and sticks of satay and small pieces of lacy, apricot fabric to decorate the tiny windows of the dormitories behind.

The air trapped in the narrow passageway between the factory and the tiny boarding rooms is still, hot and thick. On a small, clean patch of concrete Subiata and Mariam sit cross-legged and self-conscious, unwinding and retying long, black, glossy plaits, surprised at this interest in their ordinary lives.

'Honestly,' says Mariam, 'I wanted to have an experience and I wanted to avoid the village culture of marrying at a young age. From the age of twelve my parents wanted to marry me off. This is just the village culture,' she says, through an interpreter, 'if you are getting old and are still single then it is shameful.'

Mariam is the second of nine brothers and sisters. Now she is 22 years old and her young sisters in the village, already married, are lugging babies on their hips in batik slings. 'About 75 per cent of the girls from my village have gone. When I was sixteen I asked a friend to take me to Jakarta. I knew I would get a job because my friend knew someone here at the factory. Five of us went together on the bus. My father said it was okay, so long as I was only going to Jakarta because of the job. There is nothing for me to do to earn money in the village. I can just help my parents in the fields.'

A couple of her friends went back to the village to get married when their parents called them but Mariam says she will not. 'My younger sisters got married when they finished elementary school (about twelve or thirteen) and they all have children. In Jakarta I am not embarrassed to be single at my age, but when I go home to visit I am so ashamed that I don't go out of the house.'

In 1888 a daughter was born to the mistress of a petty aristocrat from the Royal Family of Jepara in East Java. Her name was Kartini. She would never come even close to realising her goals and would die by the age of 25, but one hundred years later she would still be upheld as the 'mother of the nation', a contradictory official heroine whose legacy has since been enthusiastically perpetuated by the Indonesian Government.

Kartini was different from the girls of her time because her father allowed her to go to school with her brothers until the age of twelve. In the *adat* of much of Java a woman was offered no role outside the family hierarchy: she was a daughter, sister, wife and mother. High-born women of the Royal courts of Java in particular were fiercely protected—confined to the Palace or allowed to leave only when hidden from view behind the curtain of a carriage and chaperoned by a male of suitable authority.

'Once a young girl reached puberty, she was gradually distanced from her immediate family, parents and siblings. Not long after that she was married off. And frequently, once she had children her husband took a second wife, the first wife often being regarded solely as a mother from then on,' writes Sylvia Tiwon in *Fantasizing the Feminine in Indonesia*. 'High-born women of marriageable age [once they reach puberty] find themselves imprisoned in the courtyards of their father's Palaces.'

Kartini's early years were very happy. Through her schooling she made many friends outside her home, learnt to read and write Dutch and established relationships with the Dutch wives and daughters of Indonesia's colonial administrators. She dreamed of building schools for girls, to provide others with the same key to the world she only briefly glimpsed. Her father's original decision to permit her to attend school was, Kartini writes, 'because he was an educated man'. He was worried, however, about sending his daughter to high school in the city of Semerang with her brothers and said no to her request to continue her studies. Instead he gave her books to read at home and allowed her to write letters to her friends, many of whom were Dutch. Kartini wrote to one of her friends:

> My prison is a large house, encircled by spacious grounds. But it is encircled by a high stone wall and this kept me imprisoned. No matter how large the house and garden, if you are forced to live there you will feel stifled. I remember how in silent desperation I flung myself at the eternally closed doors and against the cold stone walls. No matter in which direction I walked, I would run into a stone wall or a locked door.

The likelihood of her leaving this home was only as a wife but girls at that time rarely had any say in their choice of a husband and were often married off at a very young age to a man chosen to enhance the social or economic status of their fathers. A common Javanese saying went: 'Follow your husband to heaven, get dragged with him to hell'.

Kartini's isolation gave her much time to think, and to come up with some very radical ideas for a girl of those times. She noticed that mothers played an important role in 'creating mean and selfish men' by fulfilling the every wish of their little boys and constantly putting the boys' needs ahead of their sisters. She also noticed that the fate of a woman depended solely on the men to whom she was tied. Her own mother was the mistress of a high-ranking aristocrat but Kartini opposed polygamy because she said it caused so much pain. Of her mother she barely spoke because by doing so she would have indirectly criticised her father whom she held in the highest esteem despite his ultimate status as her gaoler. She wrote:

> When a girl walks she must do this in a very sedate fashion, with tiny, tidy steps, oh, so slowly like a snail; should you walk a little more quickly people scold you saying you are a galloping horse, and if you laugh too loudly you are scolded for showing too many teeth.

In daily life, though, it was not fathers and brothers who imposed these restrictions. Older women, including elder sisters, were often considered to exercise the main control over young girls once they had been brought into the enclosure. Younger sisters were expected to crouch down low on the floor when their elders appeared and crawl towards them on their knees, eyes to the ground.

Influences on the status of women in Java date back to the Hindu and Buddhist kingdoms that preceded the coming of Islam which, with its specific responsibilities about the role of the woman as wife, mother and homemaker, reinforced an existing patrilineal system. Dutch colonialism, with its European model of male inheritance, also reinforced the dependent status of women, but at the same time provided some education to women of the Indonesian élite.

'Old books from Java talk very specifically about the responsibilities and positions of women in relation to men. In the eighteenth century a gentleman owned a horse, a sword, and several wives—they were like chattels,' says political scientist, Dewi Fortuna Anwar. 'In Javanese society at the highest level people had a lot of privileges but their women were also the most guarded because the honour of the family depended very much on how the women behaved.'

Kartini's Dutch friends secured a scholarship for her to study in Holland, but she refused because of the impact the decision would have on her family. (It is also highly unlikely she would have been permitted to leave.)

'It is difficult to stay in the old environment, but it is impossible to venture any further. I cannot enter the new world because a thousand meshes tie me firmly to my old,' Kartini wrote. 'I long to be free, to be allowed, to be able to make myself independent, to be dependent on no-one else . . . to never have to marry. But, marry we must, must, must. Not marrying is the biggest sin for a Muslim woman, it is the greatest shame possible for a native girl and her family.'

In her father's home Kartini managed to start a small school for nine girls. She gave priority to local 'princesses' because they were the most likely to become 'victims of polygamy' as their future husbands would be of high status and thus able to take many wives. But at the age of 24 Kartini herself agreed to enter a polygamous marriage with a man many years her senior, the Head of the Rembang Regency, and already the father of six children.

She told her friends she had agreed to the loveless match because her future husband had promised to allow her to establish a school for girls. In one letter she wrote that she had concluded: 'As the wife of a Regent I will have more influence than as the daughter of a Regent'. But to realise her dreams she would 'have to be practical'. Kartini died one year later, having managed to establish a small school in her home for her husband's children and a handful of high-born girls. She died five days after giving birth to a son, from complications suffered during the delivery.

Every year the girls of Indonesia dress up for Kartini Day, wearing a pencil-thin sarong and fitted blouse that make possible only the tiny, tidy footsteps of which Kartini wrote. Ironically, Kartini herself normally rejected such confining clothing and wore loose gowns.

Over 100 years Kartini has gradually lost the title of Princess and become, instead, the 'Mother of the nation'. On the one hand she spoke up against the inequities of opportunity for women but, on the other, she eventually accepted her fate and in many ways her position reflects the contradictory position of women in Indonesia today. Legally, women have equal access to employment and over half of all adult women are now in the formal workforce. But, at the same time, the Government and the religious teachers continue to remind women of their primary responsibility as wives and mothers.

Although Java is only one of Indonesia's thousands of islands it is home to 120 million people and the dominance of the Javanese in political leadership means that Javanese culture impacts on many aspects of daily life nationwide.

In the villages, of course, women have always worked. The reality of rural life has meant that women have been forced to walk behind their men in the fields, making the kind of segregation that Kartini endured almost impossible. But within many Javanese homes the values Kartini railed against have endured in the unspoken servitude of wives and the assumption of priority in education for boys. 'It is a source of a Javanese man's status that he doesn't do housework, for example. He expects to be served,' said Dewi Fortuna Anwar.

There is ample evidence to suggest that the women

of Java continue to serve their husbands even if they hold down their own jobs. The social pressure on a Javanese woman to cook for her husband and fulfil his every need is great, just as is the pressure on her to defer to his authority in public. But, there is also ample evidence to suggest that their daughters may not follow in their footsteps. And it is here that the new economic reality of the female workforce of Indonesia's factories clashes with the old social order.

'I think women are in a strategic position in the economy now, so from a policy point of view the Government will be forced to take more notice of their particular needs,' said Dewi Fortuna Anwar, 'and I think this will also affect personal relationships. It is difficult for a man to expect to be served by a woman who has a pay check of her own and women will be less and less willing to be treated as such. Nowadays we are also seeing more and more divorces. Women who were afraid to leave their husbands are now more willing to end marriages which do not work. And at the same time we are now seeing women who are choosing not to marry at all because they enjoy their independent lifestyle.'

At the train station in the town of Solo the horses and carts still line up with the buses, taxis and cyclos to meet the early morning train. The dry season is just beginning to take hold and the sun strikes early and strong. The unloading and reloading progress slowly, like the bicycles which cruise quietly through the streets. Solo is the closest stop to the village of Kepuh that lies somewhat further to the south where the rugged, red hills, with their dry, spindly outcrops of grass tell the true story of this land.

The plains that surround Kepuh are rich and lush, the knee-deep water in the rice fields glinting in the early morning light, the dirt tracks shaded by tall, strong coconut palms. But the richness of the land is artificial. Before the introduction of irrigation this land was dry and poor, producing only one crop of rice a year from the short wet season. Life was very, very hard so the children began to leave. Now the fields produce three crops a year but there are not enough people left to work the land.

At the house of the village head, Sukardi Puroatmojo, the people have gathered this morning around prayer mats and packages of fragrant rice, wrapped up in banana leaves. His grandson has just died in childbirth. Life and death are fate, the decisions of God, he says. With the mosque wailing, he and his wife and their visitors invite us to sit and talk in the shade of the wooden verandah.

'In the past it was the man that was boss here, he had to provide the money for the family. But on the farms that money is not enough so the situation has reversed. The men stay at home and the women go because they can get a better job outside than a man,' he says. How many young girls and young mothers have left? The answer is the same. 'Banyak, banyak,' the people murmur, 'Many, many.'

'Here it is not just the young, single girls, says Sukardi, it is many of the mothers and some of the young men as well. 'The young people go to the city, then they come back to get their friends. The village girls go first and mostly they will meet a man in the city and then they don't come back. Then the married women go. Now we hire workers from poorer villages to help us work the fields.'

Ibu Surip is 52 years old. When she was married,

more than 30 years ago, she met her husband at the wedding party. He was from a different village so she hadn't even had a chance to sneak a look at her parents' choice. She laughs, everyone around her laughs. 'I just felt happy I was going to get married. I didn't think anything about that man. I just assumed that my parents chose well,' she says in her local dialect. Her husband, a farmer, took over her parents' authority as tradition would dictate. She stayed at home or helped in the rice fields and deferred to his opinions on the important matters of her life.

Four years ago Ibu Surip's daughter, Srimaryati, asked permission to leave to work in a confectionery factory in Jakarta. She was seventeen years old. 'She told us she would like to have a job of her own and said that making her own money was a better life than asking for money from her parents,' she says.

Last month Ibu Surip informed her daughter that she had already chosen a young man and was ready to arrange her marriage so now she could come home. Srimaryati said no. Everyone laughs.

'Times have changed, life has changed, so it is all right that she rejects my arrangement,' says Ibu Surip.

'The first goal used to be to get married, now it is to get a job,' says Sukardi's wife, Ibu Shinem, who is also the headmistress of the local school. So many young people have left and married outside the village, she says, that her elementary classes, that once catered for 50 small children, now have barely fifteen pupils.

Sukardi says his village believes in fate, a strong undercurrent in the teachings of Islam. So, he says, it is possible for the men to let their wives go if the opportunity is now there for a better life. In many cases married women are working in cities to ensure their children go beyond the elementary education of almost 90 per cent of Indonesia's adult workers, and are qualified for something more than industrial linework.

'The married women feel they have a responsibility to feed and educate their children. The men don't feel worried because they know they need the money,' he says. 'In the past it was embarrassing to see a man doing a domestic task. Now they cook and clean and look after the children, and they don't feel embarrassed because their lives are better.'

Along the road to the south lie thousands more rural communities just like Kepuh. It is not necessary to ask which families have lost their daughters. The panes of glass and brick walls are evidence of their success in Jakarta's factories.

At the village of Pondok, a pilot Government research project is underway. On their small wooden desks the village officials have the new census forms to be filled out this month. The forms do not ask who lives in each house. Instead, they ask who has left, how old they were when they went and where they have gone.

Bibliography

Aung San Suu Kyi, *Freedom from Fear*, Penguin, Harmondsworth, 1991

Bachofen, J. J., *Myth, Religion and Mother Right*, Princeton University Press, NJ, [1861], 1967

Barnes, Gina, *China, Korea and Japan: The Rise of Civilization in East Asia*, Thames & Hudson, London, 1993

Bhutto, Benazir, *Daughter of the East*, Mandarin Paperbacks, London, 1989

Beltran, Ruby Palmer and Javate de Dios, Aurora, *Filipino Women Overseas, Contract Workers . . . at What Cost?*, Goodwill Trading Co. Inc., Manila, 1992

Chan, Eliza, 'Gender Studies', *News and Views No. 8*, University of Hong Kong, 1995

Goonerante, Yasmine, *Relative Merits: A Personal Memoir of the Bandaranaike Family of Sri Lanka*, St Martin's Press, New York, 1988

Khin Myo Chit, *Colourful Myanmar* [Burma], Parami Books, Yangon [Rangoon], 1995

Kim, Marion, *Once I had a Dream: Stories Told by Korean Women Minjung*, Documentation for Action Groups in Asia, Hong Kong, 1992

Kintanar, Thelma (ed.), 'The Impact of Colonisation

on the Image of Women in the Hiligaynon Novel', *Review of Women's Studies*, Vol. IV, No. 2, University of the Philippines, 1994–95

——, *Review of Women's Studies*, Vol IV, No.2, University of the Philippines, 1994–95

Koo, Dr Linda, 'The Non-Status of Women in Traditional Chinese Society', *Bulletin of the Hong Kong Psychological Society*, No. 14, January, 1985, pp. 64–70

Korea Handbook, Seoul International Publishing House, Seoul, 1987

Kristof, Nicholas D. and Wudunn, Sheryl, *China Wakes*, Nicholas Brealey Publishing Ltd, London, 1994

Le Thin Nham Tuyet, *Women in Vietnam*, Foreign Languages Publishing House, Hanoi, 1978

Lieuanan, Victoria (ed.), *Women Entrepreneurs in South-East Asia*, Asian Institute of Management, 1992

Lone and McCormack, *Korea Since 1850*, Longman Cheshire, Melbourne

Mi Mi Khaing, *The World of Burmese Women*, Zed Books Ltd, London, 1984

Roces, Mina, 'Can Women Hold Power Outside the Symbols of Power?', *Asian Studies Review*, Vol. 17, No. 3, April, 1994

Sears, Laurie (ed.), *Fantasising the Feminine in Indonesia*, Duke University Press, Durham and London, 1996

Thailand: King Bhumibol Adulyadej, The Golden Jubilee, 1946–1996, Asia Books Ltd, 1996

Than Tun, Dr, *Studies in Burmese History*, London, 1964

Van Reenen, Joke, 'Central Pillars of the House: Sisters, Wives & Mothers in a Rural Community in Minangkabau, West Sumatra', Research School CNSW, Leiden, The Netherlands, 1996

Yayori, Matsui, *Women's Asia*, Zed Books, London and New Jersey, 1987

Young, Dr Lee O. (trans. John Holstein), *Korea in its Creation*, Design House Publishers, Seoul, 1994